3

BJORKLUND

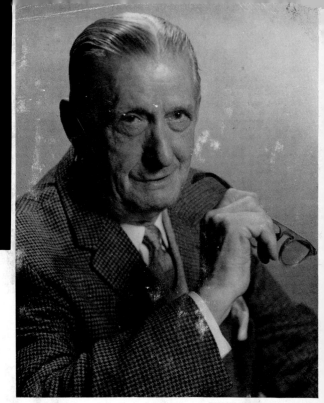

PHOTO BY WILLIAM KAHN

Harry

Sinclair

Drago

IN THE MORE THAN FORTY YEARS that have intervened since he published his first book dealing with the American West, he has never, to quote the old saying, "hung up his saddle." John K. Hutchens, in the *New York Herald Tribune*, and other reviewers have called him an "angry writer"—angry in the sense that he has never hesitated to attack and demolish the myths and legends that have so entwined themselves with the truth that we have come to accept them as history.

When his award-winning *Wild, Woolly and Wicked, The History of the Kansas Cow Towns and the Texas Cattle Trade*, was published in 1961, it was widely acclaimed, not only for its authentic story of the great cattle drives, the cow towns themselves, but for the devastating manner in which it stripped the glamor and heroics from such motion-picture and television worthies as Wyatt Earp, Bat Masterson, Wild Bill Hickok and a host of others. His *Red River Valley, The Mainstream of History from the Louisiana Bayous to the Texas Panhandle*, was equally well received. *The American Book Collector* said: "This is one of the top Western books of the year ... A lot of historians and fiction writers have pecked away at the Red River story but it took Drago to give up a turnkey job on the old rebel river."

He counted coup again in *Outlaws on Horseback, The History of the Organized Bands of Bank and Train Robbers Who Terrorized the Prairie Towns of Missouri, Kansas, Indian Territory and Oklahoma for Half a Century*, with its documented case histories that shattered many hoary old fables of the prairie bandits.

In *Great American Cattle Trails*, Mr. Drago has once more demonstrated his knowledge of Western lore. This comprehensive account of the famous trails and of the men who followed them is full of stories of hardship, danger and adventure, and it gives a fascinating picture of the growth of the United States.

GREAT
AMERICAN
CATTLE
TRAILS

GREAT AMERICAN CATTLE TRAILS

The Story of the Old Cow Paths of the East
and the Longhorn Highways of the Plains

by HARRY SINCLAIR DRAGO

Illustrated with photographs and maps

DODD, MEAD & COMPANY

NEW YORK

For

RAYMOND T. BOND

who, in the long ago, taught me
how to distinguish uninterested from
disinterested—and many other things

An Introduction and Acknowledgment

In telling the story of the old trails, the men who made them famous, the wild and woolly cow towns they spawned and the development of the unorganized range-cattle business into a multi-million dollar industry, it was difficult to avoid repeating, in some instances, what I had previously written in other books. It was not always possible, for history is history and can not be changed for the convenience of the writer.

Recently I had the honor of writing a long and (I trust) informative introduction for the handsome new edition of that Bible of the trail men, *The Trail Drivers of Texas,* in the course of of which I reaffirmed my long-held conviction that in its several hundred personal reminiscences there is more of the color, spirit and character of the men who pointed the big herds north than can be found elsewhere. It has no literary value, and was not intended to have. I have leaned on it heavily.

I also want to acknowledge my indebtedness to J. Frank Dobie for his splendid *The Longhorns* and *The Mustangs.* To say anything about the Longhorn or the Mustang without paying tribute to him is impossible; he pre-empted the field, and brilliantly too. He said he preferred to be known as a folklorist rather than a historian. Of course he was both. There is magic in what he wrote and I treasure pages that scale the heights of pure literature.

As always the historical societies of Kansas, Oklahoma, Wyoming and Montana, among others, have been helpful. No questions addressed to any one of them has ever gone unanswered. The American History department of the New York Public Library and the National Archives, in Washington, have been equally cooperative. On a more personal basis, I want to thank my old friends Peter Decker, the noted bibliophile, antiquarian and writer, Sol Lewis, the publisher, and Mike Ginsberg, the Boston bookseller, for the material and advice they have given me. There have been many others, particularly Don Ward, the editor of the *Brand Book,* for setting me straight on Jean Pierre Chouteau and the Missouri St. Louis Fur Company.

I sincerely hope that the excerpts I have used from Washington Irving's *A Tour of the Prairies* and his *The Western Journals* will induce many readers to discover their charm for themselves. For an equally enjoyable adventure, turn to the historical writings of Grant Foreman, who in his many books has told the story of Oklahoma with gusto and affection.

Harry Sinclair Drago

Contents

Illustrations

Boysen Dam and reservoir
Granville Stuart
Conrad Kohrs
Moreton Frewen
John Clay

GREAT
AMERICAN
CATTLE
TRAILS

1

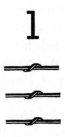

The Early Trails

TODAY, IN THE DENSELY populated Commonwealth of Massachusetts, where towns and cities crowd close on the heels of their neighbors, with the average farm limited to a hundred acres or less, there is no historical marker to say where the first cattle trail in America once wended its way. But by fitting together the bits of information that are available, a documented record of its beginnings and importance is possible.

For several hundred years or more, English farmers with cattle for sale had "walked" them to market, usually a matter of only a few miles. At first, that practice was followed by the colonials, but as the farmers of New England began to establish themselves at ever greater distances from Boston, the market for livestock that was to be slaughtered, the expression "walking" cattle did not apply. With fifty to a hundred miles to go, you "drove" your cows and bullocks, and you became a drover.

By the late 1670's enterprising cattle traders were moving out into central Massachusetts on regular buying trips, which enabled the farmer to dispose of whatever livestock he had for sale at his own doorstep. Ten years later, following King Philip's War, buyers were competing with one another in the still remote Connecticut River Valley country. Usually, each had several men in his employ, who accompanied him on his wanderings. It was their job, when a herd had been assembled, to assist him in driving the animals to Boston for slaughtering. A drive might start any place, and since there was no established route to be followed, the course a trader took was the one that suited him best.

The various trails converged, however, at Blackstone River, a few miles below preesnt-day Worcester, and became one. Running east from that point, by way of Hopkinton and Dedham and on into Boston, there was a well-beaten path, hammered down by the hundreds of barnyard cattle that had passed over it. Eventually, it acquired a name—the Bay State Cow Path. For at least a hundred years it was the principal thoroughfare of its kind between maritime Massachusetts and that part of the broad Connecticut River Valley lying within the borders of the state and for all of southern Vermont and much of New Hampshire as well. It survived the Revolution. Over it, badly needed succors of beef and farm produce reached the Continental Army besieging Boston.

In the lean years following the war there was little demand for cattle; beef became a luxury that only the well-to-do could afford. The bean and cod became staples of the New England diet. The whole complexion of the country began to change. More post roads, with fast stagecoaches to Worcester, Springfield, New Haven and way points, hacked up the old cow path. Presently, steamboats began to ply the Connecticut and other rivers. It marked the beginning of the great change that was to make Massachusetts and the neighboring states the industrial hub of the nation for half a century. The mill became more important than the farm, and to the farmer, stock raising became far less important than his fields of hard grains and tobacco.

Just when the last herd plodded over the old path is not a matter of record. When its usefulness was largely gone, its final demise was quickened by what, even then, was hailed as progress. The number of cattle that passed over it was infinitesimal compared with the thousands of Longhorns that came bawling up the Chisholm and other famous Western trails. But the life of the latter was brief, twenty to twenty-five years at most. In longevity, the old Bay State Cow Path topped them all, and by a very wide margin.

In all of the Thirteen Colonies there had always been some movement of cattle, but it was largely local. Only into Tidewater

Virginia, came livestock, sheep and hogs as well as cattle that had been trailed hundreds of miles. The drovers, buckskin-clad men and boys, had walked them every step of the way from central Kentucky, over Cumberland Gap and through the Blue Ridge Mountains. Moving across Kentucky, they had followed the Wilderness Road that Daniel Boone had received credit for breaking and which, in large part, was the original Buffalo Trace of the Cherokee Indians.

The first white man of record to attempt to explore the region that was to become the state of Kentucky was Dr. Thomas Walker. As agent and surveyor for the Loyal Land Company, a Virginia concern, he set out with a suitable expedition in the summer of 1750 to find a site for a settlement west of the Cumberlands. He failed to get beyond the mountains, and harassed by Indians, he turned back. The following year, on a similar mission for the Ohio Company, Christopher Gist, a frontiersman of distinction, who later accompanied Major George Washington on his mission to the French at Fort LeBoeuf, explored the country along the Ohio westward from the mouth of the Scioto River. His reconnaissance was important, but it was apparent from the apathy with which the Ohio Company received his report that it was not encouraging enough to warrant the risk and expense of establishing a settlement in the virgin wilderness south of the Ohio.

In 1752, John Finley, an Indian trader, descended the Ohio by canoe to the site of today's Louisville, and it was his vivid and enthusiastic description of the interior of the country that first fired Daniel Boone with the resolve to explore it. Boone was only eighteen at the time, and fifteen years were to pass before he set foot in it for the first time. Migrating from Pennsylvania in 1751, his father had settled with his family in the Yadkin Valley of North Carolina, where, young as he was, Boone soon won local renown as a backwoods hunter, trapper and frontiersman. When the call came for volunteers to accompany what was to be General Braddock's disastrous expedition against the French at Fort Duquesne, he went as a wagoner and blacksmith. Later, he spent several years in Florida, hunting and trapping. In 1767 he was back in the Yadkin Valley. He renewed his acquaintance with

Finley and induced the latter to accompany him on an extended exploration of Kentucky.

Joined by two others, they set out from Watauga, in eastern Tennessee, a tiny hamlet in the untracked wilderness, and headed northwest in the direction of Cumberland Gap, at the base of the Cumberlands. This was heavily timbered, thicket-choked Chero- kee hunting country. The only way to get through it was to follow the trace that in former years herds of buffalo on their annual migrations north and south had punched through the maze of laurel and alder thickets and entangling grapevines.

If you will glance at a map, you will find Cumberland Gap at the point where Tennessee, Virginia and Kentucky come together. If the great herds of buffalo, moving northwest out of Georgia and the Carolinas, had found the Gap the best way of getting over the spiny back of the Cumberlands, it must have been the result of much trial and error as well as animal instinct. War parties of Cherokees from the south and raiding Shawnees from beyond the Ohio had been crossing that way for centuries. White men could do no better. Though it was a means of passage, it was steep and forbidding, especially on its eastern flank. No wheel turned over it until 1795, when the state made it a wagon road (Kentucky had achieved statehood in 1792).[1]

After passing the summit of the Gap, Boone and his party de- scended the western slope of the Cumberlands without difficulty. Crossing Yellow Creek and the Cumberland River, they entered the fertile expanse of the Cumberland Valley. This was the begin- ning of what came to be known as Boone's Wilderness Road. It crossed Kentucky in a northwesterly direction in a course that led through today's Peach Orchard, Danville and Bardstown to the Falls of the Ohio. For two-thirds of the way it was the old Buffalo Trace, there for anyone to follow. But to Boone went the credit and the glory. John Finley, who should have shared it equally with him, won only anonymity.

Boone's place in history is secure. He was "a typical American pioneer and backwoodsman, a great hunter and trapper, highly skilled in all the arts of woodcraft, familiar with the Indians and their methods of warfare, a famous Indian fighter, restless, re- sourceful and fearless. His services, however, have been greatly over-estimated, and he was not, as is popularly believed, either the first to explore or the first to settle the Kentucky region." [2]

The name "Wilderness Road" has survived, but today, even in Kentucky, very few people have any knowledge of the Buffalo Trace, and not many ever heard of it. It is incredible to young and old that buffalo by the thousand once ranged Kentucky. With its numerous salt licks, the region had a powerful attraction for the shaggy, lumbering brutes. If the trail they made across the state from Cumberland Gap to the Ohio meandered crazily, it was because the herds checked their migration to turn aside to some adjacent salt lick. In the vicinity of Lexington there is evidence that they strayed as much as fifteen miles from the course to which they were committed, and to which they returned when their craving for salt was satiated.

After swimming the Ohio River, about where New Albany now stands, they continued on across Indiana and in the vicinity of Vincennes left that state and ended their migration on the grass-covered prairies of Illinois. In his journals, La Salle, the French explorer, comments at length on the great herds of buffalo he found roaming the lands of the friendly Illinois. But in October, when the trees were beginning to drop their leaves, the long and arduous return migration of the animals to their winter range in the Carolinas and below began, and suddenly where the prairies recently had been black with buffalo, only a few old and decrepit bulls remained.

Long before Boone's time, the great herds of buffalo from the south were no longer toiling over Cumberland Gap. They were never to come again, for they had disappeared from their Carolina-Georgia ranges. Their disappearance has never been satisfactorily explained. They hardly could have been killed off by hunters, surely not by Indian hunters. Unlike the white man, they killed only what they could eat. At the time of their disappearance, white hunters were not numerous enough to have accounted for their complete extinction as they did at a much later date on the plains of western Kansas and the Texas Panhandle, when the hide hunters slaughtered thousands of buffalo and left the carcasses to rot where the animals fell.

Some unknown pestilence might have carried off the great

herds. That is possible but also unlikely, since their whitening bones would have been left as a clue to their fate. No such discovery was ever reported. We know that when the first white men established themselves on the coast of Virginia, the Carolinas and Georgia a vast number of buffalo roved the upland plains east of the Appalachian Mountain Chain. It may be presumed that they had been there long enough to be regarded as native, but they were "woods" buffalo, somewhat larger and far more migratory than their cousins of the Western plains, and so classified by naturalists. The distance from their ranges east of the Appalachians to the Mississippi was less than to the prairies of Illinois to which they were accustomed to resort. Is it possible that, answering some urge known only to themselves, they migrated westward en masse through the uninhabited wilderness of northern Alabama and Mississippi, crossed the great river into Arkansas and lost their identity by infusion with the plains buffalo?

With the danger of Indian depredations removed, following the War of Independence, an extensive migration into Kentucky from Maryland, Virginia and North Carolina began, amounting, it is estimated, to between five and six thousand. While many came down the Ohio from Fort Pitt (Pittsburgh) the great majority entered the country by way of Cumberland Gap, bringing livestock with them. By 1800, cattle and hogs had multiplied to the point of abundance. But with no way of disposing of them, they were of little value. Finding a market rapidly became a matter of economic necessity for the farmers spread out over the Blue Grass.

It had to be Tidewater Virginia; nowhere else was a market to be found. According to their reckoning it was a full six hundred miles from central Kentucky to Richmond, to be reached by going over Cumberland Gap, skirting the Shenandoah foothills and trailing through the Blue Ridge Mountains into the Valley of Virginia. It took courage even to contemplate such a long and hazardous undertaking. They would be gone for four months, two months going and two months returning. But they were rugged men, and necessity was driving them.

It was no later than the summer of 1802 when the first Kentucky-bred cattle reached Tidewater. It was the beginning of a traffic that lasted for some twenty years, growing in volume as the annual pilgrimage continued, only to decline and then pass out of existence when the Kentuckians turned to a new and flourishing market that had opened in Pennsylvania.

Perhaps it is because driving livestock over Cumberland Gap was always an individual effort, unrelated to other men who were similarly engaged, that so few accounts of it have come down to us. In those that have, it is the Wilderness Road that is mentioned, not the Buffalo Trace. Apparently, even then, the old trace had faded into the recesses of history. Big Ben Holladay, the "stage-coach king," boss of the Overland Express Company, the Pony Express, California shipping magnate and railroad builder, was raised in Nicholas County, Kentucky. In his old age, he liked to recall his boyhood days on what he always referred to as "the Wilderness Road," and how he, still a lad in his teens, with his father and older brothers, had trailed their cows, hogs and some sheep through the mountains to Richmond, Virginia, walking every step of the way, back and forth, and returning with their mules laden with tea, sugar, gunpowder and other necessities.[3]

In Virginia, where historical markers are everywhere, it is remarkable that not one has been placed to commemorate the cattle drovers from Kentucky or to mark the route by which they reached Richmond and the coastal centers of the Old Dominion. And yet it was over the route they had blazed that Confederate General Felix K. Zollicoffer led his little army of seven thousand men in his attempted invasion of central Kentucky, only to be killed and have his force completely routed in an engagement with Union troops under General George H. Thomas, the "Rock of Chickamauga," at Mills Springs, in Wayne County.

Like the Bay State Cow Path, the Wilderness Road cattle trail was an east-west trail. There was a third, the Three Mountain Cattle Trail, and it was by far the most important if judged by the thousands of cattle, horses, mules, hogs, sheep, even turkeys, that were driven over it. It has been said that a herd of Longhorn cattle, from west of the Mississippi, used it in getting to market. This is to be doubted, no evidence ever having been produced to confirm it.

The Three Mountain Cattle Trail had its beginnings in Ohio, Indiana, Illinois and Kentucky. They produced an unknown number of small feeder trails, but wherever they originated, they became one when they crossed the western border of Pennsylvania. Properly speaking, the Three Mountain Trail began there and ended without leaving the state. The cattle that were driven over it were a hundred per cent domesticated barnyard cattle. The only range cattle to reach the Eastern Seaboard before the War between the States was the herd of Longhorns that Thomas Candy Ponting, Jr., drove from Baxter Springs, Kansas, to the new railhead at Muncie, Indiana, from where, after many misadventures, he landed them in New York City.

What became the Three Mountain Cattle Trail was originally the offshoot of an old Indian trail that led from eastern Pennsylvania and crossed the Susquehanna in the vicinity of today's Harrisburg, where it turned south and west down the Cumberland Valley. It was after General Braddock's defeat on his way to attack Fort Duquesne, in 1755, and the end of Indian hostilities, or what was believed to be the end, that white settlers in number began to move into the region west of the Susquehanna River and established towns, many of which survive today. Old Indian trails became roads. Though unimproved, the one leading into the Cumberland country became important and acquired the name of Valley Road. But the farther it went, the more pronounced became its swing to the south; if you were bent on traveling west, there were only two places where you could escape from the valley.

The first was at Shippensburg, where a rocky trail, known locally as the Three Mountain Road, struck off boldly for North Strasburg, Fannetsburg, Burnt Cabins and Fort Littleton. Ten miles down the valley, at Chambersburg, you had your choice of another road leading to the west. By way of old Fort Loudon it reached McConnellsburg, where it crossed the Blue Mountains and met the Three Mountain Road west of Fort Littleton. On foot or by horseback, even by Conestoga wagon if strong enough for it, you could keep on going—over the Kittatinnys and the Tuscaroras, and eventually reach Pittsburgh.

In 1810, when men and goods were moving west rather than south, the Valley Road, with the turnoff via Fort Loudon, was widened and improved and became the Pittsburgh Pike, the first toll road in western Pennsylvania. This lower road by way of

Chambersburg was longer, but the going was so much easier that it captured most of the traffic. The Three Mountain Road fell into disuse and practically lost its identity, the section between Shippensburg and Fort Littleton being commonly referred to as "the Shippensburg cutoff." But after drowsing for approximately two decades it was rescued from oblivion by the thousands of small herds of livestock that came streaming over it from the west, and was reborn as the Three Mountain Cattle Trail.

By 1820 the farmers of Ohio, Indiana and Illinois were confronted with the same problem that had forced the Kentuckians to undertake the long drive across the mountains to Tidewater at the turn of the century: they had an abundance of livestock and no market for it.

It is not to be doubted that travelers from the East carried word into the flatlands of Ohio and its neighboring states of a trail through central Pennsylvania over which livestock coming up the Cumberland Valley from West Virginia and Kentucky was being driven to the vicinity of Harrisburg, beyond which were open roads leading to the Philadelphia and Baltimore markets.

Promising as the news was, nothing was done about it until tales became common that buyers (always identified as speculators) from New York, Philadelphia and Baltimore, accompanied by their own crews for handling stock, had established themselves at Harrisburg and that the competition among them was so keen that a man could dispose of his cattle at a satisfactory price. Only then were the first small herds from the Midwest shaped up and headed for Pennsylvania.

In 1828, John Murray and his sons, from Lake County, Ohio, put a small herd over the Three Mountain Road. Very likely it was the first, though several others laid claim to that distinction. It marked the beginning of John Murray's long association with the now-forgotten trace. For thirty years and more he and his sons put cattle over the Pennsylvania mountains. In 1860, Robert Murray put the last herd through. The railroad had reached Pittsburgh; the Three Mountain Road was finished.

Historians have never given John Murray his due. He lifted trail driving to the level of an organized business. The methods he originated were adopted by the Texans in the era of the great

Longhorn drives to the Kansas cow towns, and though they improved them, they remained his debtors.

Murray realized clearly enough that although there were thousands of Midwestern farmers like himself, who had a few head of stock which they were anxious to sell, they would have to pool their cattle if they were to be trailed a long distance and disposed of at a profit. He proposed that in every community farmers with excess stock should turn the animals over to a man whom they could trust, on credit, and who would drive the assembled herd over the trail and sell it at the best possible price. Less the expenses incurred and the trail driver's percentage of the profits, what remained would be paid to the respective owners.

At a later date, this was what the trail drivers of Texas did. When a herd of two thousand or more Longhorns was pointed north, it wore the road brand of the trail driver but also perhaps as many as half a dozen ranch brands of the owners who supplied the critters. That was as far as the similarity went. The trail driver had a trail boss, who was responsible for getting the herd to its destination; he had nothing to do with the selling or the handling of money. That was not John Murray's way; with him, the boss was both trail driver and trail boss; he followed the herd on horseback, made all arrangements as he went along and had only two men on foot to act as flankers, which was sufficient to keep a herd of seldom more than a hundred and fifty farm cattle on the trail.

To anyone acquainted with the mass movement of cattle that was the rule on the great north-south Western trails, the driving to market of herds of a hundred or a hundred and fifty head would seem to have been a trifling business. The reverse was true; the Three Mountain Road was big business, and only the old Bay State Cow Path enjoyed a longer life. It was, as its name indicates, a mountain trail. Within a distance of ten miles it climbed over three paralleling ranges—Tuscarora, Kittatinny and Blue Mountain—rugged going on a rocky trail that was never more than twenty feet wide, which would have made the handling of big herds impossible. Traveling over the Pennsylvania Turnpike, today's superhighway, which closely follows the route of the old trail, you get an idea of the difficulties the drovers had to contend

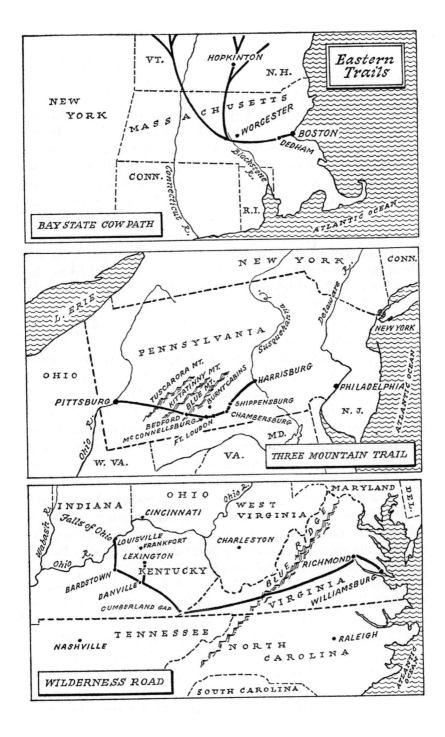

Eastern
Trails

BAY STATE COW PATH

VT. HOPKINTON N.H.

NEW YORK

M A S S A C H U S E T T S

WORCESTER BOSTON
DEDHAM

CONN. *Connecticut R.* *Blackstone R.*

R.I.

ATLANTIC OCEAN

N E W Y O R K CONN.

L. ERIE

Delaware R.

NEW YORK

OHIO P E N N S Y L V A N I A *Susquehanna R.*

TUSCARORA MT.
KITTATINNY MT.
BLUE MT. HARRISBURG
BURNT CABINS PHILADELPHIA

PITTSBURG SHIPPENSBURG
Ohio R. BEDFORD N.J.
MCCONNELLSBURG CHAMBERSBURG
FT. LOUDON
W. VA. VA. MD. **THREE MOUNTAIN TRAIL**

Ohio R. OHIO MARYLAND DEL.

INDIANA CINCINNATI WEST
Wabash R. VIRGINIA
Falls of Ohio CHARLESTON

LOUISVILLE FRANKFORT
Ohio R. LEXINGTON RICHMOND
BARDSTOWN KENTUCKY WILLIAMSBURG
DANVILLE VIRGINIA
CUMBERLAND GAP
B L U E R I D G E

T E N N E S S E E
NASHVILLE N O R T H RALEIGH
C A R O L I N A

WILDERNESS ROAD
SOUTH CAROLINA

with as they trudged over it. The tunnels which burrow through Blue Mountain, Kittatinny and Tuscarora ranges are there because when the great highway was under construction, engineers could devise no practicable way of taking it over the mountains.

Many estimates have been made of the number of cattle, horses and mules that were driven to market over the Three Mountain Trail during the years of its existence as a major livestock thoroughfare. Some of the figures given are astronomical. None can be documented. One of the most conservative commentators and best-informed writers on the Three Mountain Cattle Trail, Minnie Dubbs Millbank, has said: "It is estimated that in numbers the cattle averaged at above 175,000 a season, aggregating for the life of the trail well over five million." [4] The seasonal figure she gives seems unduly high, since snow closed the trail for at least five months out of every twelve, and every heavy summer downpour made it a quagmire in places and usually halted the movement of stock for at least a day.

If the 175,000 figure is to be accepted as a yearly average, it must be limited to the peak years of the trail, when the herds followed so closely on the heels of those ahead that the dust never had time to settle; and it must include the thousands of Kentucky-bred mules, which were in great demand in the anthracite mines of eastern Pennsylvania, and the considerable number of young farm horses, mostly from Ohio and Kentucky. Though John Murray opened the trail in 1828, it was not until the early thirties that it became a major highway for livestock. Its importance began to decline with the arrival of the railroad in Pittsburgh, in 1854, and the last six years of its existence were increasingly lean ones as freight rates were lowered and it became cheaper to ship by rail than drive over the mountains on foot.

An average seasonal figure of forty thousand and an over-all total of around three million head would seem to be a more logical estimate.

The trail began in the vicinity of Pittsburgh and ended at Harrisburg, or thereabouts. Its length, allowing for its rambling, was roughly three hundred miles, a mere fraction of the distance covered by the more famous Western trails, which in some instances had twice three hundred miles behind them before they got out of Texas. But the wealth it produced was tremendous. The cattle it delivered were not cheap. Prices fluctuated from week to week. When the market was high, a drover might get as much as forty dollars a head. Often he sold for twenty-five to thirty dollars. This was more than twice as much as beef cattle brought at the Kansas markets in the 1870's and 1880's.

The folklore of the Three Mountain Trail has largely been lost. However, from the letters that have been preserved by several dedicated historical societies, the ledgers of old taverns and the village ordinances enacted to control the drovers and their herds and to levy fines for trespassing and the destruction of property, the story of the trail can be pieced together.

It is not studded with violence; there were bitter disputes and bloody tavern brawls, but there were no killings. Drovers were often robbed. Invariably when that happened the crime occurred in one or another of the numerous taverns, some of which were deadfalls of the lowest characters. Whores of the coarsest stripe were part of such establishments, working with male confederates (sometimes the proprietor) to relieve a man of his money. Going east, a drover was comparatively safe. It was after he sold his cattle and was returning home with the proceeds in his wallet that he was the target of the blacklegs and the trollops. If he were foolish enough to engage in a drinking bout, he was almost certain to be given a Mickey Finn during the course of the evening. In the morning, when he recovered his wits, his money was gone, and there was little he could do about it. His stupidity usually cost him the confidence of the farmers who had entrusted their cattle to him and made it impossible for him to assemble another herd.

As business on the trail increased, so did the number of taverns. In the first forty miles after it emerged from the mountains, there were no less than thirty places licensed to sell whisky. But the tavern keeper's profits were not limited to what he took in over the bar. In addition to providing food, lodging and drink, he had pasturage on which cattle could be turned out for the night at so much per head. The drover had to do business with him, for there was no such thing as free grass on the Three Mountain Trail. Long before it reached Shippensburg it ran through settled, fenced-off country. When a herd was turned off the trail for the night, it had to be put on somebody's pasture, and at a fee. If the grass had been cropped down by too much usage, hay had to be purchased. As a rule, it was the enterprising tavern keepers who could supply it.

In time, the best of them became the leading men of their respective communities. The lodging they supplied was primitive (pallets on the floor of what was known as the "common room," large enough to accommodate fifteen to twenty men and usually situated to the rear of the barroom). If you didn't mind paying an extra fifty cents, you could sleep upstairs in a bed. The food was usually good; it was plain, but there was always plenty of it. A tavern that won a reputation for serving good meals soon had all the trade it could handle. The boss of a trail herd would range ahead during the afternoon and make arrangements for the night, and he would drive on an extra two or three miles to reach a favorite stopping place.

Greedy tavern keepers defeated themselves by becoming too numerous; if a trail boss could not arrive at satisfactory terms at one place, he went on to the next. It resulted in some sharp bargaining. The drover did not always get the worst of the haggling, though he was always at the disadvantage of never carrying with him any subsistence for man or beast. But traveling light enabled him to maintain a schedule of ten to twelve miles a day with cattle and twice that distance when he was driving mules or horses.

Once a herd had become accustomed to following a leader (always an ox), it moved along without giving much trouble. There were minor breakaways. They were of little consequence unless they occurred while a herd was passing through a village, when fences were knocked down and gardens trampled. One such instance took place at Orrstown and resulted in so much damage that the citizens petitioned the selectmen to prohibit the herds from passing through the village. John Orr, the tavern keeper, quelled the uprising.

Several years ago the writer had occasion to comment on the "speculators" who drove out in their gigs from New York, Philadelphia and Baltimore to intercept the herds coming into Harrisburg from the west. Part of it seems worth repeating.

"Among the speculators . . . was that professional rustic and master schemer, Uncle Dan'l Drew, who in the years to come was to cross swords successfully with Commodore Vanderbilt, Jim Fisk and Jay Gould, wreck the Erie Railroad and loot its treasury of millions. Dan'l Drew must once have been young, but as Stewart Holbrook says in *The Age of the Moguls,* no one ever regarded him as anything but old. . . . He followed the practice of having his drovers 'salt' his cattle, the day before reaching market, then letting them drink their fill, adding several tons to the gross weight of his herd. It brought into the language the term 'watered stock,' which is still with us."

The Three Mountain Trail has no fame. Today, it would be impossible to locate whole sections of it in the jungle-like maze of mountain laurel and cedars that long ago blotted out most of what used to be called the "cutoff." But though it is erased and gone, it must rate among the great cattle trails of America.

2

The Osage Trace

OF ALL THE TWELVE OR MORE wilderness outposts composing the so-called chain of forts, by which the royal governors of New France hoped not only to contain the English colonists within the coastal region east of the Alleghenies but to protect their line of communication between French Canada and French Louisiana and control the vast fur trade of half a continent, none provided a greater source of revenue than the collection of shabby log cabins lining the mud flats on the western bank of the Mississippi River, a league below the mouth of the wild Missouri, which they named St. Louis.

From its humble beginnings, it was to grow into the fur and peltry capital of America. As recently as 1960, it was still the largest raw fur market in the United States. When in 1803, as a result of the Louisiana Purchase, the French flag was run down for the last time and St. Louis passed into the sovereignty of the United States, it continued to be in spirit and custom a French town, and that was largely so half a century later.

No other unofficial capital of an industry ever controlled such a wide, seemingly illimitable empire as did St. Louis. Every Western explorer—beginning with Lewis and Clark, De Bonneville, Fremont, Parkman and others—made it their headquarters, and entwined in its history are all the great names of the American fur trade—Astor, Ashley, Manuel Lisa, the Sublettes, the Chouteaus.

By 1808, Indian traders, hunters, trappers and men bound up the Missouri with the brigades, all of whom claimed St. Louis as their home, were pushing into Texas, up the Arkansas to the Rocky Mountains and spreading out over the Upper Missouri and its tributaries. Striking west from St. Louis, they found old Indian trails leading through the virgin forests and over the hills and bluffs, for this was the homeland of the once all-powerful Osage Indian Nation that had dominated most of Missouri, Arkansas and parts of Oklahoma and Kansas. Recurring epidemics of smallpox and incessant warfare with the Pawnees and other plains tribes had weakened the Osages, but they still claimed southern Missouri as their hunting grounds. They welcomed the white traders who supplied them with what they soon began to regard as necessities, though they had lived without them for centuries.

By 1810, parties of peaceful Osages were crossing Missouri from their principal village on the banks of the Neosho River, near the present village of Shaw, Kansas, to St. Louis to trade for their peltries, beeswax and bear's grease. The trail they used soon became the main wilderness highway for white men as well as red, and the latter identified it with the name—the Osage Trace. As first used, the name undoubtedly applied only to the trans-Missouri section of the great trail, but in time it was given to the equally important north-south trail of the Osage Nation, running down through today's eastern Oklahoma to Red River.

After leaving St. Louis the trace went up the north side of the Missouri to within a few miles of Jefferson City, where it crossed the river and struck off to the southwest. It was there that diversions began to occur, some of them seasonal, due to the flooding of mountain streams in the Ozarks. Later, when the trace became part of the principal wagon road between St. Louis and the Texas frontier, and finding grass for the horses and bull teams became a factor, it left the main track whenever necessity demanded.

The Osage Nation had become a mounted tribe at about the same time as their hereditary enemy, the Pawnees. Once the Osages had the horse to give them mobility, they began raiding into Kansas, carrying war not only to the Pawnees but to the Comanches and other wild tribes of the plains. To the south, the way was open to the salt licks and salt springs of what was soon to be known as Indian Territory, and subsequently Oklahoma. On these salt-making expeditions, whole villages—men, women, children, dogs and camp impedimenta—moved over the trail.

It was a region in which game abounded. When their material needs had been satisfied, the Osages turned from work to pleasure, and the young warriors set out on horse-stealing forays across Red River into Texas. In bands of from twenty to fifty, they started from the vicinity of La Saline (now Salina), passed the future sites of Muskogee and McAlester, went through Limestone Gap and reached the Red where Ben Colbert, the famous Chickasaw full blood, was later to establish his ferry and bridge.[1]

The frequency with which these horse-stealing raids were perpetrated, plus the fact that for a quarter of a century or more they were the chief diversion of the Osage Nation, would seem to indicate that they were uniformly successful. Just when raiding parties came down the trace for the last time cannot be stated with authority. It hardly could have been later than 1820. By that time the greatness of what George Catlin, the painter, described as "the noblest of all Indian tribes" had passed. They were a weakened, subsidized people, content to be placed on a Kansas reservation.

Although disease and constant internecine warfare were the chief causes of their eclipse, there was a third factor, often overlooked—the decision of the United States government to quiet their claims to the vast territory between Kansas on the north, Texas on the south and Arkansas on the east, on which it proposed to settle the so-called Five Civilized Tribes, Cherokee, Creek, Choctaw, Chickasaw and Seminole, in return for their ancestral homelands in Georgia, Alabama and other Southern States from which, by government order, they were to be ordered to migrate.

At the peak of their greatness as an Indian power, the combined Great and Little Osage Nations claimed the lands westward from St. Louis to the vicinity of the Neosho River, in Kansas, and south to Red River and the Texas border, a distance of six hundred miles or better if measured by the course of the Osage Trace. Few Indian trails were longer, and none was to become more commercially important to the white man. It seems unnecessary to say that the Santa Fe Trail was not an Indian trail, nor was the Oregon Trial.

Paradoxically, the importance of the great trace began to manifest itself at the very time that its Indian originators were being forced to relinquish it. Very likely it was beyond the comprehension of the Osage to understand that by government edict their lands were to be taken from them and given to another tribe. Very likely they didn't believe it would happen. The first evidence they had of what was in store for them—evidence they could understand—came when the Union Mission, twenty-five miles southeast of today's Claremore, was abandoned.

Other missions had come and gone almost unnoticed. But Union was the first Protestant mission established in eastern Oklahoma, and its medical services and freely given material aid had won the high regard of the Osages. Agents of the United Foreign Missionary Society of New York had obtained the formal permission of the tribe to establish a mission in their country in 1819, but it was not until February, 1821, that the missionaries and their families, twenty-two in all, arrived and work began on the various buildings. The site chosen was adjacent to a famous salt spring to which the Osages had been in the habit of resorting for years, to make salt. It was selected with that in mind, the missionaries foreseeing the advantage of having the expected proselytes coming to them, rather than the other way around.

Native salt-making was a long, tedious process. To increase and simplify production, and at the same time win the goodwill of their converts, the missionaries purchased a great number of cast-iron kettles and had them brought up the Arkansas River by keelboat.

Speaking of this spring and the operation there, Grant Foreman, the eminent Oklahoma historian, says: "This was a famous salt spring and was mentioned in the report of Major Amos Stoddard when, in 1806, he was cataloging the resources of the Louisiana Purchase. At this spring eleaborate equipment was installed, including a furnace more than a hundred feet long to be used for heating the large number of kettles needed to evaporate the water from the salt. Many people were employed in cutting hundreds of cords of wood yearly that were used for fuel in the furnaces." [2]

Hopefield Mission, near Union Mission, was abandoned at the same time, but it had a second life when it was re-established near the mouth of Cabin Creek, a few miles south of the present town of Vinita. When Hopefield reopened, the Reverend Requa and his wife were there alone. Not only were they without assistants, they had no Indians to instruct in the path of Christianity. The Osages were gone, and the Cherokees had not yet arrived.

The question of Indian removal had been uppermost in some of the Southern states, especially in Georgia, for years. It was basically economic. The Indians owned some of the most fertile farmlands. The white man coveted them and was determined to get them, which made it a political issue. The government owned millions of acres of unoccupied lands west of the Mississippi. These were offered to the Five Civilized Tribes at a few cents an acre, in exchange for the lands on which they had dwelt for generations. As the pressure on the Cherokees and Choctaws and Creeks increased, some were induced to move. Perhaps as many as two thousand of the Five Tribes had been relocated in what we know as western Arkansas and eastern Oklahoma (principally in Miller County on Red River) before President Jackson used his high office, in 1829, to demand that all Indians in the Southern states be removed to lands west of the Mississippi. A subservient Congress made his wishes into law the following year.

Once legislation had been passed covering the removal of the Five Civilized Tribes to the unoccupied lands west of the Mississippi, the government went ahead with its plans for creating the new Indian Territory. The nomadic or seminomadic Indians (largely the Osages) were forced out, and the great tract was surveyed and cut up into tremendous reservations for the Civilized Tribes, with additional millions of acres held in reserve for them. Military protection against the wild plains Indians (Comanches and Kiowas) was promised, along with many other benefits.

It was hoped that this seeming benevolence would serve the dual purpose of making the Five Tribes more amenable to being exiled from their homelands, as well as quieting the rising clamor against removal in New England and other Eastern states, where influential newspapers in Philadelphia, New York and Boston were attacking President Jackson for fathering "this cruel and shameful blot on our national conscience."

The Cherokees were the most powerful of the Five Tribes, and they spearheaded the resistance to removal. They held out for ten years, and when they finally capitulated it was through a schism that resulted in a tribal blood feud that took the lives of hundreds before it burned out, three-quarters of a century later.

The first recorded appearance of Cherokees, Choctaws and Creeks on the Osage Trace occurred in 1829, when a delegation of chiefs from those tribes, conducted by government agents and army officers, left St. Louis and followed the famous trail across Missouri to Chief Pahu-cha's (better known as White Hair) village and the Osage Agency on the Neosho River, between Parsons and Shaw, Kansas. This was an exploring expedition to enable the Indian visitors to inspect the lands the government was offering them.

Turning south at the agency, they soon crossed the Labette River into Indian Territory and reached Cabin Creek and the new Hopefield Mission. Another thirty miles brought them to Pryor's Creek. Turning east for five miles, they arrived at August Pierre Chouteau's trading post on the Grand (Neosho in Kansas) River at La Saline (called by the Osage, Grand Saline).

Here, within a circle no more than fifty miles in diameter was what well could be called the heart of the Territory. It included the cabin where Captain Nathaniel Pryor, the celebrated frontiersman who had accompanied Lewis and Clark on their historic exploration of the Pacific Northwest, spent his last days; Chouteau's famous post at La Saline; Sam Houston's Wigwam Neosho, conveniently located near the head of navigation on the Arkansas at the Three Forks, and equidistant from the landing at Fort Gibson from which a military road had been constructed to Fort Smith, across the Arkansas line. Fort Gibson, built by Colonel Matthew Arbuckle and the 7th U. S. Infantry in 1824–25 was the first and, until the War between the States had come and gone, the most important military post in all Oklahoma, save for the three years that it was deactivated.

For ten months a year, keelboats bound up the Arkansas from the Mississippi River had no difficulty in reaching the mouth of

Grand River and even the Verdigris, half a mile further upstream, where a number of traders established posts. It was the meeting of the three rivers, the Arkansas, Grand and Verdigris, that brought the term Three Forks into use. In time it came to include much of the surrounding region.

From the Kansas line to Fort Gibson, all the lands that the visiting delegation inspected had been allocated to the Cherokee Nation. It was by all odds the fairest part of the Territory. The chiefs from that tribe should have been pleased. It is not of record that they were.

Crossing the Arkansas and swinging to the west, the inspection party cut across the lands that the Creeks were to own. The way led south then through the vast region of hills, swamps and small rivers and creeks that the Choctaws were to occupy. With its rich bottomlands, it was not unlike their native habitat in Mississippi. Reaching Red River, the delegates and their guides went downstream by boat.

The expedition had been undertaken by the government in the hope that on-sight inspection by the headmen of the various tribes would lessen resistance to the removal. It seemed to have some effect on the Creeks, for in the following spring a steamboat came up the Arkansas bringing 780 members of that tribe to the temporary Creek Agency on the Verdigris, four miles from Fort Gibson. Colonel Auguste Chouteau had recently sold his Verdigris River trading post to the government and it was now the "agency." [3] (This was only the first contingent. It was 1836 before the Creek migration was completed.)

The Choctaws gave in when the Treaty of Dancing Rabbit Creek was signed in 1832. The Chickasaws, their neighbors, soon followed them. The fierce Seminoles had to be removed by the military. But nothing could budge the Cherokees in any number until bribery and political intrigue succeeded in pitting the Lower (eastern) chiefs against the Upper (mountain) faction. The government got the signed treaty it wanted, and in 1838 the tragic "Trail of Tears" of the Cherokee Nation began, winding through Tennessee, Kentucky, the southern tip of Illinois, across Missouri, northeastern Arkansas and finally for two hundred miles down the Osage Trace. Winter of a nature to which the Cherokees were not used overtook them on the way. Of the twelve thousand who were herded west, hundreds of the elderly and very young died of starvation and exposure.

Long before the Five Civilized Tribes were settled on their new reservations, the Osage Trace had become more than a strictly Indian highway. As early as 1822 the migration of settlers from Missouri and Illinois to Texas had begun. It was to continue to grow from year to year until the eve of the War between the States. In March, 1845, it was reported that a thousand white-topped, ox-drawn wagons had crossed Red River into Texas in six weeks.

In October, 1832, Washington Irving, the celebrated author, came down the Osage Trace in the company of Henry L. Ellsworth, who had been appointed one of a board of three commissioners "to visit and examine the country set apart for emigrating Indians, west of the Mississippi." [4] Two of Irving's friends were in the party, as was Colonel A. P. Chouteau, the undisputed lord of the wilderness realm. After being treated to his hospitality at La Saline, they went on to Fort Gibson, where a company of Mounted Rangers, under Captain Jesse Bean, was detailed to act as military escort to the Ellsworth party on its projected journey westward beyond the Cross Timbers, where Oklahoma City now stands, then south across the North Fork of the Canadian, the South Canadian and Red rivers. Ellsworth meant to work northeast from there, through what came to be called the Chic and Chock country (Chickasaw and Choctaw), and return to Fort Gibson.

This must have been the most comic and ridiculous official government junket ever undertaken. It accomplished nothing. Had Commissioner Ellsworth never left Washington, there must have been days when he could have seen more Indians sight-seeing in the Capitol than he encountered on the plains and prairies of Oklahoma. Luckily, he found a few Creeks when his command was almost at the point of starvation and its horses so played out that many had to be abandoned. There was no discipline: Everybody got lost; the hunters often disappeared for a day or two; the members of Ellsworth's immediate party, off hunting, sometimes failed to return to the encampment before midnight. As for the Rangers, they were raw young men recruited from the frontier farms and villages of Arkansas and Missouri who had not the slightest conception of military discipline. Being the neighbors of their officers, they regarded them with the familiarity of equals and companions. They had no uniforms or commissary and were unsoldierly enough to leave Fort Gibson without knives and forks.

The Ellsworth expedition has been called a military mission. Actually, it was little more than a hunting party, in the course of which many deer, several elk, many wild turkeys, a skunk or two and several buffalo were killed. John Francis McDermott says, "They saw not one hostile Indian, nor gathered any significant information about the terrain, nor marked a road, nor accomplished anything except to wear out a few horses and run short of food." But he hastens to add that far from being a meaningless comedy of errors, it gave us two imperishable pieces of Americana from the notebooks and pen of that great American genre word painter, Washington Irving: *A Tour on the Prairies* and *The Western Journals of Washington Irving*, the latter containing some of the material found in the *Tour* and much that is new.

Irving had left St. Louis on September 15, spent a month coming over the Osage Trace to Fort Gibson, and from there set out on the circular tour of the prairies with Ellsworth that ended with his return to Fort Gibson on November 8.

No one before him had tried to describe the great trace and the wilderness through which it ran. There is no better way to see and know it than through his eyes. Winding through the Ozarks, fording rushing mountain streams, penetrating virgin forests of hardwoods, are only the frame for more intimate pictures, a bivouac, for instance: "About 3 o'clock encamping in some beautiful place with full appetite for repose, lying on the grass under green trees— in genial weather with a blue, clouldless sky—then so sweet sleeping at night in the open air, and when awake seeing the moon and stars through the tree tops—such zest for the hardy, simple, but savory meats, the product of the chase—venison roasted on spits or broiled on the coals—turkeys just from the thicket—honey from the tree—coffee—or delightful prairie tea. The weather is in its perfection—golden sunshine—not oppressive but animating—skies without a cloud—or if there were clouds, of feathery texture and lovely tints—air pure, bland exhilarating—an atmosphere of perfect transparency—and the whole country having the mellow tint of autumn." [5]

The weather changes, and a violent thunderstorm breaks. "The rain comes rattling upon us in torrents and spattered up like steam along the ground; the whole landscape was suddenly wrapped in gloom that gave a vivid effect to the intense sheets of lightning, while the thunder seemed to burst over our very heads, and was reverbrated by the groves and forests that checkered and skirted the prairie. Man and beast were so pelted, drenched and confounded, that the line was thrown into complete confusion; some of the horses were so frightened as to be almost unmanageable, and our scattered cavalcade looked like a tempest-tossed fleet, driven hither and thither, at the mercy of wind and wave." [6]

Irving's pungent description of the scene on the morning of the Ellsworth expedition's departure from what loosely could be called "civilization" is photographic in its details:

"Having crossed the ford (below the falls of the Verdigris) we soon reached the Osage Agency where Colonel Chouteau has his offices and magazines, for the dispatch of Indian affairs, and the distribution of presents and supplies. It consisted of a few log houses on the banks of the river, and presented a motley frontier scene. Here was our escort awaiting our arrival; some were on horseback, some on foot, some seated on the trunks of fallen trees, some shooting at a mark. They were a heterogeneous crew; some in frock-coats made of green blankets; others in leathern hunting-shirts, but the most part in marvellously ill-cut garments, much the worse for wear, and evidently put on for rugged service.

"Near by these was a group of Osages; stately fellows, stern and simple in garb and aspect. They wore no ornaments; their dress consisted merely of blankets, leggings and moccasins. Their heads were bare; their hair was cropped close, except for a bristling ridge on the top, like the crest of a helmet, with a long scalp lock hanging behind. They had fine Roman countenances, and broad deep chests; and, as they generally wore their blankets wrapped around their loins, so as to leave the bust and arms bare, they looked like so many noble bronze figures. The Osages are the finest looking Indians I have ever seen in the West. They have not yielded sufficiently, as yet, to the influence of civilization to lay by their simple

Indian garb, or to lose the habits of the hunter and the warrior; and their poverty prevents their indulging in much luxury of apparel.

"In contrast to these was a gayly dressed party of Creeks. There is something, at the first glance, quite oriental in the appearance of this tribe. They dress in calico hunting shirts of various brilliant colors, decorated with bright fringes, and belted with broad girdles, embroidered with beads; they have leggings of dressed deer skins, or of green or scarlet cloth, with embroidered knee bands and tassels; their moccasins are fancifully wrought and ornamented, and they wear gaudy handkerchiefs tastefully bound round their heads.

"Besides these there was a sprinkling of trappers, hunters, half-breeds, creoles, negroes of every hue; and all that other rabble rout of nondescript beings that keep about the frontiers, between civilized and savage life, as those equivocal birds, the bats, hover about the confines of light and darkness." 7

Irving does not mention that Paul Liquest, Colonel Chouteau's brother, was the agent and that the subagency was soon to be deactivated. Very likely he knew, but he was far more interested in catching the life and color of the place.

"The little hamlet of the Agency was in a complete bustle," he noted. "The blacksmith's shed, in particular, was a scene of preparation; a strapping negro was shoeing a horse; two half-breeds were fabricating iron spoons in which to melt lead for bullets. An old trapper, in leathern hunting frock and moccasins, had placed his rifle against a work-bench, while he superintended the operation, and gossiped about his hunting exploits; several large dogs were lounging in and out of the shop, or sleeping in the sunshine, while a little cur, with head cocked on one side, and one ear erect, was watching, with that curiosity common to little dogs, the process of shoeing the horse, as if studying the art, or waiting for his turn to be shod." 8

Quite apart from demonstrating that Irving was as much at home in depicting the life and homespun characters of the frontier as the rustics of his native Hudson River, these charming glimpses of the day-to-day scene are more revealing than pages of historical statistics. Nowhere is this truer than when the expedition is returning to Fort Smith, ragged, half-starved, some of the weary horses no longer able to carry a rider. On turning a thick clump of trees, a frontier farmhouse is discovered.

"It was a low tenement of logs, overshadowed by great forest trees. . . . Here was a stable and barn, and granaries teeming with abundance, while legions of grunting swine, gobbling turkeys, cackling hens and strutting roosters swarmed about the farmyard.

"My poor jaded and half-famished horse raised his head and pricked up his ears at the well-known sights and sounds. He gave a chuckling inward sound, something like a dry laugh; whisked his tail, and made great leeway toward a corn-crib; and it was with some difficulty [that] I could steer him up to the door of the cabin."

Captain Bean, Ellsworth and several others had gone on ahead of Irving.

"A single glance within was sufficient to raise every gastronomic faculty. There [they] sat around a three-legged table, crowned by a broad and smoking dish of boiled beef and turnips. I sprang off my horse in an instant and entered this palace of plenty. A fat good-humored negress received me at the door. She was the mistress of the house, the spouse of the white man, who was absent. I hailed her as some swart fairy of the wild, that had conjured up a banquet in the desert; and banquet it was in good sooth. In a twinkling, she lugged from the fire a huge iron pot. . . . Placing a brown earthen dish on the floor, she inclined the corpulent cauldron on one side, and out leaked sundry great morsels of beef, with a regiment of turnips tumbling after them, and a rich cascade of broth overflowing the whole. This she handed me with an ivory smile that extended from ear to ear; apologizing for our humble fare, and the humble manner in which it was served up. Humble fare! Humble style! Boiled beef and turnips, and an earthen dish to eat them from! To think of apologizing for such a treat to a half-starved man from the prairies; and then such magnificent slices of bread and butter! Head of Apicius, what a banquet!" [9]

Irving was soon homeward bound, down the Arkansas by steamboat. Behind him he left a frontier that was to change beyond his recognition, and quickly. By the time the *Tour* came from the press in 1835, the Osage Trace had become a commercial highway linking the Midwest with Texas. Officers returning to St. Louis from Fort Gibson reported that daily they had passed hundreds of emigrant wagons and trains of heavy ox-drawn freighters bound for Texas. At the Three Forks, wagons were often backed up for a mile, waiting to be ferried across the Arkansas.

Heretofore, the traffic had been almost exclusively one-way, from north to south. That began to change, and by 1836, the freighting outfits were returning laden with hides, peltries, cotton and wool. Soon thereafter, herds of half-wild Texas mustangs, being driven north for sale on the Missouri market, were disputing for the right-of-way.

What followed was inevitable. In eastern Texas (western Texas was still largely a vacuum) there was a superabundance of Long-horn cattle. New Orleans was the only market, small and easily glutted. Though the way was long, the prospect of driving their surplus cattle up through the Nations to Missouri and finding a better market appealed to the Texans. As yet, there was no rail-road west of the Mississippi, and wouldn't be for another fifteen years, but St. Louis had rail connection with the East and was shipping livestock. So, for the first time, Texas cattle were pointed north. They were put into the water at Rock Bluff Crossing, a few miles below Colbert's Ferry on Red River, and by way of Boggy Depot, Limestone Gap and old North Fork Town reached the Three Forks.

They came by the hundred at first. It was a modest beginning but it heralded the birth of one of America's great cattle trails. Year after year, in increasing thousands, herds of Longhorns were to come bawling "up through the Nations," a colloquialism that became part of Texas speech. Though there were places where the trail herds cut away from the old trace for short distances, they always returned to it until they were as far north as Cabin Creek. There they originated a cutoff to the northeast that brought them to where the Pacific Railroad was to establish the town of Sedalia in 1860, a saving of sixty miles.[10] It quickly became the established thoroughfare between St. Louis and Texas. Troops passed over it, going and coming from army posts in Texas; so did government freighters. When the Butterfield Mail Route was established in 1858, it was the route its speeding stages followed.[11]

If ten years before Washington Irving saw the Osage Trace it had begun to lose its identity as an exclusively Indian trail, ten years later its character had changed almost completely. By 1844 it had even lost its name. In the conversation of men, by letter, in newspaper accounts and government documents, what had been the Osage Trace became the famous Texas Road. In places the scars it cut deep in the prairie sod of eastern Oklahoma are still visible.

3

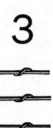

The Texas Road

NO OTHER CATTLE TRAIL played so important a part in the history of the country through which it passed as the Texas Road. It was not, of course, exclusively a cattle trail—which was singular in itself—but the estimated two hundred thousand Longhorns that were driven over it in the approximately twenty-one years in which it flourished fully establishes it as one of our great cattle trails. It was the one great highway of Indian Territory, and so strategically located that in peace and war it inevitably played a major role in the life of the country.

When the early Texas drovers brought their herds up from Dallas over the surveyed Preston Road to Red River and crossed at Rock Bluff Crossing, the trail north from the river was well established as the Texas Road. If in the last few miles it reached Red River over several different branches, those branches met and became one, long before they got as far as Boggy Depot, on Clear Boggy Creek, a matter of less than fifty miles. Why they invented a new name for the route they followed up through the Nations has never been satisfactorily explained. They labeled it the Shawnee Trail—and that too is a mystery, for it was never a Shawnee thoroughfare.

"Just when or how some began to call it the Shawnee Trail is uncertain," says Wayne Gard in his excellent *Chisholm Trail*. "The name could have been suggested by an Indian village, called

Shawneetown, on the Texas bank of the Red River just below the trail crossing. Or by the Shawnee Hills, which the route skirted on their eastern side before crossing the Canadian River."

No one has offered a better explanation. You will find the Shawnee Trail mentioned only sparingly in *The Trail Drivers of Texas,* which would indicate that it was never widely accepted.

It is worthy of note that the Missouri, Kansas and Texas (the Katy), built in 1872, the first railroad in the Territory, closely followed the route of the Texas Road. Today, U. S. Highway 69 affords the motorist a direct road to Texas, often in sight of the old Texas Road. Thus the Texas Road, the Katy and Highway 69, which enter Oklahoma together at its northeastern corner, cross the Red River into Texas together.

Though nothing remains today of Auguste Pierre Chouteau's headquarters at La Saline, it was too famous in the early days of the Texas Road, and before, to be passed by unnoticed. It is not enough to say that Auguste Chouteau and his father were the wealthiest and most successful Indian traders of their day.

The history of St. Louis and the Chouteau family are synonymous, for the Chouteaus were prominent among its founders, and Major Jean Pierre Chouteau, Auguste's father, the organizer of the St. Louis-Missouri Fur Company, usually called just the Missouri Fur Company, had established St. Louis as the fur capital of the country. Outmaneuvered by the redoubtable Manuel Lisa, the bold adventurer, explorer and trader, of Spanish ancestry, in his bid to have his exclusive license to trade with the Osages residing within the borders of what was then known as Upper Louisiana renewed, Chouteau and his son, August Pierre Chouteau, to circumvent the situation, induced three thousand Osages to move down the Neosho (or Grand) River to the great salt spring in the vicinity of today's Salina, Oklahoma, and trade with them there.[1]

A post was established on Grand River, despite the fact that when Missouri Territory was organized by act of Congress in 1812, it was given jurisdiction over a vast territory beyond its present borders. The location was ideal but it attained no importance. Back in his stronghold at St. Louis, the elder Chouteau continued to pull strings, and in 1817, Frederick Bates, secretary of the Missouri Territory, issued a license to trade in the name of Colonel

A. P. Chouteau and his partner Joseph Revoir and establish posts wherever they pleased. It was a sweeping victory for the Chouteaus.

Contrary to popular conception, Revoir, an Osage half-blood, had begun trading at Grand Saline, and he remained in charge until he was killed in 1822 by Indians as the result of a personal feud. It was then that Auguste Chouteau took over and began the extensive improvements that soon made La Saline the foremost trading post on the Texas Road.

Like his father, he was a man of dominating personality, a shrewd trader and organizer. Respected by the Indians and rival traders, he achieved the status of a wilderness potentate. Though he is usually accorded the title of colonel, it appears to have been only honorary. His wife, Rosalie, was an Osage full blood. By her he had numerous children.

It was Auguste Chouteau who shipped the first load of furs down the Arkansas and Mississippi rivers to the New Orleans market by keelboat. The venture was so successful that he followed it by building a flatboat capable of carrying up to twenty tons. It reached New Orleans safely with its rich cargo of beaver, otter, bear and deer pelts. The boat, of course, had to be sold for what the timber would bring. As other traders established themselves at the Three Forks, they followed the same practice, two or three often shipping their furs together.

When shallow-draft steamboats began to appear on Western rivers, the flatboat era ended. As early as 1826–67, steamboats were coming up the Arkansas to the Three Forks. In New Orleans newspapers, steamboats began advertising regular sailings between that city and what was called "Creek Agency" (the Falls of the Verdigris). They brought upstream a general cargo of merchandise suited to the Indian trade and returned with assorted furs and buffalo hides, the latter just beginning to have some commercial value.

At La Saline, Auguste Chouteau allowed himself all the luxuries obtainable in the wilderness. He was famous for his hospitality. Irving saw it in its glory. In his *Journals,* he says:

"He [Chouteau] lived a care-free life. His residence was a double log house with a large passage through the center, from which a stairway ascended to the second story, and the whole was covered with whitewash. A piazza extended across the front with buffalo and bear skins draped over the railing, while one end was loaded with harness, where cats and dogs were sleeping together. One room, the treasure house of the establishment, contained his guns, rifles and traps.

"In a large yard in front of the house a number of Indians were roasting venison under a tree; negroes, half-breeds, and squaws welcomed the distinguished visitors; negro girls ran about giggling while others took and tethered the horses. Numerous dogs and pigs, hens, flying and cackling, turkeys, geese, and ducks, all fat and happy, sounded a noisy welcome, and made the scene one of animation and color. The guests passed to their supper through the open hallway where Indians sat on the floor; and such a supper! Venison steak, roast bear, fricaseed wild turkey, bread, cake, wild honey, and coffee served by Masina, the half-breed sister of Rosalie, Chouteau's Osage wife, as curious Indians peered at them through the window." [2]

Irving was only one of many noted guests who enjoyed the hospitality of La Saline. Thomas Nuttall, the famous English naturalist, came up the Arkansas in 1819, and was delighted with the country and enthusiastically predicted that with the advance of civilization a great city would arise at the Three Forks. Others were of the same opinion. As far back as 1805, Meriwether Lewis had recommended the site to President Jackson for a trading post.

Auguste Chouteau died in 1838. "He was heavily in debt, and his slaves, stock and merchandise were mostly attached or stolen." [3] It has been said that his financial straits were due to mismanagement and his unquestioned extravagance. There were other reasons, not the least of which was the great panic that had swept the United States in 1837. It had hastened the decay of the Chouteau empire. Too, the once seemingly inexhaustible supply of furs was drying up. Locally, there were more Indians in the country than ever, but the Five Civilized Tribesmen were not hunters. Far to the west, the Wichitas, Caddos and other nonmigratory tribes were being so harassed by the wild Plains Indians that they had few furs to barter. It was now on the rich beaver country of the Rocky

Mountains and the Northwest that the attention of the fur market was fixed.[4]

At least Auguste Chouteau was spared the indignity of living beyond his time. His era was gone or rapidly going, and changes were coming with which he was not fitted to cope. By 1842, the Texas Road was feeling the impact of the thousands of Longhorns that were being driven north to Missouri and the fringe of eastern Kansas Territory. In 1849, La Saline was to be inundated by the hordes of men and women rushing to the newly discovered gold diggings of California. "So many people gathered here in 1849, in connection with the emigration," says Foreman, "that a post office was established at the place that year and called Saline." He continues, "After crossing the bridge at Salina, there may be seen immediately on the lower side a marked depression in the bank which indicates the approach over which wagons reached the ford and ferry boat crossing the stream years ago." [5]

This has become a locally accepted legend which ignores the fact that the river bank was very likely first broken down by the herds of northbound Texas cattle.

The story of the thousands of Argonauts who reached the diggings by way of the Isthmus or around the Horn is a familiar one, but enough has never been said about the thousands who converged at Fort Smith, Salina and North Fork Town and blazed a southern overland route across present-day Oklahoma, the Texas Panhandle, New Mexico and Arizona to the California gold fields. In the winter of 1848–49, while California-bound emigrants were organizing themselves into companies for their mutual safety on the trail and electing officers, another stream of gold seekers poured down the Texas Road, crossed the Grand River at La Saline and rendezvoused at North Fork Town, where an east-west trail from Fort Smith intersected the Texas Road.[6]

North Fork Town became the recognized jumping-off place for California. There the various companies joined hands for the long and perilous trek westward. This concentration of emigrants grew to the point that in 1853 the government established a post office there, called Micco, after a Creek chief. By then the route west was commonly referred to as the California Road or Marcy's Road.

A few weeks after news of the gold strike at Sutter's Creek was received in the East, small parties of adventurers had set out for California from Fort Smith. Some of them had been attacked by Comanches, Kiowas and Southern Cheyennes, their camps burned and horses run off. In Fort Smith, the gathering horde appealed to Washington for adequate military escort. The powerful Southern bloc in the Congress, which was urging that a survey be made of a route for a railroad from the Mississippi to the Pacific Ocean, made political hay out of the request by granting it at once, stipulating, however, that the military escort thus provided, in addition to safeguarding the migrants, should survey a possible railroad route.

To Captain Randolph B. Marcy, recently returned from a successful reconnaissance of west Texas and the Rio Grande, then stationed with the 5th U. S. Infantry at Fort Towson, Indian Territory, went the command. Early in April, 1849, he led an expedition of 479 emigrants up the south side of the Canadian, surveying the proposed railroad route as he advanced, and reached Santa Fe without what he calls "grave incident." Traffic over the California Road increased, and so did the depredations of the Plains Indians. The situation grew so menacing that the War Department hurriedly decided to establish a fort at a spot where it was most likely to protect the wayfarers bound for California. Again it was the experienced Marcy who was ordered to locate the new post.

The site he selected was two miles north of the Canadian, near the present village of Byars. He named it Camp Arbuckle, in honor of General Matthew Arbuckle, who as Colonel Arbuckle had built Fort Gibson.

That winter Congress appropriated money for the construction of a line of forts across Texas, from Preston, on Red River, quartering across the plains to Dona Ana, on the Rio Grande. In the spring, the War Department abandoned the California Road in favor of this shorter and protected new road. As part of the grand scheme, Camp Arbuckle was moved southwest to a point on Wild Horse Creek near its junction with the Washita and renamed Fort Arbuckle. In its new location not only was it to be part of the chain of military posts that were to be built, but in conjunction with

Fort Washita, it was hoped, it would be able to discourage the constant raiding of the Comanches into the Chickasaw Reservation to burn growing crops and farmhouses, destroy livestock and carry off Chickasaw women into slavery.[7]

Following the death of Auguste Chouteau, John Ross, the principal chief of the Cherokees and leader of the Non-Treaty faction, and his brother Lewis acquired most of the Chouteau holdings. Chouteau's passing had no effect on the growing importance of the Texas Road. Freighters and emigrant families bound for Texas were passing in an almost unbroken stream, and from the other direction came more and more herds of cattle. To avoid slogging through the mud and water that collected in the depressions during the spring rains, the traffic turned aside, and these turnouts often proved to be so advantageous that they were used in dry weather as well. In places the trail widened to several hundred yards.

By 1842, five and six herds a day were reported passing Fort Gibson. They were comparatively small herds, seldom more than four hundred head. The trail crews were small also, four or five men at most. The chuck wagon had not yet been invented. Some of the outfits carried their belongings in a two-wheeled cart drawn by a span of mules. Usually, a pack animal sufficed.

At the Three Forks, the Texas herds were intercepted by army contractors supplying beef to the military posts. Over the years, thousands of cattle changed hands there and ended up at Fort Gibson, Fort Smith, Fort Scott, in Kansas, and other garrisons. Thousands were sold, range delivery (on the spot), and were driven to Indian reservations for the government beef issue. For ten years or more it was an extremely profitable business for the Texans. But as it grew in volume, it began to be preyed on by border ruffians, so-called Jayhawkers.

It was a region without any semblance of law. A herd would be stopped and toll demanded, either in cash, which the party of the second part seldom had, or in cattle. The demand made was graduated according to the strength of the trail outfit to resist. The small outfit was helpless, and it was not unusual for a score or two of steers to be cut out and driven off by the thieves. The big outfits, who were strong enough to fight, and usually did, fared much better. The story is told of a whole herd being hijacked as it crossed the Labette River, on is way to Fort Scott, with the owner and his two men being lashed to trees to prevent their following. North of Big Cabin, a trail outfit found three Jayhawkers dangling from the convenient limb of a hackberry tree.

"Waste no time palavering; shoot first and make it count," became the rule of the Texas men. It curbed the stealing of cattle but did not stop it completely. Even as late as 1861, when the Pacific Railroad had reached Sedalia and the herds were being pointed there, they were still being stampeded and cattle stolen. Long before that, the trail drivers on the Texas Road found themselves caught in another and widely different trap against which it was impossible to fight.

Ninety per cent or more of the cattle that were driven up the Texas Road reached Red River by way of the Preston Road, a surveyed road between the river and Dallas. As has been stated, they were put into the water at Rock Bluff Crossing, where, depending on the stage of the unpredictable Red, they either swam or walked across. The crossing was a natural one. On the Texas side, a cleavage in the limestone bluff ran down to the river, and the low bank on the other side enabled cattle to walk out unhindered. When Ben Colbert established his ferry in 1852, cattlemen continued to use toll-free Rock Bluff Crossing, with a saving of twelve cents a head.

They had learned several years back that Benjamin Franklin Colbert was not the only member of the Five Civilized Tribes shrewd enough to match wits with the white man. During the time in which the emigrant Indians were getting settled in their new homes, they had been content to demand a steer or two for the privilege of permitting a trail herd to cross their lands. Charles Leflore, a Choctaw, appears to have been the first to realize that he could do better than that: the trail herds were trespassing and he proposed to exact a toll or fence them off. Limestone Gap was situated on his headright. Sending a herd down the Gap was a convenient and timesaving way of getting through the Limestone Hills. He put up a stout fence and gate and demanded a toll of ten cents a head for passage. The drovers protested, but they paid it.

It was only the beginning. The Tribal Council soon took this lucrative shakedown out of the hands of private individuals and made it the business of the Choctaw Nation. Presently, a toll of fifty cents was demanded, and collected, for passage across its lands. The Creeks adopted the same policy. The Cherokees felt justified in stepping up the price to seventy-five cents. Cattlemen railed at what they called the "exorbitant" tolls and tried to escape paying them but without much success. The Civilized Tribes had their own law and courts. Each of the big three, the Choctaws, Creeks and Cherokees, had its own mounted police, and they were efficient, especially the Cherokee Light Horse. To save time and avoid fines, the drovers paid the tolls. Coupled with the fees paid to Texas cattle inspectors and the inevitable losses a trail herd suffered, it made driving cattle three to four hundred miles and selling them in Sedalia for twelve to fourteen dollars a head something less than a bonanza.[8]

The life and death of most cattle trails followed a very similar pattern; they came into existence because of the driving need of stockmen to find a market, and their demise came when a better way of reaching that market was found. The Longhorns that were driven up the Texas Road introduced an element that was new and previously unheard of into the long-distance moving of livestock. It was to puzzle and bedevil the range cattle business, farmers with dairy herds, government officials, both state and federal, and to result in years of violence and bloodshed.

Trail herds had often broken down fences, trampled gardens and destroyed growing crops. The crime with which the Texas Longhorn now stood charged was not something that could be easily remedied. In his hulking carcass he carried the deadly germs of an infection that was fatal to native Shorthorn cattle, the Missourians claimed; where he passed or grazed, he poisoned the grass, and domestic stock put on it took sick and died in three weeks. The cattlemen didn't know what this mysterious malady was. No one knew, though it was given half a dozen names. This, of course, was America's first bout with tick, Spanish or, as most often called, Texas fever.

By 1856, what was known as the Fever War was in full swing in the counties of southwestern Missouri. One county after another

put an embargo against the introduction and passage of Longhorn cattle. Enforcement was too costly and led to too much cor-
ruption to be effective; inspectors could be and were bribed. Texas
cattle continued to be driven through Missouri. In 1861, a state-
wide ban against Texas cattle became law, and machinery was set
up to enforce it. Railroads were forbidden to transport cattle from
one county to another.

With Missouri closed to them, the Texans trailed their cattle
up through eastern Kansas to the newly completed Hannibal and
St. Joseph Railroad on the Missouri River. The financially shaky
Hannibal and St. Joe took a chance and hurried the critters across
the state to Quincy, Illinois. But that avenue was closed almost
immediately, for Kansas no sooner achieved statehood in 1861
than it outlawed the entry of Longhorn cattle.

Herds of Longhorns were seen moving back and forth along the
Kansas–Indian Territory border for weeks, trying to get through.
Turning back as far as Three Forks and North Fork Town, they
were pointed west for the booming Colorado gold camps, following the abandoned California Road up the North Canadian. It
perhaps was just as well, for in the increasing frenzy of the Kansas-
Missouri Border Wars, Kansas was no longer safe for Southerners.

Trailing cattle across the Indian Territory and through the
Oklahoma Panhandle to Colorado was not a trifling business. It
continued through the war years that were soon to follow. Taking
the average of the various estimates that have been made, no less
than 200,000 head reached the Denver region. Some of them were
Indian cattle, stock-raising having become one of the principal
pursuits of the Cherokees.

Before considering the role the Texas Road played in the War
between the States, an incident occurred in December, 1855,
which, although I have mentioned it elsewhere, is worth repeating
if only because of the calibre of the men involved. Down the new
military road from Tahlequah, the Cherokee capital, and on down
the Texas Road to Honey Springs, North Fork Town, Boggy
Depot and Fort Washita, came the recently created 2nd U. S.
Cavalry on its way from Jefferson Barracks, St. Louis, to man the
new Texas posts. There were ten companies, numbering 750 men,
800 horses, 25 wagons and 600 mules—a military caravan several

miles in length. And its officers? They were to become the flower of the armies of the Confederacy: Albert Sydney Johnston, Robert E. Lee, Fitzhugh Lee, J. E. B. (Beauty) Stuart, William J. Hardee, Earl Van Dorn, Theodore O'Hara, John B. Hood, Edmund Kirby Smith—and for the Union, the future "Rock of Chickamauga," George H. Thomas.

The coming years were to prove that seldom, if ever, had there been such a concentration of military genius and leadership in one regiment.

4

War on the Texas Road

ALL OF THE MAJOR ENGAGEMENTS of the War between the States occurred east of the Mississippi River. It was there that the great armies maneuvered, alternately advancing and retreating as the casualty figures mounted into the tens of thousands. It explains better than anything else why so little attention has been given to the struggle west of the river, particularly in Indian Territory, where North and South and their respective Indian allies waged one of the bitterest chapters of the great conflict. Homes and villages were ravaged and so much livestock destroyed that starvation and near-starvation were widespread.

The total number of men engaged could scarcely have been more than twenty-five thousand, but they spread destruction by torch as well as bullets. When it was all over, the Cherokee Nation lay desolate, for to them the war between the Union and the Confederacy provided the climax to the bloody and bitter feud that had divided the tribe since the days of the Removal. To dismiss the sanguinary struggle that was fought up and down the Texas Road as no more than a series of skirmishes of no real importance would be a gross error.[1]

With the beginning of hostilities, the Secretary of War recalled the garrisons manning the Texas posts. Riddled by desertions, which included officers and men who had cast their lot with the South, the remainder were marched north through Indian Ter-

ritory to Fort Leavenworth, Kansas. The next precipitate act of
the Secretary was to withdraw the garrisons from Forts Towson,
Washita, Cobb, Arbuckle and Smith (Fort Gibson had been
abandoned in 1857), the reason given being that it would be impossible to supply them. It was a foolish and disastrous decision.
It left Indian Territory open to the Confederacy and had a far-
reaching effect on the Union sympathizers among the Five Tribes,
many of whom felt they had been deserted and saw no way to turn
but to the South. This was particularly true among the Creeks.
The Choctaws, slaveholders themselves, and the Chickasaws were
solidly for the Confederacy. The Cherokees were about evenly
divided, and among them, as has been stated, it was a strictly
factional division that followed the line of the old feud between
the No Treaty Party, led by Chief John Ross, of the Upper Cherokees, and Elias Boudinot and Stand Watie of the Lower, or so-
called Treaty Party, in which hundreds of Indians had been
murdered.[2]

While the North did nothing to win the allegiance of the Five
Civilized Tribes, the South made constant overtures, promising
among other things that an Indian state would be set up; that they
should have equal rights with the whites and be able to vote in
national elections. All this was to be granted as soon as victory was
achieved. The Confederacy had an able advocate in Robert M.
Jones, a half-blood Choctaw and the richest Indian of his time,
who had been appointed Indian delegate to the Congress of the
Confederacy by President Jefferson Davis. Before leaving for Richmond, Jones arranged the coup that made Stand Watie the principal chief of the Lower Cherokees and gave him his commission
as colonel of the Cherokee Mounted Rifles.

The South found a brilliant, loyal and resourceful leader in
Stand Watie. He was born Stand Oowati in 1806, on the Coosa-
wattee River, near present Rome, Georgia. When or why he
shortened his name has escaped history. Many photographs of him
are in existence, usually showing him in his Confederate uniform
—a rather stout man of less than medium height, with a strong nose
and implacable eyes.

Chief Ross, knowing his life was in jeopardy with his enemy's
rise to power, retired from his capital at Tahlequah and found

refuge among the Upper Cherokees, his stanch supporters, and declared for the North, in return for which he was undoubtedly assured of the support of the Union forces (Kansas militia) guarding the border.

Fort Towson and Fort Washita became Southern strongholds. At Boggy Depot, the headquarters of the Confederates was established, and great quantities of supplies were gathered there. Texas troops arrived to join Stand Watie's Indians. Though white officers took command, Stand Watie ravaged the country with the Indian Brigade, a strong outgrowth of the former Cherokee Mounted Rifles, and took possession of Fort Gibson. Its psychological importance was great, but physically it was in deplorable condition, unfit to withstand artillery. Surmising that they would not be there long, the Confederate force did nothing to improve its defenses. The expected happened, and when a Union force of several Kansas militia regiments and a Missouri battery, accompanied by several hundred Osages, came pounding down the Texas Road, Stand Watie withdrew without risking an engagement. He retired to a position across the Arkansas River and built a stockade which he named Fort Davis for the president of the Confederacy.

With Fort Gibson back in Union hands, hundreds of noncombatant Cherokees known to be followers of the Ross faction sought safety there. It immeasurably increased the difficulty of maintaining the post, which had to depend on the supplies reaching it from Baxter Springs and Fort Scott, Kansas, for its subsistence. In a determined effort to cut its communications and starve it out, Stand Watie began attacking the supply trains moving down the Texas Road under military escort.

In engagements at Poison Creek, Bird Springs and Webbers Falls, he met with some success, but he overstepped himself at Cabin Creek, where the creek crosses the Texas Road, when he attacked a government train of several hundred wagons under escort of a regiment of cavalry and six companies of infantry. He had with him less than half of the full strength of the Indian Brigade. The size of the escort surprised him, but instead of holding off until he was reinforced, he closed in and got a mauling. A few months later, on July 1–2, 1863, while the fate of the Confederacy was being written across the continent in the battle raging at Gettysburg, he was defeated for the second time at the Cabin Greek Crossing.

A few weeks later, Colonel Douglas H. Cooper—who played a leading role in what has been called by some the first battle of the Civil War fought in present-day Oklahoma and the Round Mountain Massacre by others, in which 250 or more starving, unarmed Creeks, trying to escape to Kansas and the protection of the Union Army, were slaughtered and other hundreds herded back to the Creek reservation—was elevated to the rank of Major General, C.S.A., and named commander-in-chief of all Confederate forces in Indian Territory. With a few hundred Texas volunteers and a thousand Choctaws and Chickasaws he marched up the Texas Road to Honey Springs, the site of the village of Oktaha, on Elk Creek, fifteen miles south of Muskogee. There he built warehouses and filled them with supplies and ammunition.

Including the Cherokee Brigade, he had about four thousand men in his command. At Fort Smith, General Cabell was under orders to join him with another thousand men on request. Confident that he had troops enough to take Fort Gibson by assault, Cooper disclosed his ambitious plan to his staff and ordered Cabell to join him. Stand Wati opposed the undertaking. From a personal reconnaisance he knew that the defenses of Gibson had been improved and that the garrison had an abundance of ammunition. Cooper refused to be dissuaded, and as he awaited the arrival of General Cabell, Union scouts picked up news of the proposed attack. General James G. Blunt was dispatched from Fort Scott with troops and artillery, and making a forced march, reached Fort Gibson on the evening of July 16. Crossing the Arkansas River during the night, his command augmented by most of the Fort Gibson garrison, he reached Honey Springs and had his cannon planted and troops dispersed by daylight.

General Cabell with his Fort Smith column had not yet effected a union with Cooper. The latter, instead of dropping back and waiting longer, gave the order to attack. At eight o'clock, the battle was joined. The Confederates charged across Elk Creek but met such stubborn resistance that they were forced back into the timber that fringed it, from which, though suffering heavy casualties, they refused to be dislodged until noon. They began a hasty retreat down the Texas Road in the early afternoon, but not before they burned their wagons and warehouses. Blunt remained on the field, burying his own and the enemy dead.[3]

For the South, it was a disastrous defeat. Cooper was removed from his command and Stand Watie, raised to the rank of Brigadier General, was named commander-in-chief of all Confederate forces in the Territory. He reorganized the Indian Brigade and began an effective guerrilla campaign. But there was little to fight for. With the fall of Vicksburg and Lee's defeat at Gettysburg, it was obvious to all but the most rabid Southerners that the war was lost.

With Indian stubbornness, Stand Watie persisted, and on September 19, 1864, at the spot on Cabin Creek where he had previously met defeat on two occasions, he captured a Union supply train valued at $1,500,000.

On September 12, a government train of 205 wagons, loaded with supplies, left Fort Scott for Fort Gibson. In the train were an additional 90 wagons carrying sutlers' supplies, also four army ambulances and several score of ox-drawn ricks carrying three thousand tons of hay, the whole under the escort of 260 men of the 2nd, 6th and 14th regiments of Kansas Cavalry, commanded by Major Henry Hopkins of the 2nd Kansas.

With him, Stand Watie had General R. M. Gano and the full Indian Brigade, numbering about 1,500 Indians and Texans, supported by a battery hidden in the timber. The battle began at two o'clock in the morning and lasted until evening.

Although about a hundred wagons and some of the escort managed to break through the line of fire and reached Fort Gibson safely, it was a resounding disaster for the Federals, the worst they suffered during the war in Indian Territory. What the Rebels could not carry off, they destroyed, burning the hay, shooting the oxen and scattering the mules they could not use.

The Five Civilized Tribes were as weary of the war as the rest of the country. But it dragged on. There was little left that could be destroyed. Weeds began to grow on the once busy Texas Road. The only cattle driven up from Texas in the past three or four years had been for Confederate troops. Since Union gunboats had seized control of the Mississippi, following the capture of Vicksburg, it was the only movement of Longhorns out of that state. During the first years of the war, great herds had been driven to Shreveport, Louisiana, to be slaughtered and the carcasses shipped down Red River and across the Mississippi to feed the Confederate forces in the Southern States.

With Stand Watie pursuing a meaningless scorched-earth policy, the war ended with Lee's capitulation at Appomattox on June 9. It was not until June 23, two and a half months later, that Stand Watie rode into Doaksville and laid down his arms—the last of the Confederate generals to surrender.

But if there was peace elsewhere, there was none in Indian Territory. With victory for the North, Chief John Ross became the virtual spokesman for the federal government, and he did not intend that there should be peace among the Five Tribes except on his terms. The Cherokee country had been laid waste largely by the Choctaws. Determined that they should pay for it, Ross decreed that they must divide their lands with their former slaves, take them into the tribe and give them equal rights. The rich and powerful Choctaw Nation was forced to submit.

Though John Ross had his way about it, it cheated him out of what he really wanted—the crushing of his old personal enemy General Stand Watie, for the Choctaws rallied behind the General. Coupled with the support of the Lower Cherokees, it made him so powerful that Ross realized that he dared not touch him. And yet, six years later, when Stand Watie died suddenly while on a visit to his old home on Honey Creek, the Ross faction was suspected of having had a hand in it. He is buried in the old Polson cemetery, a few miles south of Tahlequah. Close by are the graves of John Ridge, John Ridge, Jr. (uncle and cousin to him), and Elias Boudinot, his university-trained brother, all three of whom were assassinated one night in 1839, at the direction, it was charged, of Principal Chief John Ross. Whether true or not, the murdering of the three men was avenged many times over. Giant Tom Starr, head of the powerful Starr clan and the father of Sam Starr, who married Belle Starr, boasted that he and his brothers alone had snuffed out the lives of twenty-one Ross adherents in retaliation.[4]

In the courthouse square in Tahlequah there is a statue of

Stand Watie. If he was a bitter foe, he was also a loyal friend. Whatever his shortcomings, he was a remarkable man whose name must forever be associated with the history of the Texas Road.

There was another, a man born of a Scotch father and a Cherokee mother in Tennessee in 1805. Though he was to remain unknown until his name was given to the greatest of all American cattle trails, his career as a wilderness and cattle trader began at Fort Smith, the Three Forks and old North Fork Town. He was honest, industrious, surprisingly well educated for his time and situation, and until the day he died, he had the respect of all who knew him. He was Jesse Chisholm.

He bought cattle that came up the Texas Road and trailed them northwest to various Kansas military posts, including Fort Scott, Fort Riley, Fort Harker and Fort Zarah. On at least one occasion, he drove a herd to Colorado. He also did some contracting of beef for Kansas Indian reservations. His activity as a cattle trader is usually overlooked, but there is documentary evidence that it contributed to some of the confusion (not yet dispelled) concerning the true and original Chisholm Trail, with which his name will always be associated.

Jesse Chisholm was in his mid-thirties when he began his adventurous career as a pack-animal wilderness trader, purchasing his trade goods from the cluster of frontier merchants who had established themselves at the Falls of the Verdigris, and then striking up the North Canadian, blazing a trail that some years later became more or less the route of Captain Marcy's California Road. He was soon trading as far west as today's Blaine County, Oklahoma, with the Wichitas and Caddos. On the North Canadian, a few miles from what became the town of Greenfield, he opened his first trading post. It was a temporary location, and he abandoned it some time later for a more favorable site at Left Hand Spring, six miles east of Greenfield.

That he became well-acquainted with the Kiowas and Comanches as well as the nonmigratory tribes is attested by the fact that at the government's great Medicine Lodge Creek, Kansas, peace conference with all the Plains tribes, in 1867, he acted as interpreter for the Kiowas, Comanches and Southern Cheyennes. Marveling at Chisholm's linguistic ability, Commissioner of

Indian Affairs Taylor asked him how many Indian languages he could speak. The modest answer was, "Only six." [5]

Though it is not to be supposed that they were his only contacts with the so-called wild Indians of the Plains, his repeated meetings with them at Edwards' Settlement and Trading Post on the south bank of Little River, near its confluence with the South Canadian, which flourished for years as the favorite trading place of the Comanches and Kiowas, were the most important. Built across Little River from the site of old Fort Holmes, which had been established in 1834 and abandoned several years later, it was for years the most important and prosperous post west of Fort Smith. Chisholm not only lived there on several occasions but married Edwards' white Creek daughter.

He was prosperous enough to build a new post at Left Hand Spring. A short distance downriver from it, he laid out a ranch, with house and barns. His principal business was now with the Wichitas. Their relations became so friendly that he was adopted into the tribe. That he was not motivated by any thought of material gain in affiliating himself with the Wichitas was amply proven in the years that followed. They hunted in season, but they also tilled the soil. Never a warlike people, they could not contend with the ferocious Comanches and Kiowas. Their situation worsened with the coming of the war and the withdrawal of all Union troops from the Territory for their loyalty was to the North.

Southern agents moving among the Plains tribes had no difficulty in whipping them into raiding the Wichita and Caddo villages, leaving a red trail of destruction wherever they struck. For those who escaped their wrath the only salvation lay in self-imposed exile from their lands. They gathered up their belongings, burned their thatched houses and retreated into Kansas. Jesse Chisholm and his family went with them. They settled on the Neosho River in Woodson County. This was in 1861. Three years later, they relocated on the rich bottomland between the Little Arkansas and the Arkansas, where the two rivers gradually come together. Again Jesse Chisholm moved with them.

"Early in the spring of 1864," says A. T. Andreas in his *History of Kansas*, published in Wichita in 1883, "the Wichita Indians and affiliating tribes, who had been driven from the Indian Territory in the winter of 1861–2, and who had made temporary homes in Woodson County (Kansas), removed from there and established a camp at the mouth of the Little Arkansas. The name of their camp was Wichita, from which the present city of Wichita derived its name. They remained until the fall of 1867, when they returned south."

What he is saying is that a new agency had been created for them on the Washita River, which the government had designated as the Wichita Agency.

"With the Wichitas (when they removed from Woodson County) came Jesse Chisholm," Andreas continues. "He built his house on the stream which derived its name from him (Chisholm Creek), and moved in with his family.[6] He also established a ranch between the two rivers (the Little Arkansas and the Arkansas), three miles above their junction. . . . In the spring of 1865 Mr. Chisholm located a trail from his ranch to the present site of the Wichita Agency on the Washita River, Indian Territory, distance of 220 miles. This trail subsequently became and is still known as the 'Chisholm Trail.' "

He is correct; it was the original and only real Chisholm Trail. But this calls for some explanation. That can come later. For now, let it be said that Jesse Chisholm never referred to the path he blazed as the Chisholm Trail, nor did any of his contemporaries, for it did not come into use until he had been in his grave for six months. The only name he ever heard for it was Chisholm's Wagon Road. His purpose in breaking out the road was to make it possible for him to get his wagons to his old trading post and ranch at Left Hand Spring and on to the new Wichita Agency. Cattle had nothing to do with it. For this we have the word of James R. Meade, at times his employee, partner, friend, the man who knew him best.

Jesse Chisholm was not a surveyor, not an engineer, but in blazing a trail through the wilderness he had the frontiersman's uncanny knack of being able to get from one place to another by the easiest and most practicable means. It is a tribute to his path-finding ability that when the Chicago and Rock Island Railroad

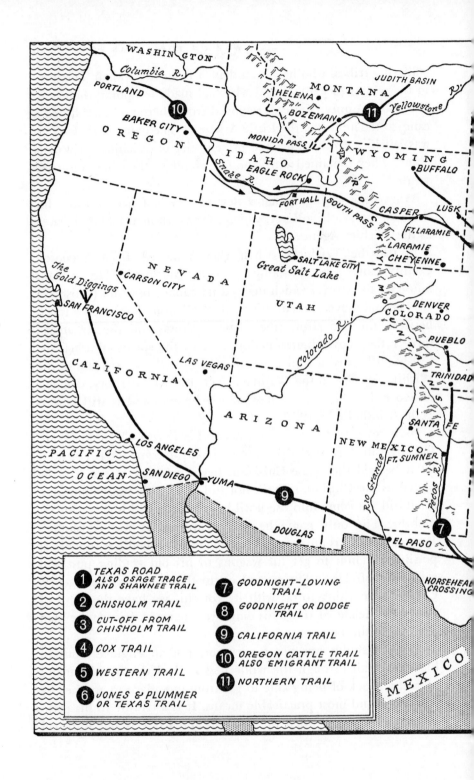

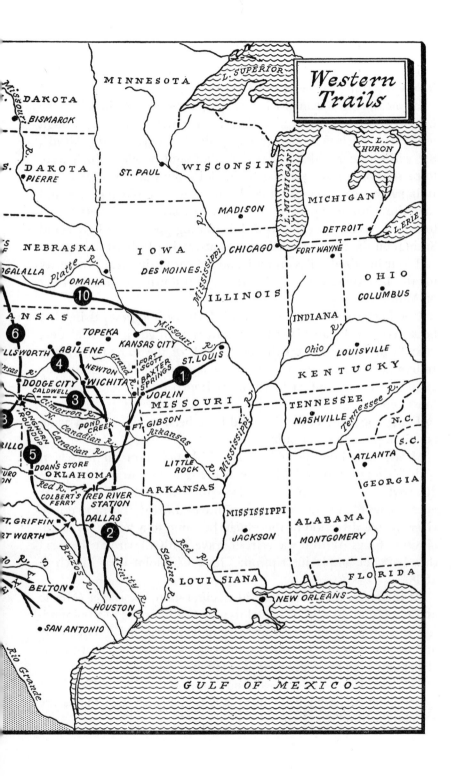

Western Trails

built south through Oklahoma in 1891, it could do no better than follow the trail that bears his name.[7]

In measuring the man's integrity and the respect in which he was held, it is worthy of note that the first wagons he got through to the new Wichita Agency carried goods belonging to Jim Meade, the white trader, valued at several thousand dollars, which were to be sold on a profit-sharing basis. Chisholm's bartering with the Indians was so successful that he soon was employing two and sometimes three experienced drivers to assist him in getting his four-mule teams over the road. His trading post at the Left Hand Spring, on the North Canadian, was attracting Indians from three and four hundred miles around, and he was tasting real prosperity for the first time, when death struck him down without warning on March 4, 1868.

Jim Meade's moving account of Jesse Chisholm's passing has been accepted by all historians. Andreas, who got it from Meade, says: "Chisholm died on the north fork of the Canadian in the Indian Territory March 4, 1868, of cholera morbus, caused by eating bear's grease that had been poisoned by being melted in a brass kettle."

Today the cause of death would have been ascribed to an acute attack of ptomaine poisoning.

Meade tells how he arrived at Chisholm's post on March 7, with his wagons loaded with goods for him, and found the place deserted, ". . . where a few weeks before there had been a great encampment." There were signs of hurried flight. Turning down-river, in the direction of the ranch, he came to a newly made enclosure of logs. Within was a fresh grave, with a board at the head that bore the smple inscription: "Jesse Chisholm died March 4, 1868."

At the ranch Meade found Bill Greiffenstein, the trader (Meade and Greiffenstein were destined to play leading roles in the founding and building of the future city of Wichita), a Dr. Greenway and several others. The Indians, fearing that they were about to be struck down by some mysterious pestilence, had fled.

"So Jesse Chisholm died, a good man, honest, honorable [I am quoting myself] who little suspected that history was to reserve a niche for him." [8]

The exact location of the grave was soon forgotten, and it remained neglected for more than half a century, until in 1930, Joseph B. Thoburn, the revered Oklahoma historian, Alvin Rucker and T. U. Taylor, former Dean of Engineering, University of Texas, after studying the published memoirs of Jim Meade, visited the Left Hand Spring and from Meade's description located the grave.

There, in December of that year, the students of the Greenfield High School erected a wooden cross in Jesse Chisholm's memory. It stood for nine years before the base rotted away and the marker tumbled into the weeds and high grass.

In April, 1939, Taylor interested some of his friends in putting up a permanent monument. It is a concrete monolith, the sand and water that were used being carried from the Left Hand Spring. It bears the following inscription:

> JESSE CHISHOLM
> Born 1805
> Died March 4, 1868
> No One Left His Home
> Cold Or Hungry

5

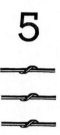

The Texas Fever Scourge

ALMOST FIFTY YEARS AFTER Missouri first barred the door against the Longhorn as the carrier of a mysterious disease to which it was immune itself but which was fatal to Shorthorn cattle, Theobald Smith, a young and unsung scientist in the U. S. Department of Agriculture's Bureau of Animal Industry, after three years of endless, original field and laboratory experiments, solved the killer enigma that was Texas fever—the greatest enemy with which the cattleman and the trail driver ever had to contend.

No one whose livelihood depended on cattle escaped its menace. Sooner or later, it rang down the final curtain on every north-south cattle trail in America. No matter where in Texas a trail herd of Longhorns was shaped up and pointed north for the lucrative Kansas, Nebraska, Colorado and Wyoming markets, the trail driver who had gathered them from different ranches and owned them (usually on credit) and his trail boss and trail crew were acquainted with the difficulties that lay ahead, with some or all of which they would have to contend. Maybe there would be dry stretches on the trail, without water for man or beast, blizzards, stampedes, thieving Indians; rivers might be transformed into raging torrents, cattle drowned and men swept to death at the crossings. They had the fortitude to face up to and usually overcome such dangers and calamities, but when state-wide embargos on Texas cattle stopped them at the border and closed the trails, there was nothing they could do. Trail driving was finished.

Outbreaks of Texas fever were widespread. Some were of epidemic proportions. Perhaps the worst occurred in Champaign County, Illinois, where several thousand Longhorns, purchased in Abilene, Kansas, were being fattened for slaughter on the same pastures on which domestic cattle were grazing. With the coming of warm weather, the native stock began to sicken and die. Newspapers screamed "Texas fever." Farmers, fearing they would lose their whole herds, hurriedly shipped their cows to market. They were already infected, and many died in the cars. In New York State, Governor Fenton appointed inspectors to quarantine all cattle arriving from the West and asked his legislature to ban the sale of Texas beef in the butcher shops.[1]

Tolono, Illinois, was the focus of infection. In that township nearly every cow of domestic blood died. All of central Champaign County suffered almost equally. The federal government sent out so-called experts to control the epidemic and discover its cause. It was a case of the blind leading the blind; they didn't know what they were looking for and would not have recognized it if by some miracle they had found it.

Considering the important part Texas fever played in the eventual closing down of the great north-south cattle trails, it seems pertinent to examine it at some length. It had many names: Spanish fever, tick fever, Longhorn fever. Call it what you would, there was no chance of your being misunderstood.

From the first, it was generally agreed that in some way the deadly killer was the harmless-looking tick that buried itself in the hide of the cow and turned its blood to water. Not one tick, but hundreds—thousands! But that was as far as agreement went. No one could explain why the adult Longhorn from the brush country of south Texas, though heavily infested with ticks, was immune to Texas fever. But why were the cattle immune? The best explanation advanced was that they had been attacked by the disease as calves. Having survived, they were henceforth immune. That was partially true. Stockmen would have been more correct if they had said that successive generations of the Longhorns forebears had been attacked and that the survivors had slowly built up an immunity that extended over a century or more, perhaps from the time that Andalusian (black Spanish) cattle had been brought to this continent.

How the disease was communicated to tick-free cattle by the Longhorns was explained in a dozen different ways, all of them very wide of the mark. When, in an effort to improve the quality of their cattle, some of the big Texas outfits imported white-faced Herefords and turned them out to range with native stock, they took sick in several weeks and were dead a month later. Again the old explanations were advanced. Some thought that dead ticks had dropped off the Longhorns on the grass and that the new-comers had eaten them and become infected. Others were sure it was something in the saliva the Longhorns left on the grass, or maybe in their urine or dung.

One of the absurdities that became widespread was that Brahma cattle imported from India and unloaded at Galveston (or was it Corpus Christi?) were responsible for Texas fever. Of course, there were hotbeds of Texas fever all through the South, from North Carolina westward, where Brahma cattle were never seen. That was acknowledged by those who believed in the validity of the Brahma theory, and their explanation was that the Texas tick had been born across state lines to the Old South by winds, birds or some other means. The dissenters shook their heads, but they were faced with a knotty argument they could not prove was fallacious, for the Carolina tick and the Texas tick were identical—which may make you wonder (and at the same time explain) why splenic fever in cattle came to be known from the coastline of the Atlantic to the Rio Grande of New Mexico as "Texas fever," to which by no stretch of the imagination was it indigenous.

When one Northern state after another began putting embargos against Texas cattle into law, no one was more affected than the stockman of central and south Texas. No one knew more about splenic fever than he, which was little enough, but he could not be talked out of his long-held conclusion that the tick was at the bottom of his troubles.

College professors, turned government inspectors, were telling him that Texas fever was a hot-weather disease. He refused to be-lieve it; down on the Gulf Coast, where it was always warm, his

Longhorns, who were lousy with ticks, were just as healthy in July and August as at any other time of the year. And yet it was a fact that herds that left Texas late in the summer and ran into cold weather before they reached Ogallala, Nebraska, where they were held for a month or more before being trailed north to stock the new ranges in Wyoming, were tick-free when they reached their final destination. It proved beyond reasonable doubt that the little red-brown killer could not survive temperatures that dropped to the freezing point.[2]

The Executive Committee of the Wyoming Stock Growers' Association made much of it and informed its members that Texas fever could be controlled if Texas cattle were not permitted to enter the Territory until they had been "wintered" for at least sixty days. "Wintering" Longhorns was not something new. Joseph McCoy, who fathered the Texas cattle trade in Kansas with his market in Abilene, in 1867, had used it as his principal argument to persuade the Illinois Legislature, which was about to ban all Texas cattle, following the epidemic in Champaign County, to exempt cattle that had been "wintered north of the 37th parallel" (the boundary between Indian Territory and Texas to the south, and the state of Kansas).

McCoy was afraid that another epidemic of Texas fever would spell ruin for the Kansas market. He commented bitterly that the "wintering" law was being circumvented by the basest sort of trickery:

"One of the provisions of the law was that the owner of a herd of Longhorns must appear before a notary public and swear under oath that his cattle had been 'wintered' somewhere in Kansas. They then could be shipped into Illinois 'under seal.'

"It was astonishing the following summer how many 'wintered cattle' arrived in Abilene. In fact it was difficult to get a steer or cow, four or five years old, without it having been 'wintered' somewhere. As to those 'certificates under seal', there was no trouble to procure them in abundance of a hatchet-faced, black-headed limb of the law. . . . For months he had been oscillating between beggary and starvation, and was only too glad of the opportunity to 'manufacture' certificates by the dozen or cartload, for a small consideration."[3]

How to control Texas fever had become the desperate need of the livestock industry. Until it could be controlled, there was no hope of eradicating the disease. Not only were the legislatures of Illinois, Missouri, Kansas, Colorado, Wyoming, Utah and New Mexico enacting restrictive measures, largely meaningless, into law, but it had become the grave concern of the federal government.

In the twenty-five years that had passed since Kansas became the hub of the Texas cattle trade, no one had come close to finding a solution to the problem. No matter by what trail a herd of Longhorns came north to market, it had to enter or cross Kansas somewhere. What Kansas did was the key to the whole mass movement of cattle.

Soon after Kansas was granted statehood, in 1861, it banned the entry of Longhorn cattle. That law was repealed a few years later (1865) and a new one took its place. But it applied only to the eastern counties. "West of the first guide meridian west of the sixtieth principal meridian," it read, all restrictions against Texas cattle were lifted. It cut the state in two about sixty miles west of Topeka. "By common consent everything west of Topeka was dismissed as 'no-good' country, semi-arid, sparsely populated, and it was generally agreed would never amount to anything. There were a few straggling settlements; Salina, making a brave effort to establish itself as a farming community, was the most important." [4]

Twenty years later, Kansas presented an entirely different picture. Settlers, homesteaders, discharged soldiers, had been streaming in. Land was cheap and easily acquired. In every direction the plow was turning under the prairie sod, and where in 1865 only a handful of domestic Shorthorn cattle grazed there now were thousands. The Shorthorn Breeders' Association had become a militant organization, and teaming up with the grangers, it had the votes to pass the legislation both wanted. Their common enemy was the Longhorn and the Texas cattle trade. On March 12, 1885, a bill for the purpose of quarantining the entire state against Texas cattle became law.

Though its proponents claimed it was not as all-sweeping as that, in effect it amounted to a total blockade, and it was accomplished in one sentence:

"No person or persons shall, between the 1st day of March and the 1st day of December of any year, drive or cause to be driven into or through any county of this State, or turn or cause to be turned or kept upon any highway, range, common or unenclosed pasture within this State any cattle capable of communicating or liable to impart what is known as Texas, splenic, or Spanish fever."

Violators were to be fined not less than $100 and not more than $2,000 "or be imprisoned in the county jail not less than thirty days and not more than one year, or by both such fine and imprisonment." Since the trail-driving season was encompassed in the closed months, it meant only one thing: total blockade. Sheriffs, under sheriffs and constables were authorized to arrest all offenders, and since they were to share in the fines to be assessed, the law was enforced. "Justices of the peace within their respective counties shall have criminal jurisdiction in all cases arising under the provisions of this act." [5]

At first, some of the big Texas outfits coming up the Western Trail to Dodge, or going on up the Jones and Plummer Trail to Ogallala, refused to believe that they couldn't get through. They soon discovered their mistake. The law had brought trail driving within the state of Kansas to an end.

With no more cattle coming from the South, Wyoming stockmen, with the cooperation of the Union Pacific Railroad, arranged to have Texas cattle brought to Ogallala by rail. It was a long, roundabout and costly operation, and it was flying in the face of what they had learned about the beneficial effect of subjecting Southern livestock to cold weather. By rail, Longhorn cattle were arriving in Nebraska in half the time it took them to plod up the long trail at twelve to fifteen miles a day. The result was ruinous. Here is an excerpt from the report of the Secretary of the Wyoming Stock Growers' Association:

"It will be remembered that when we separated in April, the experiment of bringing cattle from Southern Texas to Ogallala, Nebraska and neighboring stations on the Union Pacific was about to be tried. The first shipment unloaded in May and others followed for two months. From these points they were driven north and northwest. The result was disastrous and realized fully the opinion expressed by our Territorial veterinarian, Dr. Hopkins.

Within a few weeks the disease [Texas fever] showed itself viru-
lently among the Nebraska cattle which grazed near these unload-
ing points, and large numbers died. Cattle which were brought
west from the Missouri River and grazed temporarily in the vicinity on their way westward, caught the infection, notably one lot of
fifty bulls, all of which died within a month from the time of exposure to the contagion. The trail taken northward by the animals
which had come by rail to Ogallala became infected, especially
the watering places and bed grounds, and the herds which followed later, both importations from Iowa and herds from Northern Texas (the Texas Panhandle), lost large numbers. Later on,
the same route was followed unwittingly, and in the opposite
direction by many bunches of beef cattle going southward to the
railroad for shipment to Chicago. The time was very short for the
development of disease in these cases, yet nearly every bunch lost
from one to a dozen on the cars or in the Chicago yards.[6]

"To ascertain beyond doubt the true cause of death your committee sent the veterinarian into the field . . . and kept him there
for some weeks. . . . The evidence everywhere showed unquestionably splenic fever. This fever is disseminated in the dung and
urine of the Southern Texans and the virus or poisonous germ is
inhaled by the native cattle grazing over these excretions."

How wrong he was! So were the others who wrote learnedly
about Texas fever. In twenty-five years, no one had come even
close to discovering the   truth. The following by Dr. James V.
Hopkins, Territorial Veterinarian of Wyoming, is typical of the
nonsense that was being purveyed by responsible men. "Texas
fever," he says, "is an enzootic disorder, probably due to the food
on which southern cattle subsist, whereby the systems of these animals become charged with deleterious principles, that are afterwards propagated and dispersed by the excreta of apparently
healthy animals."

That such opinions were the rule rather than the exception is
reflected in the lengthy report (192 pages) of Joseph Nimmo, Jr.,
Chief of the U. S. Bureau of Statistics, a government document,
published in 1885. This *Nimmo Report,* very rare today, has been
accorded the distinction of being named "one of our four most
important cattle books" by Ramon F. Adams and other leading

authorities. Nowhere else has such a mass of information dealing with the range and ranch cattle traffic of the Western, Southwestern, and Northwestern states and territories been assembled. Since he is dealing with the economics of the cattle trade, he dwells at length on the losses due to Texas fever and the quarantine laws enacted to control its spread. It is when he expresses his opinion in regard to the cause and nature of the disease that he goes astray.

"Its cause and pathology are as yet involved in mystery," he says. "A few general facts of commercial significance, touching the manifestation of Texas fever, appear, however, to be pretty well established. . . . The Southern Texas cattle on their way north, in most cases, suffer a constitutional disturbance apparently attributable to change of food and climate, but it is said that usually they are not affected by what is distinctively known as Texas fever. This appears to involve the apparent paradox of their imparting a disease which they themselves do not have.

"The theory now generally held is, that the cause of the disease exists in a latent state in the cattle of Southern Texas, under conditions of climate and food which produce no impairment of the health of the animal, but that during migration to the north, such latent cause of disease passes off in fecal matter, and is inhaled or taken into the stomachs of the northern animals when they feed upon the ground over which the Texas cattle have passed."

He was only parroting the gibberish of men who were no better informed than he. Having said that the cause of Texas fever was as yet involved in mystery, he should have stopped there. He was a good public servant, intelligent and industrious, but what the country needed was a Leeuwenhoek, a Pasteur, or Robert Koch— and it found him in Theobald Smith.

"It was Theobald Smith," says Paul de Kruif, "who made mankind turn a corner. He was the first, and remains the captain of America's microbe hunters. He poked his nose—following the reasoning of some plain farmers—around a sharp turn and came upon some amazing things . . . to show why northern cows get sick and die of Texas Fever . . . why southern cows trail along with them a mysterious death for northern cattle." [7]

He had a bachelor of philosophy degree from Cornell University, a doctor of medicine from the Albany Medical College.

He studied mathematics and German. What he really wanted to pursue was science, peer through microscopes, to learn ways to paint bacilli, to breed them true, to shoot them under the skin of animals, to hurry off to Germany and cast himself at the feet of the great Koch, as other young Americans of his inclination were doing. But he had to look for a job. Presently he found one, humble and poorly paid in what de Kruif calls "the feeble, struggling, insignificant, financially rather ill-nourished, and in general almost negligible Bureau of Animal Industry."

Through the long, hot summer of 1888, Dr. Smith and his assistant, bachelor of agriculture Killborne, ran tests on the livers and spleens of cows that had died of Texas fever and were shipped to them packed in ice. To clean up after them, they had an ex-slave named Alexander. In an attic room of the old Department of Agriculture Building, facetiously labeled a laboratory, Smith sweltered with the others. In the spring of 1889, Dr. Salmon, the chief of the bureau, wangled an appropriation out of the department and declared an all-out war on Texas fever. From him, Theobald Smith learned what the cattlemen of south Texas had been saying for years, namely that the tick was the cause of the disease. Smith reasoned that if that was what men who had spent their lives with Longhorns thought, it was worth investigating. It started him on the greatest tick hunt in history.

He read the Nimmo report and everything else bearing on Texas fever on which he could get his hands. It led him to several conclusions on which, right or wrong, he based his continuing research. He accepted the theory that the tick was the villain; that the adult Longhorn was immune to its blood-sucking; that the insect, unable to withstand freezing or near-freezing temperatures, dropped off the animal on which it had been living, and presumably died after it struck the ground.

He discovered nothing to make him change his mind. It left him a long way to go. He was looking for microbes now, but he couldn't find them. He built himself an outdoor laboratory. It was just an open field outside of Washington that he fenced off into four compartments. One day seven thin but perfectly healthy cows from North Carolina were brought up the Potomac by boat and unloaded. All seven animals were infested with ticks. Smith and Killborne placed four of the cows in Field No. 1. The remaining three were put in Field No. 2. Healthy Northern cattle were brought in. Three were put in Field No. 1 with the North Carolina cows. It was only the beginning of the experiment Smith was conducting. He and Killborne spent three days picking the ticks off the three cows in Field No. 2 and destroying them. It was laborious, nasty work, the insects often squeezing to messy pulp before they let go.

When the cows in Field No. 2 were tick-free, Theobald Smith put two healthy Northern animals in with them. Now he was ready to prove whether or not the tick was the assassin. All he could do was wait.

August was only a week old when one of the Northern cows in Field No. 1 began to show ticks. In a day or two, they appeared on all three. They stood with humped backs and refused to eat. They were burning up with fever. Then one died. The next morning all three were stretched out on the ground, dead.

In Field No. 2, where (mistakenly) he believed there were no ticks, the two Northern cows remained bright and healthy. Smith had his answer, or part of it. But he wasn't stopping now. He removed the two Northern cows from Field No. 2, and while the floor of the barn ran red with his post-mortems, he watched the Southerners from which he and Killborne had picked the ticks. Ten days later, they were festooned with ticks—ticks so small that the two men had not found them. They were adults now. The females began to swell up with the blood they had sucked from the unmindful cows. Swollen to the point of bursting, they dropped off the animals to lay their eggs on the ground, two thousand or more, and die, their life's work completed. Smith gathered eggs and waited for them to hatch. In less than three weeks he had myriads of crawling, lively baby ticks in his glass jars.

In Field No. 2 he penned up the Southern cows in a small enclosure and littered the grass with his ticks. He knew they had to find sustenance in a day or two or die. Most of them perished, but thousands scurried up the legs of the cows to bury themselves in the hair, get a firm grip on the hide, grow fat, spend their brief life-span and die. Smith wanted to learn more, so he introduced his young ticks to a healthy Northerner. In jig-time the cow showed signs of Texas fever, and in nineteen days was dead.

The result astounded Theobald Smith. It convinced him that it was the hungry baby red-brown tick that was the killer, not the bloated adult. It sent him back to his microscopes; not to examine more diseased spleens and livers, for it was settled in his mind that they were only the effect, not the cause, of Texas fever. It left him with only one direction in which to turn. After four and a half years of closing in on the enemy, he had to risk success or failure on a guess, a surmise: it had to be a microbe in the blood itself that was responsible for the fatal anemia.

He took a healthy heifer and exposed it to ticks. Day after day he examined samples of its blood. As the heifer sickened, he saw the blood change color, lose its rich red and become thin and darkish. He hurried back to his attic with samples of the blood between little pieces of glass. Under the microscope it went, and sure enough!—here were twisted, jagged, wrecked blood corpuscles instead of good even round ones with edges as smooth as a worn dime. And inside these broken cells—it was fantastical, this business—were the little pear-shaped microbes!

Theobald Smith's report—you can find it in the National Archives—"showed mankind an entirely new and fantastic way a disease may be carried by an insect. Wipe out that insect, dip all your cattle to kill their ticks . . . and Texas Fever will disappear from the earth." [8]

Of course, dipping cattle in a trough filled with a solution of creosote is mandatory in most states today. The trail herds are no more, the quarantine laws against Texas fever have long since been repealed, and the menace it once posed no longer threatens the cattle industry.

6

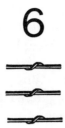

The Longhorns Leave the Texas Road

IT WAS SOME MONTHS AFTER the close of hostilities between the North and South before the Texas Road began to show signs of returning to life as an important frontier highway. The War Department had taken possession of and garrisoned all the old military posts in the Territory, with the exception of Fort Cobb, which had been burned, and the Texas forts. The Quartermaster's Depot at Fort Smith had to keep them supplied. Daily, army freighters rolled over the military road to Fort Gibson and down the Texas Road to Boggy Depot and points beyond.

They accounted for most of the traffic at first. By late fall, Sawyer and Ficklin's El Paso Stage and Mail line was operating again, with triweekly coaches for El Paso and San Diego. But where there had been a constant passing of emigrant wagons, with their canvas tilts, bound for Texas, there was only an occasional "mover." Though the war was over, the bitter hatreds born of it were very much alive. Whenever a Texas-bound wagon passed the Three Forks, it was safe to venture that the lanky grim-visaged owner, cracking his long whip as he walked beside his oxen, and his family were Southern sympathizers escaping from one of the Missouri counties that had been laid waste by Union guerrillas. Big as it was, there was no room in Texas just then for Yankee newcomers.

Nowhere was "reconstruction" being applied with a heavier hand than in Texas. The state was bulging with cattle as never before. During the war, very few of them had been "worked." They had multiplied. No one could say how many were running wild on the plains and down in the prickly pear thickets of the *brasada,* most of them unbranded. Fifteen million was believed to be a conservative estimate. Very likely, twenty million would have been a more accurate figure. Without a market, they had little value. Thousands were slaughtered for their hides and tallow, which had to be carted to one of the Gulf ports and shipped by boat to New Orleans. The owners received a net return of only three or four dollars per head. That men were ready to toil for such miserable wages was only because Texas was economically prostrate. In east Texas, the ex-slaves refused to work cotton; the state's only visible asset was cattle.

Texans had backed the South with their wealth, and at war's end they were caught with a lot of worthless Confederate currency; there was very little "hard" money in the state. What was needed were hated Yankee dollars. So, in the summer of 1866, trail herds of Longhorns began going up the Texas Road again. They were sent up with big crews, for there was every reason to believe they would run into trouble at the Kansas line. The ban against Texas cattle of 1861 had been repealed, but the new law of 1865 was just as strict. The Texans could pay the Indian tolls in cattle, and they were prepared to use the same medium of exchange to bribe border inspectors. What they didn't know was that the chaotic conditions prevailing in the southeastern corner of Kansas would be in their favor.

In a treaty concluded at Canville Trading Post on September 29, 1865, the chiefs of the Great and Little Osage tribes were beguiled into agreeing that "having now more lands than are necessary for their occupation, and all payments from the Government to them under former treaties having ceased, leaving them greatly impoverished, they were desirous of improving their condition by disposing of their surplus lands." [1] No time was lost in removing the Osages to a new reservation across the Kansas border, in Indian Territory. [2]

Another chunk of Cherokee country had been whittled off for a few hundred Delaware and Quapaw Indians. In the report of the U. S. Commissioner of Education for 1872, the number of Delawares is set down at 311, Quapaws 225—a miserable remnant of two once great tribes. The history of the Delawares is well-known; the Quapaws have been more or less neglected.

To understand to what low estate the latter had fallen it is necessary to go back to the days of the early French explorers, Joliet, Marquette and Charlevoix, to whom they were known as the Arkansa, living in villages at the mouth of the Arkansas River, which they controlled. In his *Historical Journal of a Voyage Down the Mississippi,* Father Charlevoix describes them as numerous and warlike, "the tallest and best-shaped of all the savages of this continent." Later, Antoine du Pratz, in his *Histoire de la Louisiane,* says much the same thing, remarking that "they were the first tribe that had succeeded in conquering the fierce Chickasaws."

The removal of the Great and Little Osages and the opening of their ceded lands to settlement was followed by a congressional act providing for the sale of these public lands (half a million acres), "to Aid in the Construction of Certain Railroads."

It brought several thousand settlers rushing into the fertile Neosho Valley for cheap land. As for the prospective railroads, they were slugging it out with one another as they raced for the border in a desperate effort to grab the fabulously rich government land grant that was to go to the road that first crossed into Indian Territory. The little town of Baxter Springs, that believed it was squarely on the border but wasn't, began to boom. For approximately twelve months it became, surprisingly enough, the most important cattle market in all Kansas. Even more surprisingly, most of the herds that went through Baxter Springs to northern railheads were Texas Longhorns. They did not come off the Texas Road. The Texans had detoured to the west for fifty miles and followed the Verdigris River into Kansas. When they drove into Baxter Springs it was with what were supposed to be "wintered" cattle from the Western prairies. They had properly notarized papers to prove it. Farmers, fearful of another outbreak of Texas fever, who dared to raise their voice, were threatened into silence by the toughs employed by the saloonkeepers of Baxter Springs, of whom there were no less than twenty-six. In fact, the town boasted that it had a saloon for every hundred men who set foot on Military Avenue, its only thoroughfare. Baxter Springs is seldom named among the lawless and much publicized cow towns of Kansas, but judging by the number of shootings and killings that occurred there, it was as tough as Abilene, where, according to the *Topeka Commonwealth,* "hell was in session twenty-four hours a day."

It was at Baxter Springs that one of the tragic misadventures of the war occurred on the morning of October 6, 1863.[3] Quantrill and his guerrillas attacked the small Federal garrison there, consisting of a company of cavalry and a company of colored infantrymen, while part of the small force was away on a foraging expedition. After a sharp exchange lasting less than half an hour, Quantrill withdrew, having lost two men and killing nine Federals. As he was withdrawing, Major General James G. Blunt, accompanied by his staff, a regimental band and a detachment of troops, on his way from Fort Scott to his new command at Fort Gibson, approached Baxter Springs. Mistaking the departing raiders for a welcoming committee, he was quickly surrounded and almost all of his small detachment captured.

According to the testimony of eyewitnesses (all of them prejudiced, it must be admitted), Quantrill shot all his captives, including the wounded. Blunt, who escaped with a handful of men, reported: "I soon discovered that every man who had fallen, except three who escaped by feigning death, had been murdered, all shot through the head. The brigade band, teamsters, and all headquarters clerks who were first captured were murdered the same way."

The Baxter Springs Massacre, in which ninety-eight men died, would not have occurred except for his blundering. Blunt went on, however, to prove himself a competent commander. It was he who defeated Stand Watie and Cooper in the battle of Honey Springs.

By trickery, outright skulduggery and a fanatical determination not to give up in face of seemingly insurmountable odds, the Missouri, Kansas and Texas Railroad (the Katy) was the first to cross the border into Indian Territory. It remains one of the most exciting chapters in railroad building.

Though the Katy was safely across the line and apparently had won the tremendous land grant (1,600,000 acres, or thereabouts) if it could hang on to it, it now appeared that the Congress had granted the Santa Fe and the Missouri River, Fort Scott and Gulf (the Border Tier Railroad) the right to build west through Indian Territory. The Santa Fe was no menace, but the little Border Tier road had been acquired by James F. Joy, the politically powerful railroad magnate who controlled the Chicago, Burlington and Quincy, the Michigan Central, the Hannibal and St. Joe and the Kansas City, St. Joseph and Council Bluffs.

His purpose in buying the Border Tier road was perfectly obvious to the officials of the Katy. The Atlantic and Pacific (today's Frisco) was one of the important cogs in Joy's blossoming railroad empire. Its rails were already laid this side of Sedalia. When his construction crews suddenly began heading west with a great burst of activity, it became plain enough that Joy meant to effect a junction with the Border Tier and use it to take him into Indian Territory. President Levi Parsons of the Katy and Bob Stevens, his general manager, realized that when that happened the Atlantic and Pacific would be right on their heels. The expected happened.[4]

The immediate objective of the Katy was the old plank cabin that stood on the level prairie between the forks of Big Cabin Creek.[5] There the old military road from Fort Gibson to St. Louis struck off from the Texas Road. Stevens intended not only to establish a major supply dump at Big Cabin, but to intercept the freight and passenger traffic coming up from Texas and carry it the rest of the way north on Katy rails. His plans received a jolt when he learned through his spies that the Atlantic and Pacific was "comin' a mile a minute" and meant to cross the Katy right-of-way at Big Cabin and shut him off.

Parties of armed men began to roam the prairies by night. Atlantic and Pacific location stakes disappeared. Miles back behind its end of track, rails were torn up, ties stacked and burned.

Andy Peirce, the A. and P.'s counterpart to Bob Stevens, realized without stopping to catch his breath who was behind the trouble he was having. He was willing to slug it out with the Katy on its own terms, and so was Joy. Several hundred St. Louis roughs were hastily shipped out to Indian Territory. The stage was set for unbridled violence. Raiding back and forth became a nightly occurrence, heads were cracked in pitched battles, men were killed and anything that would burn was fired.

The weather became abominable. Rain fell in torrents for days, washing out new roadbed and turning creeks into raging torrents. But with bulldog tenacity and the connivance of some powerful Cherokees, Elias Boudinot, Jr., and General Stand Watie among them, the Katy drove into Big Cabin and kept on going. It was never to be out of trouble all the way to Red River and Texas. Its construction crews fell ill of what was call the "ague" as they hacked their way through the sweltering bottomlands and swamps. There were constantly recurring difficulties with the Indians, but the major source of trouble was the hordes of renegade whites who established themselves at every new railhead to steal whatever could be moved, destroy what could not, and prey upon the graders and track-layers. Murder went unpunished, for it was a country without law.

At the time of the Removal, the government had written into the treaties that white men would not be permitted to dwell in the Territory. That had quickly become a dead letter, for which the Indians themselves were to blame for allowing white men to marry into the tribes, thereby gaining legal residence and sharing in government gratuities. Thousands did. Most of them were off-scourings of Natchez and other Mississippi River towns. Others, "wanted" men who were on the dodge, found a safe refuge until Isaac Parker, the famous "Hanging Judge," and his hundreds of deputy U. S. marshals began to dig them out and bring them to trial in federal court at Fort Smith.[6]

Usually, the advent of a ralroad brought civilization of a sort to the surrounding country. That was not true of the Katy. Twenty years after its completion, if you moved a few miles away from it, to right or left, you were in a sparcely populated, backwoods wilderness.

Of course, the Missouri, Kansas and Texas Railroad had swallowed the old Texas Road and made it little more than a memory. Where a railroad ran there was no need or place for ox-drawn wagons, speeding stagecoaches and bawling herds of trail cattle. Picture if you will the thousands of Longhorns, the hundreds of wagons piled high with baled cotton, that had been moving north for almost two years to meet the monster that was advancing toward them from Kansas, first at one railhead, then at another, the distance always growing shorter, until no more railheads were left and the iron horse was in Texas.

It was on Christmas Day, 1872, that the first Katy train steamed across Red River into the new, railroad-owned town of Denison. The venerable Texas Road was finished, but it did not mean that trail driving had ended. To the contrary, more Longhorns were going north than ever before, but they were crossing at Red River Station, a hundred and twenty-five miles west of Rock Bluff Crossing. For the past four years the number of herds going up the Texas Road had been dwindling. A new trail to the thriving Kansas market had been opened, and they had been turning to it. It had many advantages. Prices were better; there were no Indian tolls to pay, no Texas fever ban and no mobs of armed grangers to turn a herd back. The trail was well grassed and watered, and it was shorter. History was to remember it, for it was the famous Chisholm Trail, destined to be the greatest of all American cattle trails.

The crossing was wide at Red River Station, but cattle did not have to swim all the way. A shelving sandbar ran out from the northern bank. When they reached it, they could walk out. On the Texas side, a wide chute, boxed in by high walls, led down to the water's edge. Once the leaders were in it, a herd could be pushed across without much difficulty.

Usually the Red was just a sluggish stream that could be crossed anywhere if the quicksands were avoided; but following several days of heavy rains in the Wichita Mountains, to the northwest, it became a raging torrent that no trail boss in his right mind would attempt to cross. Some did. It happened more than once. Cattle and men were drowned. It was as nothing when measured against the not less than two million Longhorns and the thousands of trail hands that crossed there safely. Red River Station was the greatest of all cattle crossings. Never before nor since has the world seen its like. Through its portals passed the mightiest mass migration of cattle that history has ever witnessed.

Contrary to the impression given by most writers that it was just a lucky spot on the river, with possibly a store and a saloon,

Red River Station was an established frontier town long before the Longhorns came to overwhelm it with their dust and bawling. To trace its history, the clock has to be turned back to the time when France was in possession of Louisiana and the Spanish throne claimed everything west of the Sabine River. It may be, as tradition has it, that Coronado crossed the Red River there in 1514 in his search for the fabled Seven Cities of Cíbola. Its recorded history goes back as far as 1720. In that year, Sieur de Bienville, the Governor of Louisiana, sent Chevalier Charles Claude Du Tisne and an armed force up Red River with orders to "proceed to its headwaters and disperse any Spanish force you may encounter, occupying the rightful lands belonging to our sovereign and most noble King." [7]

Counting the twisting and turning of the Red, Du Tisne did not get within seven hundred miles of its headwaters. No one was to get there until the Marcy expedition, in 1852, located the springs from which it rises in Palo Duro Canyon. But discovery was only incidental to the French Governor's real purpose in dispatching an armed force up Red River. There was no established boundary between French and Spanish possessions. Through Indians, the Governor of Louisiana learned that Spain had built a bastioned fort of great strength at Nacogdoches (Texas), fifty miles west of the Sabine River, to guard against French encroachment, and further, were constructing several military posts on Upper Red River.

Du Tisne's force was small, less than a hundred, but they were seasoned men, former *coureurs de bois,* from French Canada. It was June, and with game and berries plentiful, they were able to live off the country. Staying close to the river, they trudged forward through an untracked wilderness in which they found no evidence of the presence of white men. They were four hundred miles above Fort St. Louis, the northernmost French outpost (about where Shreveport was to stand), when just beyond the mouth of Salt Creek they encountered two adobe forts and a corral of pickets over which flew the Spanish flag. The small, level plain on which the outpost stood was the field where one day thousands of Longhorn cattle were to be held prior to being driven across the river.

The twin forts, Fort San Bernardo and Fort Teodoro, were garrisoned by three hundred men, officered by Spaniards, the rest either Mexicans or Indians who had been recruited from the Mission San Antonio. Though France and Spain ostensibly were at peace, Du Tisne ordered his men to fire on the forts. It was returned with vigor enough to convince him that he was badly outnumbered. Even so, he might have carried the place by storm. He wasn't tempted to try, for although his men had few equals as bush fighters, out in the open they were of little account. After some sporadic shooting, he withdrew as night came on and began a long retreat down the river.

Looking back on the history of the forts, it would appear that Spain could have remained there indefinitely. But the post was abandoned a few months later and the garrison marched back to San Antonio, presumably to check the raiding of the Lipan Apaches. Wind and rain soon crumbled the adobe walls of San Bernardo and Teodoro, and a few years later no evidence remained of Spain's brief occupancy of the spot—only the name survived, Spanish Forts, or oftener just Spanish Fort. You will find it on many old maps, situated on the south bank of Red River, in Montague County, Texas.

White settlement of Red River Valley was slow. Some of it came from the South, but many of the families that had come down the Texas Road in their covered wagons had taken up land in the river counties and were scratching a living out of their valley farms. Where an enterprising merchant set up shop and attracted trade from the surrounding country, a settlement was likely to be born. By 1850, at least fifty families were living at what was known as Spanish Fort, or just "the Station." When it acquired the name of Salt Creek is not known, certainly prior to the War between the States, and it was so designated by the Post Office Department as late as 1873.

In 1861, the grassy swale on which the Spaniards had built their adobe forts became the scene of military activity for the second time. With the beginning of hostilities between the North and South and the withdrawal of U. S. troops from the Texas posts, the frontier was left exposed to raids by the wild tribes of the Plains. So many horses were stolen, houses burned, settlers and their families murdered, that a company of a hundred militiamen, half of them mounted, was mustered in at Gainesville, under command of Captain John T. Rowland, who was ordered to build a stockade, with suitable headquarters, at an advantageous location. The site he chose was the one once occupied by the old Spanish forts. It had the distinction of being the most northwestern military outpost of the Confederacy.

The men were rough, bearded frontiersmen, without uniforms and strangers to army discipline, but they had been weaned on a rifle. And as the old saying had it, "They could smell an Injun before they saw him." They surprised and annihilated several parties of raiding Comanches. This brought a measure of safety to the valley. Settlers who had fled to Gainesville began to return to their homes, at what they called "the Station." The term became so widely used to designate Salt Creek that the settlement adopted the name. Later, for better identification, it was changed to Red River Station.[8]

In its original location it was adjacent to the slope that ran down to the ferry that one-legged Henry Heaton, an old-time freighter, had established. When the big herds began going up the Chisholm Trail in 1868, it was down this slope or swag that they reached the river. In what was more or less a matter of self-preservation, Red River Station picked itself up bodily in 1870 and moved to a newly surveyed townsite, three-quarters of a mile to the east, on the high bluff overlooking the bend of Salt Creek. Its existence was brief, but such old records as survived the disastrous fire of 1884 show that title was taken to over a hundred town lots.

With millions of dollars on the hoof flowing past its door, Red River Station prospered for a time. Daily stage service to Gainesville was inaugurated. Jim and Molly Love's hotel became famous from San Antonio to Abilene. In Molly Love the cowboy had a friend, and tales of her hospitality and generosity became legendary. She fed them when they were broke and nursed them when they were sick. Returning busted after a spell of riotous living in one of the Kansas cow towns, their spirits revived as they crossed the old Rebel River (the Red). That was where the North ended and God's Country began, which oftener than not meant putting their feet under Molly Love's table again.

Most of the Texans who went up the trail were veterans of the late war. A few of them still wore some part of their old service uniforms—patched pants, a shabby jacket or battered campaign hat. For the first time Red River Station saw Confederate gray. "Hearts overflowed at the sight," says Glen O. Wilson, in the *Southwest Historical Quarterly*.[9]

Red River Station is gone, obliterated. In the cemetery on the bluff above Salt Creek old toppled-over headboards could be found, buried in the weeds, until a few years ago. They have disappeared, reduced by recurring brush fires to ashes which the winds have blown away.

Most authorities agree that 1871 was the peak year of Red River Station's importance as a cattle crossing. As such it had a comparatively long life, beginning with the 1868 season and ending with the virtual abandonment of the Chisholm Trail in 1884–85. During the years of the great Longhorn exodus from Texas, there was excitement at Red River Station, and tragedy, but remarkably forty years of research does not reveal that they were accompanied by violence and gunsmoke—a conclusion that is confirmed by that Bible of trail-driving, *The Trail Drivers of Texas*, a monumental collection of the personal experiences of the trail drivers themselves, gathered together and first published by the Old Trail Drivers' Association in 1920. In it you will find a hundred references to Red River Station, but not one of the trail drivers recalled having had any trouble there. Salty old Ben Borrum seemed to offer a satisfactory explanation. "The Station was a good place for a trail boss to weed out his troublemakers and turn them adrift. If we had any differences to settle, we waited till we got where we was goin'."

The one thing most of them recalled was the great tie-up that occurred there in the spring of 1871, when sixty thousand Longhorns and three hundred and fifty or more men waited for the rampaging river, "which seemed to be a mile wide with the brown flood lashed into waves as white as a wagon sheet," to become passable. It had been raining for days, a steady downpour. "Fully thirty outfits were stacked up there. Some had been waiting for more than a week, unable to cross."

The confusion grew as more and more outfits drove up from

the South. "Cattle were soon backed up for forty miles, the bosses keeping their crews in the saddle day and night, sleep forgotten, as they struggled to make good their claim to a little grass and breathing room."

Mark Withers, of Lockhart, Texas, was there. Young as he was, he was already a veteran of the trail and on his way to becoming one of the important figures in the Texas cattle trade. In *Red River Valley* I published his account of the Red River Station incident as he recalled it after a lapse of many years. It is a colorful and informative footnote to history, and with the reader's indulgence, I would like to repeat it.[10]

"We left Caldwell County with twenty-two hundred head of mixed cattle. Five hundred of them were mine. I had the rest on credit. It was the wettest spring I can remember, and we had trouble all the way, rain every day; we didn't know what it was like to roll up in a dry blanket at night. When we reached the Colorado, it was so high we had to swim it. We hit the Brazos about four miles west of Waco. It was on a big rise and we had to swim the herd again. I knew if we didn't run out of the rain we'd never get across Red River.

"We came up west of Gainesville and had just crossed into Montague County when we began to hear cattle bellering. It was far off, but it never stopped. It was like a wall of sound, two or three miles wide. It continued through the night and grew louder as we drove on north the next day. By landmarks I recognized, I knew that with conditions normal we were still two days from Red River Station. In the afternoon, we saw cattle ahead of us, two or three big herds and by the way they were spread out we knew they were being held. We stopped where we were and I rode on alone to find out how bad the situation was. I knew it must be the river that was holding things up, but I wasn't prepared for what I saw and was told. Some wild estimates put the number of cattle concentrated there at 75,000. I believe 60,000 would be more like it."

As for the river, he described it as a foaming brown torrent.

"The litter of heavy brush and broken trees sweeping by gave you the feeling that, for hundreds of miles, everything that grew along both the North Fork and the Prairie Dog Town fork had been plucked out by the roots and sent swirling and bobbing down river, leaving both branches scoured clean."

He moved his herd back two miles that evening to better grass, where it would be easier to hold. In the morning, he rode down the cut to the Station.

"A number of men were gathered there. Shanghai Pierce was the only one with whom I was well acquainted. He was doing a lot of talking, and he wasn't whispering. What he was saying made sense, as it usually did. He wanted everybody to drop back ten to twelve miles, arguing that if a run started, with all the outfits packed in together, there would be hell to pay and we would all get hurt—in the pocketbook. That no one was going to get across for days was plain enough, but nobody would listen to him. They had already been waiting so long that they weren't interested in dropping back and losing their turn in getting over when that became possible."

The rain stopped that afternoon and the following morning broke bright and clear, with a warm sun shining. Viewed in that light the Red looked less forbidding. For days, a little outfit from Refugio County, with an all-Mexican crew bossed by a "white" man, had occupied a favorable position on the open field at the head of the wide break in the limestone bluffs that opened the way to the river. To their right they had what remained of an old rail fence, now hidden in a hedge of *bois d'arc,* which made holding easy on that side. On their left they were somewhat protected by a cabin, built of pickets and now fallen to ruin, and the picket stockade that had once surrounded it, relics of the War between the States when the Confederacy had stationed the company of militia there.

In the late afternoon, when the glint was gone from the water, the Mexicans drove a small bunch of steers down the cut and put them into the water. A rider went in with them and tried to get them pointed for the opposite bank. The current caught them almost at once and began to sweep them downstream. A submerged log shot to the surface, struck the Mexican's horse and pitched him into the river. Frantically he tried to grab a steer by the tail, but missed. A second rider tried to save him. Both were lost; so were the cattle.

The weather continued fine, and the various outfits began to hope that they could put their cattle across in another day or two. They were hoping for too much. Without reason, a herd got up two nights later and started to run.

"It carried another herd with it," Withers recalled. "It was only the beginning. In no time at all they were all running and milling. It was after daylight before we got them held, and we had a tangle of cattle and brands on our hands that would be hard to describe. In my personal experience I never knew of a man on the ground being run over by a Longhorn, but when a steer went down in a jam like that he seldom got up.

"We all had losses that night, some of them were pretty heavy. The only way we could unsnarl that mass of cattle was to go to work as though we were on a roundup, everybody cutting out his own stuff and holding it at a safe distance. It took us ten days to get them straightened out. When it came our turn to cross the river, it was a millpond."

7

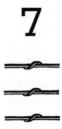

The Longhorn and the Mustang

IN THE PERIOD BETWEEN 1843–44 AND 1888, which covers the beginning and end of trail driving on north-south Western trails, every herd, with the exception of the cattle that were driven out of the Texas Panhandle into Colorado over the Goodnight-Loving Trail, had to cross Red River somewhere, and they were exclusively Longhorns—millions of them. Anything like an accurate figure will never be known. A government estimate, published in 1884, placed the number of Texas cattle that had entered the state of Kansas at between four and five million. My own careful tabulation, based on figures gathered from many sources, indicates that this estimate was overgenerous; at best the total was somewhat less than four million.

Car loadings at Abilene, Ellsworth, Newton, Wichita, Caldwell and Dodge City hold a surprise, establishing beyond question that of all the Texas cattle driven into the state, less than 40 per cent were shipped out by rail. The rest were trailed north to stock the ranges of Nebraska, Wyoming, Montana and Dakota, or went to the military posts or to Indian reservations.

Estimates of the number of range cattle in Texas at the close of the Civil War run all the way from six to fifteen million. The tax returns of 1867 place the figure at six million. That most cattlemen trimmed the figures they submitted for tax purposes can be taken for granted. Actually, few could say in all honesty how many head they owned—or claimed to own.

It wasn't only cattle that were pointed north. George W. Saunders, the famous stockman and founder of the Old Time Trail Drivers' Association, says that no fewer than a million mustangs were trailed out of Texas and sold to Northern ranchmen for range work. During the first years of the Kansas markets, there was no demand for them; they were small, intractable and not as desirable as native stock. "In 1871," he related, "we brought back over the trail 150 cow ponies and several chuck wagons from Abilene, Kansas, belonging to Choate and Bennett and W. G. Butler; but later, after ranches were established throughout the Northwest, those ranchmen learned that our Spanish ponies were better for their range work than their native horses and after that cow ponies were ready sale and the cowboys came home by rail or boat.

"Later there was a demand for Texas brood mares. This proved a bonanza for Texas ranchmen as our ranges were over-stocked with them and they were almost worthless. I drove 1,000 in two herds to Dodge City in 1884. It was claimed that 100,000 went up the trail that year, and more than 1,000,000 went up the trail from the time the horse market opened until the trail closed." [1] (That would be 1889, four years after Kansas had shut the door on Longhorn cattle.)

In a very true sense the Longhorn and the mustang must be regarded as inseparable; together they wrote a wide slice of American history. Without them it would have been very different.

The Longhorns have often been placed in the category of semi-domesticated animals, an opinion seldom shared by men who depended on them for their livelihood and who, presumably, were best acquainted with them. The mustang gave man an ascendancy of a sort over the Longhorns; he could herd and drive them but he could not break their will nor reduce them to the humble state of Durhams, Herefords and other breeds of range cattle. The Longhorn was dominated by its ingrained compulsion for freedom, and it could not be bred out. Invariably, if given the opportunity, he quickly reverted to his feral state. He could scratch a living where other cattle would have starved; his hoofs were hard, and distance meant nothing to him when he was going to water—often thirty-five miles or more. In his semiwild state, he was a savage fighter, fearing nothing that walked on four legs.

When man pitted the mustang against the Longhorn, it was a case of steel meeting steel, for in spirit they were two of a kind. The foremost historian and storyteller of the Southwest, J. Frank Dobie, has told the story of the Longhorn and the mustang with great understanding and feeling. In his *The Mustangs,* he dwells at length on the indomitable spirit and pride of the mustang, the true *mesteño,* from which came the Texas cow pony. "The best ones," he says, "were tameless, and swift, and proud. Their essence was the spirit of freedom." [2]

That was equally true of the Longhorns. To this writer, who knew them before their glory was completely gone and they had become museum pieces in the fenced pastures of rich men, Dobie's description of them stirs memories:

"Tall, bony, coarse-headed, coarse-haired, flat-sided, thin-flanked, some of them grotesquely narrow-hipped, some with bodies so long that their backs swayed, big ears carved into outlandish designs, dewlaps hanging and swinging in rhythm with their energetic steps . . . with their steel hoofs, their long legs, their stag-like muscles, their thick skins, their powerful horns, they could walk the roughest ground, cross the widest deserts, climb the highest mountains, swim the widest rivers, fight off the fiercest bands of wolves, endure hunger, cold, thirst and punishment as few beasts of the earth have ever showed themselves capable of enduring." [3]

Without them the Chisholm Trail would have had no reason for its existence. Before attempting to untangle the trail's muddled history, the history and background from which the mustang and the Longhorn sprang should be examined. They were exclusively of Spanish origin, and their forebears were first brought to the New World by Columbus on his second voyage and turned out on Hispaniola (Santo Domingo). The cattle multiplied rapidly in that lush country. Some were soon moved to Cuba, where ranches were established, undoubtedly the first on this continent.

In 1521, Gregorio de Villalobos sailed from Santo Domingo to the mainland (Mexico) with a number of young cows and bulls sufficient to establish a beef herd. It may be presumed that he took horses with him also. If so, they were not the first to reach the mainland, for Hernando Cortes had horses in his train when he began his conquest of Mexico, in 1519. When Cortes established his hacienda at Cuernavaca (horn of the cow), he imported a great number of cattle from his ranch in Cuba. Nineteen years later, when Francisco Vasquez de Coronado set out from Mexico City to find the mythical Seven Cities of Gold, he was accompanied by three hundred white adventurers, several hundred Indians, and herds of horses, sheep, goats, swine and five hundred head of cattle. The animals, gathered in the province of Jalisco, were to be slaughtered for food as the expedition required and were not taken along for purposes of propagation. Undoubtedly, Coronado's cattle were the first to enter what today is the United States. Mention is made of his having as many as one thousand horses with him.

Allowing for the number of animals that had been slaughtered, or abandoned because of exhaustion, and those that had broken away, he was still well-supplied when, proceeding eastward, he entered what is now Texas. It was the custom of the Spaniards, and later of the colonial Mexicans, to leave most of their male animals uncastrated, and spaying females was unknown to them. It meant that such as escaped in what we know as Arizona, New Mexico and west Texas were fertile. They should have propagated in their wild state. That they failed to do so was undoubtedly because they were killed off by Indians.

There can be little question but what the great French explorer, René Robert Cavelier, Sieur de la Salle, was the next to bring Spanish cattle into Texas in 1685, when, missing by hundreds of miles, the mouth of the Mississippi for which he was searching, he established his ill-fated colony on the shore of Lavaca Bay. Before sailing from Santo Domingo, he had taken aboard chickens, swine and cattle. It was his declared intention that the majority should be allowed to propagate. His colonists were soon starving, however, and eventually everything went into the pot.

Cattle came to Texas to stay with the establishing of the missions. Captain (given the rank of general by some) Alonso de León, Governor of Coahuila, made four journeys into Texas, beginning in 1687, bringing cattle and horses with him. In 1690, he and Father Damian Massanet established the missions San Francisco and Santa Maria on the Neches River, near the Louisiana line. They had several hundred head of branded, semidomesticated cattle with them. They were turned out to graze. Reinforcements from below the Rio Grande arrived that year. For the first time, Spanish cattle were firmly established in Texas.

The following year Texas was proclaimed a province and Domingo Terán los Rios was named Governor. In 1691, when he came north to take office, he brought with him a great number of domestic animals. The incessant raiding of Lipans, Comanches and Apaches brought the first attempt to establish a government to an end two years later. When Terán los Rios returned to Mexico he left cattle and horses behind, to wander ownerless over the plains and in the brush. They multiplied into the thousands. Twenty-three years later, 1716, when the Spanish began their first serious attempt to establish missions and colonists in Texas, the padres and their charges were amazed at the number of cattle they saw—old branded *mesteños* (mustangs) running with countless wild *cimarrones*. As used by them, the term *mesteños* applied to cattle as well as horses.

More and more missions were established, beginning at Corpus Christi and swinging around the Gulf Coast in a belt seldom more than a hundred miles wide. Some ground was broken and crops planted, but it was around the cow that their economy revolved. It was their only medium of exchange; it supplied them with meat, hides, tallow, rawhide and other by-products. It is not necessary to pursue the often disastrous story of the missions. That is something unto itself. What is important is the change that the Mexicans who gathered at those outposts of religion and civilization saw in the cattle they hunted. Even an ignorant peon, if he were past middle age, knew that there were two breeds of so-called Spanish cattle, and he could remember when there was a marked difference between them.

The "black Spanish" (Moorish) cattle were smaller, more difficult to control than the "brown Spanish" (Castilian). It wasn't their black color that made them more valuable; from them you got fighting bulls. In Spain the two breeds had been kept segregated. The *hacindados* had followed that practice in Mexico. Here, in Texas, where they had been running together for a quarter of a century, they had become one, with the characteristics of the black predominating in everything but size. These were big cattle, with long horns, something no one has explained satisfactorily. They were mean, would attack when cornered and, despite their seeming clumsiness, had the agility of a deer. When enraged, they had the ferocity of a grizzly. If you got a rope on one in the prickly pear thickets, the only way you could drag it out was to chain it to a tame ox.

"Black cattle" were, as might be supposed, predominantly black, and they were marked by what Texans (and Mexicans) called a "lobo stripe"—a stripe usually white but sometimes brown or yellow—running down the back from neck to the tail. The early crossbred Texas cattle, mixed in color, retained the stripe, not as marked as in the true "black cattle" but still an identifying stripe.

In attempting to trace the bloodlines of the Longhorn some commentators have stressed the fact that after Mexico won its independence from Spain in 1821, there was an influx of settlers from the United States into Texas, largely from Arkansas and Louisiana, who brought with them some scrub cattle, known as "Arkansas travelers" and "canebrake splitters," originally from British stock, such as Ayrshires and Durhams, and their strain was eventually reflected in the Spanish cattle of Texas. Since they were so few in number and their habits such as to prevent them from mingling with range cattle, it is to be doubted that they had any recognizable effect on the Longhorn. Half a century later the Brahma from India was introduced to give native cattle more weight. The cross accomplished its purpose, but it did not change the appearance of the Longhorn noticeably.

When the Moors invaded Spain, they brought the original "black Spanish" cattle with them. They were the aristocrats of the bovine world of Andalusia just as surely as the heavy-horned Castilians were the peasants. By welding the two breeds into one, Nature produced an animal better suited to the country which it was to inhabit (Texas) than anything man could have contrived. It matured slowly, and as a beef critter it was not at its best until it was seven to eight years old. Few will deny that the Hereford produces a better grade of meat, but until the white-faced cattle took possession of the ranges from Texas to the Canadian border and pushed the Longhorn into the discard, his reign was undisputed. How long this period lasted depends on when you have it begin. It ended some time before 1900.

In the fifteen years from 1821 to 1836 when Texas was under Mexican rule, its reservoir of cattle steadily increased, despite Indian raids and the thousands that were killed for their hides and tallow, which was the extent of their value. This increase explained why they were spreading out to the north and west from the country below the Rio Frio and the Nueces River and were being seen as far to the northwest as the Upper Brazos and the Red River country.

Naturally the percentage of unbranded, ownerless cattle increased. It became a range axiom among Anglos that unmarked cattle belonged to you if they were found grazing on land which you claimed. It often required some violent persuasion to make a neighbor believe it.

The Texas Revolution, which began on October 2, 1835, while the delegates to a meeting called to form a provisional government were still deliberating how to proceed, and ended with General Sam Houston's crushing victory over Santa Anna at San Jacinto on April 21, 1836, was followed by years of border warfare between Texan and Mexican cattlemen. Texans raided into Mexico to steal cattle, and the Mexicans retaliated in kind. It was a reflection of the racial hatred engendered by the slaughtering of the garrison at the Alamo and of Fannin's command two weeks later. A century was to pass before this hatred died out.

Texas was admitted into the Union as a state in 1845. The United States claimed the Rio Grande as the boundary with Mexico. This led to the so-called Mexican War of 1846–48 and victory for the Americans. When it was over, Texas was left with its old problem—millions of cattle and no way of disposing of them.

It will never be known when or where the name longhorn (with a lower case "l") was first applied to Texas cattle. Before the name became standardized, it had several variations. It could have originated in Illinois. Even before that state was crisscrossed with railroads, a thriving livestock business was concentrated there. It wasn't restricted to cattle. From three or four neighboring states horses and mules were brought in to be sold, turned out on the prairies to recuperate and then driven on to Ohio and points beyond. This activity was centered in Champaign and Vermilion counties, which placed it advantageously midway between the Chicago and Cincinnati markets.

It was to Champaign County that Thomas Candy Ponting, Jr., Isaac Funk, Edward Piper and other dealers drove the cattle they had purchased west of the Mississippi. Who arrived with the first Texas cattle is not known. Very likely it was Ponting, for he returned to Baxter Springs, Kansas, repeatedly to buy cattle. In 1846 Piper arrived with a herd of a thousand "long-horned" cattle that had come up the Texas Road and which he had bought at Baxter Springs. Usage soon shortened it to longhorn—always prefixed with Texas. This was long before the War between the States, which Mr. Dobie cites as about the time the name Longhorn came into general use. He, of course, uses the capital "L," which designates it as a distinct breed, which it was, in quite the same way as the Hereford, the Durham and others. If that is the point he makes, I quite agree with him.

The mustang (Texas cow pony) has never achieved that distinction. He responded favorably to the new grass he ate, the water he drank and the air he breathed—perhaps in one or all he found some chemical element that fortified him—and quickly became as indigenous to his environment as the Longhorn.

The ancestry of the Texas cow pony is not difficult to trace. When the Moslems crossed the Strait of Gibraltar in 710 to conquer the Spaniards and to hold dominion for seven centuries, they rode the finest horses ever seen on the Iberian Peninsula. Their mounts were part Arabian and part Barb, both hot-blooded breeds. The latter, sometimes called the African Arabian, from the Barbary States, was somewhat larger than the true Arabian, but he was his equal in fire, intelligence, speed and stamina. Though in appearance the Arabian purebred was his superior, they had many characteristics in common.

At no time did the Moors have more than nominal control of the entire Iberian Peninsula. In the Basque provinces of the mountainous north, the native Spanish horse, the *criolla,* continued to be bred. They were mostly duns, smaller than the Moorish horse, but agile and sturdy. To say that they were from the north of Europe, of Visigoth (west German) origin, is very likely true. The Visigoths were in Spain as allies of the Romans for centuries prior to the Moslem invasion.

The centuries of occupation by the Moors were marked by almost continuous war. It was fought exclusively on horseback, and the superiority of the Moorish horses was very often the margin of victory. It can be presumed that to maintain that advantage the Moors did their best to keep their Arab-Barb stock from falling into the hands of the Spaniards. The nature of the conflict made that impossible. Cross-breeding of the Arab-Barb stock with the dun *criolla* became inevitable. It improved the latter, and with the passing of the centuries the half-breed *mestizo* became the true Spanish horse.

Eventually the Mohammedan empire in Spain began to crumble, due as much to dissensions among their own princes as to the war the Catholic sovereigns, Ferdinand and Isabella, waged against them. In their last extremity the Moors' one remaining stronghold, the state of Granada, was subjugated, and they were forced to turn their faces back to Africa. It was January 2, 1492, the year that Columbus sailed on his first voyage to the New World, an event that, stripped of the romantic nonsense with which legend had cloaked it, was undertaken by the Crown in the desperate hope that the voyage might, if successful, relieve the deplorable condition of the monarchy's treasury. The rest is history. The following year, on his second voyage, the horses that Columbus brought to Hispaniola were the Spanish *mestizos,* and no breed could have been better adapted for the role it was to play in the years that followed.

The *mestizos'* performance as a cow pony needs no adjectives. That is the role in which it is celebrated in song and story—so much as to largely obscure the fact that this horse was the catalyst that changed the course of history of the American West. He gave the Apaches and the Plains Indians mobility, without which they would have been quickly subdued by the white man. That the fierce Apaches, had they been horseless, would have been more troublesome than the semisedentary Navajos, who greatly outnumbered them, can be doubted. Likewise the tribes of the great

Sioux Nation would have been chained to the watercourses without the horse.

In 1539, a year prior to the Coronado expedition, Ferdinand de Soto, Governor of Cuba and former Governor of Peru, had landed in Florida from Cuba with "a roving company of gallant freebooters, in search of fortune," numbering about six hundred, a third of whom were mounted, the chronicle stating that they had "about two hundred horses and a drove of hogs." Eleven years before that, Pánfilo Narváez came ashore in Florida with a small party of adventurers, among whom was the celebrated Cabeza de Vaca, and some forty horses.[4] Disaster overtook them. Hostile Indians killed most of their horses. Retreating to the coast, slaughtering their own animals to avert starvation until none or only one, as some have it, were left, Narváez and his men sailed away, skirting the Gulf Coast as far as the Mississippi.

De Soto's fate was equally disastrous. He was searching for gold, which he failed to find; instead, disease and Indian arrows cost him half his force. They ate their hogs and tried to save their horses, but most of them wore out and had to be killed. Indians got some and, presumably, others broke away. If the few horses that won their freedom were able to survive and multiply, their offspring never became numerous enough to overrun the Gulf Coast regions of Florida, Alabama and Mississippi.

After two years of aimless wandering, lost beyond his comprehension, De Soto led his men, less than a hundred by now, and the few emaciated horses left to him, out of a cypress forest to the muddy bank of the Father of Waters. History records him as its discoverer. The Spaniards crossed the great river on rafts, and after another two years of fruitless looking for treasure, a few of De Soto's ragged followers reached Mexico City. They had no horses and had not left any living ones behind. De Soto was not with them. He had died, and his body, weighted with stones, had been lowered into the depths of the river with which his name will always be associated.[5]

It was much more than mobility that the horse gave the Plains Indians and all the other Western tribes with the exception of the Indians of California, who never favored it, though it had been introduced into that country at an early date by the *conquista-*

dores. What it really did was to change the whole pattern of their lives. At first they hunted and stole them for meat. When Juan de Oñate took possession of New Mexico in 1598 under a grant to colonize it at his own expense and established his capital at San Juan pueblo, he brought an immense number of cattle, horses, sheep and goats with him. The horses soon began to disappear. Imitating the Spaniards, the Apaches mounted them and rode them to their camps, where they were killed and roasted whole.

The Apache never lost his taste for horseflesh. But he began putting them to better use when he discovered that the horse gave him mastery over the buffalo. Just when the Comanches, Pawnees, Kiowas and Southern Cheyennes acquired the horse is not known. It may have been a century later, but it is an established fact that within the next two hundred years, the Sioux, Crows, Blackfeet and other northern tribes were mounted.

The horse became the Indian's most valuable possession; he rode it into battle, counted his wealth by the size of his pony herd. To give himself greater honor, he engaged in horse-stealing expeditions against enemy tribes. He knew no sport to compare with it.

His favorite horse was his war horse; he rode it only when he went into battle. Early commentators mention that the Pawnees, to protect their prized horses armored them with a breast shield of dried buffalo hide.

The calico or paint pony, highly prized by the Sioux and other Plains tribes for its gaudy coloring, undoubtedly originated with the Nez Percé, who shared the great valley between the Cascade Mountains and the Bitter Roots with the Palouse, Flathead, Cayuse and Walla Walla. Of Shahaptian stock, the Nez Percé were the most intelligent of all Indians living west of the Continental Divide.[6] They were the first native Americans to practice selectivity in the breeding of their horses, which could be counted in the thousands. In their Journals, Lewis and Clark call the horses of the Nez Percé the finest they had seen.

Just when the Nez Percé began breeding for color is not known, but the results were amazing. Their basic stock was the Spanish *mestizo.* It may have been their only stock, though the possibility exists that there was an infiltration of British blood from the horses that Hudson's Bay Company brought into the Oregon country. More likely the colors and combinations of colors that were produced were a throwback to the ancient Barb strain in the *mestizo*. In the 1840's, the Americans streaming into Oregon "were struck by the looks of some of these Indian ponies, golden, duns splotched with white patches."

The trailing of Oregon cattle across Idaho to Wyoming (about which more will be said later) began in the early 1880's. John K. Rollinson, in his excellent *Wyoming Cattle Trails,* records a conversation with Jack Porter, a salty Wyoming cowboy, who was in Baker City, Oregon, in 1883 and about to head east with a large herd.

"A couple or three of us, myself included, had bought and traded around, and each got two or three Nez Percé [pronounced "nezpurse" by him you may be sure] Indian ponies, which were plentiful about the Grande Ronde and Powder River (Oregon) valleys. . . . These Nez Percé horses were very good animals, in fact, very superior Indian horses. They were prettily built, had good endurance, good dispositions, and were generally 'showy,' as they were appaloosas with coats of various colors and spots of different shades. They were buckskins with dark markings, and zebra marks on the withers and legs, as well as pinto-marked horses of different coats and different colored spots or markings. There were also palomillos and palominos. . . . A rangeman would rarely ever buy a horse for his cavvy unless it was a 'straight-colored' one. Our cavvy, like most others, was composed of bays, browns, grays, sorrels, blacks, whites and roans. A dun or a buskskin were considered white men's horses, too." [7]

Fancy-colored ponies were to give to your best girl or sell to a Cheyenne bartender.

8

The Chisholm Trail

IF YOU HAVE REASON TO BELIEVE that you know what you are writing about, it would appear to be a very simple matter to say where a trail began and where it ended without being contradicted. That is not the case when the trail happens to be the Chisholm Trail. It has been moved east and west and extended north and south in so many so-called authentic accounts that it is impossible to follow their conflicting geography. The initial source of much of the misinformation was the old-time trail drivers themselves.

It began with the first convention of the Old Time Trail Drivers' Association, held in Houston, Texas, 1916. I quote from the secretary's report: "The Association went into a discussion of the origin, start, route and terminus of the 'Old Chisholm Trail.' There was found to be a considerable difference of opinion as to details pertaining to this famous historic highway, and it was finally decided to leave the subject for further discussion at the 1917 convention."

A committee was appointed to pursue the matter, and the following year a report was made by W. P. Anderson, the Kansas Pacific R. R. agent at Abilene in 1868–89, which was accepted and endorsed by the association, and I shall never cease to wonder why. How men, who had been going up the trail two, or even three, times annually for a dozen years and should have been acquainted with every mile of it, could have given Anderson's letter their approval passes belief. It is a mishmash of errors, even to Chisholm's name, which is given as John, not Jesse. Anderson has the trail beginning at the mouth of the Grand River (the Three Forks), which is a hundred and sixty miles east of the Chisholm Trail to the Kansas market. He makes an east-west trail of it, running all the way out to Colorado. He even has it crossing Red River at Doan's Store, far to the west of Red River Station. The trail that crossed there was the Western Trail to Dodge City.

Here is Anderson's report, in part:

"The original Chisholm Trail was named after John Chisholm who was a Cherokee cattle trader, who supplied the government frontier posts with their cattle supply in the early part of the occupation of frontier posts and during the Civil War."

The above is largely untrue; Chisholm was not primarily a cattle trader. There is no record of his having supplied cattle to the military posts in Indian Territory.

To continue with Anderson:

"The first diversion from this trail was where the trail left the Sedalia trail for Baxter Springs. It was originally used by this same John Chisholm, the Cherokee Indian cattle trader, to supply Ft. Scott, Kans." The cattle driven to Fort Scott during the war came from the vicinity of today's Wichita, not through Baxter Springs. "The basic ground for the commencement of this trail was probably about the mouth of the Grand River where it emptied into the Arkansas. The most prominent branch of this trail runs directly up the Arkansas River to Fort Zarah, which was about a mile east of where Great Bend, Kan., now stands. From along this trail there were diversions by those cattle that went into the army supply at Fort Riley, Fort Harker, near Ellsworth, Fort Hays, near Hays City, Fort Wallace, now Wallace, Kan., the main base being in the Arkansas bottom on what is now called Chisholm Creek near the present city of Wichita, the trail continuing on west as far as Fort Bend (Bent's Fort) and Fort Lyon in Colorado, for the delivery of these cattle, hence all cattle trailed from Texas across the Arkansas River would, perforce, strike at some point the old Chisholm Trail, and hence practically all cattle, whether by Colbert's Ferry, Red River Cross or Doan's Store, or elsewhere intermediate, would naturally use some part of the original Cherokee Indian Chisholm Trail on some part of its journey to Western Kansas." [1]

All this is preposterous. No Texas cattle were trailed into central Kansas prior to the herds that reached Abilene in the fall of 1867. By then the Kansas Pacific Railroad was reaching for the Colorado line and the Santa Fe was building toward Newton. Forts Zarah, Harker and Wallace were still being garrisoned, for the Indian situation in the western part of the state was still grave, but the cattle that were supplied those posts did not come from Texas.

The herds that reached Abilene in 1867 wandered about the prairies for days after crossing the Arkansas at Chisholm Creek. There was no trail for them to follow. In the spring of 1868, Joseph McCoy sent out Tim Hersey, a surveyor, and a party of men to throw up mounds of earth, topped by a Lone Star flag, between Abilene and the Arkansas River, to direct the herds that he expected to come up from Texas that season. The only Chisholm Trail in existence at the time was the original Chisholm Wagon Road from the Arkansas River to Wichita Agency on the Washita.

If you can find a map published by the Department of the Interior General Land Office in 1876, you will see a trail running northwest from Fort Gibson and intersecting the wagon road at about what was then Round Pond Creek (Pond Creek) which is labeled "Chisholm Cattle Trail." It has led many commentators, Anderson among them, to err in designating it as part of the Chisholm Trail. The confusion regarding it was multiplied many times over, until wherever a herd was pointed north it was said to be going up the "Chisholm Trail." Nowhere was that as true as in Gulf Coast Texas. There was magic in the name. There was money at the end of it. No less a writer than Louis Nordyke, in an article written shortly before his death, declared that the Chisholm Trail had really been named for Thornton Chisholm, a prominent Gonzales County, Texas, cattleman, who "blazed the trail from below San Antonio to Red River." [2] He was echoing an old argument that there were two Chisholm Trails: one running up from the Gulf Coast to Red River, and another from there to the market in Kansas. It was never taken seriously.

"Going up the trail" and "We pointed them north," became

commonplaces of Texas speech, and they always meant the same thing: Kansas! Whether the various trails came up west or east of San Antonio, they began to merge as they neared Fort Worth— still just a miserable collection of saloons, dance halls and gamblers, either ankle-deep in dust or wallowing in mud, depending on the season—and became one as they neared Red River Station.

The extent of Jesse Chisholm's contribution to the trail that bears his name was his wagon road from the site of present Wichita to the new Wichita Agency on the Washita River. He is credited by some with having broken a trail the rest of the way to Red River. No documentation for it has ever been offered. He had no need for such a trail. The credit for breaking that portion of it rightly belongs to Buffalo Bill Matthewson, buffalo hunter, guide and pack-horse trader. McCoy tells how Matthewson met up with three Californians, Colonel O. W. Wheeler, Wilson and Hicks at Fort Arbuckle. They had purchased several thousand head of Longhorns in Texas and had put them across Red River at what McCoy calls Red River Crossing, which may or may not have been Red River Station. In its low stages the Red could be crossed in many places. This was in July, 1867. It was the intention of the three men to drive their cattle across western Kansas and the Colorado plains into Wyoming and over South Pass to old Fort Hall, and then on to California.

It is of record that at least two herds had successfully negotiated that long, roundabout journey. Some knowledge of the country through which they passed was necessary; Wheeler and his partners did not have it. By their admission they were lost by the time they wandered into Fort Arbuckle. Beginning at the time of the great gold rush, thousands of Longhorns had been trailed to California (to be covered later), which was accomplished by pointing west from the Rio Grande across hazardous Apache country and parched deserts.

Matthewson's presence at Fort Arbuckle has often been ascribed to his having two young white boys with him that he had ransomed from the Comanches and was returning to their parents in Texas. He agreed to guide the "lost" Californians to Chisholm's post on the North Canadian, from where they had Chisholm's wagon tracks to lead them into Kansas. They were on the Kansas prairies within a few miles of Abilene when they learned that a market was being opened there. "Due to the incessant rains and the grass turning soft, their cattle were in poor condition," says McCoy, "but I offered them a fair price, which they accepted. Two days later they drove into the newly-finished shipping pens. It was really the first herd that came up from Texas and broke the trail." [3]

Though it was the "first herd that came up from Texas," it was not the first herd of Longhorns to reach Abilene. At the time, thousands of Longhorns were being held in Indian Territory. They had been brought that far north without a definite destination in mind. The owners were still marking time as they moved back and forth, trying to find a way of slipping into Kansas and a shipping point. McCoy sent William H. Sugg into the Territory, with which he was acquainted, to induce the owners to drive their cattle to Abilene. That many did is attested by the fact that although the season was already far advanced, 35,000 head were shipped from there by rail that year.

Ironically, the first herd to reach Abilene was owned by three Northern men, not Texans, Smith, McCord and Chandler, who had bought the cattle from the Texans who had trailed them from their home range below Red River. There is further irony in the fact that the two men whose names are so closely linked with the Chisholm Trail never met. If Chisholm was its father, then just as surely Joseph G. McCoy was its godfather. You may read that McCoy hired Chisholm to drum up business for his cattle market. It is a fabrication; Jesse Chisholm was in his grave less than a year after McCoy saw Abilene for the first time. Such fabrications are easier to understand than the misinformation that crept into print regarding the location of the trail itself.

In 1883, when cattle were still moving over it by the thousands, Andreas, in his *History of Kansas,* marked "the true and original Chisholm Trail" as beginning at Wichita and running south to Red River Station on Red River. The trail north from Wichita to Abilene, known originally as the Abilene Trail, had lost its identity as such and by general usage had become the Chisholm Trail. In Texas, the name had been put on the main trail and the feeder trails that wound up from the south to Red River Station. But these appendages, north and south, were not part of the "true and original" Chisholm Trail that several million Longhorns and thousands of mustangs carved deep in the prairie sod of what was once Indian Territory. Andreas logs it as follows:

"The principal points on the trail are Wichita, Clearwater, Caldwell, Pond Creek, Skeleton Ranch, Buffalo Springs, mouth of Turkey Creek, Cheyenne Agency, Wichita Agency, and Fort Sill." [4]

He is in error in placing Fort Sill forty miles southwest of Wichita Agency on the main stem of the Chisholm Trail. A military road branched off there for Fort Sill, but it was not used as a cattle trail nor was it the route by which the post received most of its supplies; they came from Sherman, Texas, by way of Doan's Store on Red River.

Sam P. Ridings, in his *The Chisholm Trail*, accepts Andreas' logging and has the trail running south from Wichita Agency to Red River by way of the Little Washita, Rush Creek, Monument Rocks, Stinking Creek and Beaver Creek. Wayne Gard, in his later and excellent *The Chisholm Trail*, pinpoints it from Red River to the Arkansas River bottoms at Wichita. As has been said, if you drive from north to south across Oklahoma today on Highway 81, you will be either on the Chisholm Trail or seldom farther away from it than Walter Perry Johnson, a husky Kansas farm boy of enduring fame, could throw a baseball.

In mentioning Monument Rocks (called Table Rocks by some) Wayne Gard says: "A high point near this site became known as Monument Hill or Monument Rocks. This was a mesa whose almost flat top was strewn with slabs and boulders of reddish sandstone. As markers for the trail, some of the early drovers made two piles of these boulders, about three hundred feet apart. These piles were about ten feet across and twelve feet high. . . . Men on the trail could see these markers for ten to fifteen miles in either direction."

These "monuments" were well-known. They were in the vicinity of the bed-grounds at Stinking Creek (so named because the water was slightly impregnated with sulfur) . Water, grass and firewood always being found there, trail crews tried to reach it on their second night north from the river. If they needed markers to follow, it seems that the droppings of the herds that had gone up the trail ahead of them would have supplied a map that they could follow unerringly. It has led me to believe that building the "monuments" was begun as a lark, and that they were added to, a slab or two at a time, in the same spirit, by successive trail outfits.

Among the army of trail men, most of them young, it is to be doubted that many, from boss down to nighthawk and cook's swamper, were aware that they were taking part in the greatest mass movement of cattle the world had ever known. Its like had never been seen before and would not come again. The trailmen were working for wages, most of them, and it was hard, often dangerous work. However, it wasn't all blizzards, rain, stampedes, raging rivers; there was some fun in it, and the men extracted what they could as they left Texas behind and drove north. There was Will Foster, of San Antonio. He had hired out to Colonel W. M. Todd, who had a herd of thirteen hundred straight steers that he was putting through to Abilene. George Nail was Todd's trail boss. A man had to have a sense of humor to appreciate some of the incidents of that drive.

"Colonel Todd was drinking all the time and was very disagreeable," Foster recalled. "It caused George Nail to leave us. Everyone in the outfit was sorry to see him leave as he was a fine man and one of the best cowmen I ever saw. Things went from bad to worse and when we camped near Red River Station I quit and went to town ahead of the herd. The river was very high. People tried to get Todd to wait until the water went down. None of the men would lead the herd. The cattle got about to the middle of the stream and went to milling. Todd began calling for me. He had long white hair and was wild for a short time. He turned to Al Meyers, my pardner, and said: 'You know where Foster is. Tell him I will give him anything in the world if he will save my cattle for me.'

"I stripped and went to them. I got off my horse and right on to the cattle. They were so jammed together that it was like walking on a raft of logs. When I got to the only real big steer in the bunch I mounted him and he pulled for the other side. The others followed. When he got near the bank I drifted down the stream to my horse. It must have been about 9 o'clock, on the 8th day of

June, 1871. I kept the herd together all day until nearly sun-
down; no hat, no saddle—just my underclothes. The mosquitoes
almost ate me alive." [5]

He got back at Colonel Todd two days later.

"When we camped at Monument Rock, me and Al pitched the
old geezer's tent over a bed of polecats and when he went to bed
I tied down the front flap. It wasn't long before hell broke loose
inside. Fighting to get out, the Colonel pulled down the tent. He
cursed all of us to a fare-thee-well—not me particularly, but he
knew. Next morning to show he could take a joke, he ordered me
to ride to Fort Sill for the mail—thirty-five miles through Indian
country." [6]

Bill Jackman, a well-known trail boss of Caldwell County, had
an experience as he was nearing the Washita River, in Indian
Territory, with a herd of stock cattle, that got a wide telling. It
was the custom for a trail outfit to pick up cattle that had been
lost from herds ahead of them and carry them along until they
were overtaken, or even all the way to the end of the trail.

"One afternoon a band of about forty Indian warriors including their squaws, rode up and the chief handed me a letter. It
read:

" 'To the trail bosses:
This man is a good Indian; I know him personally. Treat
him well, give him a beef and you will have no trouble in
driving through his country.'

Ike T. Pryor.' "

Colonel Ike Pryor was destined to become one of the giants of
the Texas cattle trade.

"We had picked up a good steer the previous day. I knew from
its road brand that it belonged to Ike. I rode into the herd and cut
it out. They killed the steer then and there and had a big feast.
We went on north in peace, thanking Ike for his good advice." [7]

If your acquaintance with old-time Texas trail driving is limited
to what you have seen in the movies or on television, you have
undoubtedly concluded that what it amounted to was this: a
rancher having rounded up the cattle he wanted to sell, greased

the chuck wagon (or a two-wheeled cart in the early days), took to the trail with his ranch crew and eventually arrived at one or another of the Kansas cow towns and disposed of his beeves at a profit. In the beginning, that wouldn't have been too wide of the mark, but when trail driving became a business, it was a vastly different operation.

The professional trail driver was in many ways a cattle broker. He contracted with various ranchers for their cattle, which were to be delivered to a spot named by him, where his trail crew took over, road branded them and, when the combined herds had been shaped up, began the long journey north.

More often than not, the trail driver took possession of the cattle on credit. The cattle were counted and a price agreed on. It was on those figures that an accounting would be made five to six or even seven months later. If the rancher was taking a gamble, the trail driver was taking an even greater one. He had to bear the expenses of getting the cattle to market, make good the losses a herd might suffer, whatever the cause—stampedes, Indians, drowning at the river crossings, sickness—and finally face the greatest gamble of all, a fluctuating market. If he found it depressed and had to hold his herd on the Kansas prairies for several months, waiting for it to recover, his margin of profit could diminish to the vanishing point. When he got back to Texas and cast up his accounts, he might find that half a year's work had gone for nothing.

Elsewhere I have told the story of young Sol West, of Lavaca County, who received a thousand steers from his brother's firm, McCutcheon and West, on credit, and put them on the trail for Ellsworth. Bad luck dogged him all the way. A blizzard caught them as they were driving north from the forks of Rush Creek. With the coming of night the temperature hit bottom. His horses, sixty-five head, froze to death. He had to trade with the Indians for several mules and a horse or two before he could move his herd. He reached Ellsworth on May 20. It was two months later before his cattle were in condition to be sold. When he returned home and turned over to his brother his receipts and a list of expenditures, together with what cash he brought back, the figures showed after careful accounting that the net profit on the year's work was $1.50. "When my brother handed me the seventy-five cents that was my share," Sol recalled, "he inquired as to whether I expected to buy a herd of my own, or start a bank with it." [8]

Trail driving made millionaires of a few, rich men of many and left others bankrupt. Little Colonel John Meyers, Seth Mabry, Eugene Millett, the Slaughters, the Driskills, Dewees and Ellison, Lytle and McDaniel, Miller and Mayberry, the Blockers, the Rachal brothers and Ike Pryor were among the score or more who risked big and won big. Of course, as the old saying had it "they knew cow," but they had to face the element of chance and the vagaries of the weather same as other men. Once they had become successful they could withstand the setbacks and losings that spelled failure for lesser outfits. In the peak years of the Chisholm Trail they often had three, or even four, herds moving over it at the same time. The record was set by Millett and Mayberry in 1876 when they trailed a hundred thousand head to Dodge City and Ogallala.

A big owner seldom if ever accompanied one of his herds. When a herd had been shaped up, he would turn it over to an experienced trail boss whose authority became absolute until the cattle reached their destination. The owner's parting words were likely to be, "I'll meet you in Abilene," or wherever the herd was bound. When he had dispatched the three or four herds he was sending up that season, he would take a stage to the nearest railroad and by some roundabout traveling be waiting in Kansas for his cattle to arrive.

When he was thirty miles or so from town, the trail boss would send a rider in to locate the owner, who would come out the following day to meet the herd. A spot would be selected on the prairie where the animals could be held to recuperate for several weeks. In due course, buyers would be brought out and a sale effected. If it was "range sale," which meant that the cattle were to be driven to one of the military posts, a reservation or on into Nebraska, the buyer's men took charge of the critters. If they were to be shipped out by rail, the trail crew drove them to the railroad pens.

The trail boss could now relax for the first time since leaving Texas. He had been entrusted with the equivalent of $50,000, and despite difficulties (there always were some), he had delivered it on schedule, or approximately so. He didn't expect to be thanked for what he had done, and he seldom was. He was as responsible for the owner's prosperity as the owner himself, for he was the peg on which successful trail driving depended. It followed that many of the prominent owners, men like Ike Pryor, George Saunders and Mark Withers, were former trail bosses.

From the opening of the Chisholm Trail in the fall of 1867 to its virtual abandonment in 1884–85, it is reasonably safe to say that it was used almost exclusively by Texans. The exceptions were a few Californians and Missourians. How the trail crews were recruited for the herds that went up in 1867, I do not know, but they were Texans, and when they returned home they found it a mark of some distinction to be able to say that they had been all the way up to Kansas and back. In the spring of 1868 McCoy sent William Sugg, Colonel Hitt, an old friend from Illinois, and Charles F. Gross into Texas to spread word of the cattle market that had opened at Abilene. They were received with enthusiasm, due to the good reports Texas owners had brought home from their experience there the previous fall. Men who declared their intention of pointing a herd north were deluged by young Texans anxious to "go up the trail." Many were still in their teens.

It was from such raw material, along with a sprinkling of veteran cowboys, old enough to have worn Confederate gray, that the early trail crews were born. With few exceptions, they were all steel and whipcord, and they set the pattern for those who followed them—brave, courageous, reckless, unmatched in loyalty to their outfit, wild as eagles when they rode into a cow town at trail's end with money in their pocket. Whisky made fools of them. Perhaps that was why so many sang the remorseful old song:

> I'm only a cowboy,
> I know I done wrong.

9

McCoy's Abilene

THOUGH THE Union Pacific, Eastern Division, Railroad did not change its corporate name until May 31, 1868, it was popularly known as the Kansas Pacific almost from the time it laid its first mile of track. It was to cross Kansas to Denver, turn north and connect with the main Union Pacific at the new town of Cheyenne, Wyoming. Leavenworth was designated as its eastern terminal. As soon as it had absorbed the infant Leavenworth, Pawnee and Western, it headed up the Kaw Valley in earnest. "With state and federal aid assured, and an aditional plum of a million acres in land grants awaiting it if it reached the Colorado line in three years, it was no 'paper' railroad as so many were; this one would be built." [1]

It reached present-day Manhattan and turned up the Smoky Hill River. A few weeks later it was running trains as far west as Junction City. This wasn't a railroad junction—not yet—just the meeting of two rivers, the Smoky Hill and the Republican. No one was following its progress as reported in the newspapers more closely than young Joseph G. McCoy, the junior member of the firm of McCoy Brothers, livestock dealers, of Springfield, Sangamon County, Illinois. He says of himself and his brothers: "One thousand head of native cattle costing from $80 to $140 per head, was not an unusual week's shipment. When it is remembered that three shipments were on the road at the same time during all the season, it will be seen that their resources, financially, were not limited." They were also shipping mules, sheep and hogs as well.

His interest in the Kansas Pacific Railroad sprang from his talks with Charles F. Gross, a native of Springfield, only twenty at the time, who had returned to Illinois in the fall of 1866 after spending the previous ten months in Texas. Young as he was, Gross had served as a telegraph operator with the Union Army in the last years of the war. When hostilities were over, he was one of a group sent out to run a survey for a military telegraph line from Shreveport, Louisiana, to the mouth of the Rio Grande at Brownsville, Texas. His tales of the thousands of cattle and horses he had seen running wild, or half wild, on the plains and in the brush country of the Lone Star State, almost without value because no market could be found for them, fired McCoy's imagination. "It isn't a matter of price," Gross told him. "How to dispose of them at any price is the problem." Bill Sugg, who had trailed a herd of Longhorns out of the Red River country and managed to get them through the Texas fever blockade to Springfield, confirmed what Gross was saying.

"To establish a northern market at some accessible point to which the Texas drover could bring his stock unmolested and be reasonably sure of finding a buyer, became a waking thought, a sleeping dream," says McCoy.[2]

His brothers, William and James, gave him some encouragement. He was twenty-nine at the time. By his own description, he was a tall, gawky, shabbily dressed country bumpkin when he took a Missouri Pacific train at St. Louis for Kansas City. From a firm with which McCoy Brothers did business, he got a letter to the Kansas Pacific agent, across the river at Wyandotte, to whom he disclosed his plans. The agent was interested enough to hand him a round-trip pass over the road to Junction City, then the end of track, to look for a possible site for his market.

Of Junction City, he says: "Junction City was visited and a proposition made to one of the leading business men to purchase of him a tract of land sufficiently large for building a stockyard and such other facilities as were necessary for cattle shipping, but an exorbitant price was asked, in fact a flat refusal to sell at any price (for such a purpose) was the final answer."

Without looking further for the moment, McCoy returned to St. Louis and conferred with the president and directors of the Kansas Pacific. They were interested enough in his scheme to agree to install switches and a siding wherever he located, and pay him five dollars on every carload of cattle shipped from his yards. They would not, however, invest a dollar of railroad money in the enterprise. It was as much as he had expected to get. If he had been a better businessman and less a visionary, he would have got the terms in writing. Years later, he could say truthfully that the Kansas Pacific repudiated every promise it ever made him.

When he visited the president of the Missouri Pacific to ask for favorable freight rates between Kansas City and St. Louis, he met a humiliating reception. He was told, he recalled, "It occurs to me that you haven't any cattle to ship and never did have any; and I, sir, have no evidence that you will ever have any. I think you are talking about freight rates for speculative purposes. Therefore, you will get out of this office, and let me not be troubled with any more of your style."

He was to make the Missouri Pacific eat humble pie before he was through with it.

Chagrined but not discouraged, McCoy went to the general freight agent of the financially shaky Hannibal and St. Joseph Railroad, which crossed Missouri to Quincy, Illinois. It was in desperate need of eastbound freight. He was greeted with open arms and received very favorable rates to Quincy and Chicago. It proved to be the most fortuitous arrangement the Hanibal and St. Joe ever made.

McCoy hastened back to Springfield to attend to what he says were "business matters." Very likely they concerned the finances he was going to need. By the time he got back to Kansas, the Kansas Pacific had passed Abilene (putting up a plank signpost for a depot) and Solomon City and was reaching for Salina. On horseback, he rode west, looking for a site. He does not appear to have given more than a passing thought to Abilene. He says: "Abilene in 1867 was a very small, dead place, consisting of about one dozen log huts, low, small, rude affairs, four-fifths of which were covered with dirt for roofing; indeed but one shingle roof could be seen in the whole city. The business of the burg was conducted in two small rooms, mere log huts, and, of course, the inevitable saloon also in a log hut." [3]

Near Solomon City an excellent site for a stockyard took his eye; but on conferring with several leading citizens it was made painfully clear to him that Solomon City regarded with horror the idea of turning the town over to Texas cattle and Texas cowboys.

Salina was even more opposed to the idea. In blunt words he was told, "Salina would never stand for it." It left him nothing to do but turn back to Abilene. Abilene would stand for anything.

It was the middle of June already. If Abilene was to attract Texas drovers that season, there was no time to lose. From Charles and Mary Thompson, McCoy bought 250 acres at the northeastern edge of the settlement. Land was cheap. He also purchased a tract east of town. (It was to become notorious a few years later as "McCoy's Addition" or "Devil's Half-acre.") On the north side, he bought some lots on which to build his home.

The surrounding country was well suited to his purpose; it was sparsely populated, well watered and grassed, an ideal holding ground for thousands of cattle. Wayne Gard speculates that in selecting Abilene for his cattle market McCoy *perhaps unwittingly* violated the Kansas statute of February 26, 1867, banning the entry of Texas cattle east of the 6th principal meridian, which was approximately a mile west of Ellsworth, and sixty miles west of Abilene, making it deep inside the proscribed zone. If McCoy did not know it in the beginning, he surely was aware of it when he went to Governor Samuel J. Crawford as construction of his shipping yard began, to get him to sanction what he was doing, his argument being that the cattle reaching Abilene would come up west of the settlement and would not injure the interests of Kansas farmers and stockmen. Ignoring the fact that the enterprise was in obvious violation of state law, Crawford gave it a rousing endorsement in what he called "a plain, vigorous letter, commending Mr. McCoy's scheme and the location he had selected." He added, "I approved of the undertaking in a semi-official manner. I regard the opening of that cattle trail into and across western Kansas of as much value to the state as the Missouri River." In some quarters, he was criticized for his stand, but it never became a political issue nor was McCoy ever brought to court over it.

Though Abilene had some advantages, it posed some problems that, in view of the limited facilities he had at his command, must have seemed almost insurmountable. Land there was, and nothing else—no lumber, no hardware, and no skilled labor. He needed masons, carpenters. They had to be brought in from as far away as Topeka and Leavenworth. Pine lumber was freighted in from Hannibal, Missouri; hardwood from Lenape, Kansas.

Tim Hersey, a civil engineer, Abilene's leading citizen, who was to serve McCoy in many ways, had the stockyards, office and an eighty-room hotel staked off before material began to arrive. There was no hope of having the hotel ready for occupancy that season. It was when the stockyards neared completion that, as previously noted, McCoy sent Bill Sugg into Indian Territory to induce drovers to come to Abilene. From Springfield, he brought out his friend Charlie Gross to handle his accounts. The Kansas Pacific had put in switches and half a mile of siding and promised to build transfer and feed yards at Leavenworth. This was the first of the many promises on which they defaulted. McCoy built the accommodation at Leavenworth at his own expense. It was with some satisfaction that he could write:

"In sixty days from July 1st, a shipping yard that would accommodate three thousand cattle, a large pair of ten-ton Fairbanks scales, a barn and an office were completed, and a good three-story hotel well on the way to completion."

As soon as he was assured that herds of Longhorns were being pointed for Abilene, he invited half a hundred Iowa and Illinois cattle traders and feed lot operators to what he described as "a monster cattle auction." This was the first evidence of his unsuspected gift of showmanship. The Kansas Pacific humored him to the extent of building a small boxlike depot and installing William P. Anderson as agent. Stock cars were shunted onto the Abilene siding. Adjacent to the unfinished hotel, a large tent was erected, in which a banquet of the choicest viands and beverages was to be served his guests.

The auction was a huge success, sales were brisk and the prices received—ranging from fifteen to twenty-five dollars—were beyond the expectations of the sellers. Happily, McCoy reports: "On the morning following the banquet, September 5, the iron horse was darting down the Kaw Valley with the first trainload of cattle that ever passed over the Kansas Pacific Railroad, the precursor to many thousands destined to follow."

To repeat the figure given by McCoy, thirty-five thousand head were shipped by the end of the season. He doesn't say how many were consigned to McCoy Brothers. Certainly very few. His role was largely that of a commission man, his fee being paid by the seller in return for the facilities he provided. He also received a commission from livestock dealers for whom he acted as shipper. In addition there was his arrangement with the Kansas Pacific. It was a profitable business. McCoy was not forgetting grudges. Of the considerably more than a thousand carloads of cattle that left Abilene, all but seventeen went over the Hannibal and St. Joe on the same terms; the Missouri Pacific got the rest.

It brought an agent of the Missouri Pacific to Abilene to solicit business. McCoy was ready for him. Gleefully he records how he flung at him, almost word for word, the humiliating dismissal he had received in St. Louis that spring. "I told him it just occurred to me that I had no cattle for his road, never had, and there was no evidence that I ever would have, and would he please say so to his president."

Flushed with success, he ordered an addition built to the still unfinished hotel which would enable it to accommodate a hundred and twenty guests. With its plastered walls, laundry, parlor and its expensive furnishings, it was to be the finest hotel on the plains, its bar stocked with imported wines, the finest liquors, the choicest Havana cigars, and its food equal to the best to be found in St. Louis. He named it simply the Drover's Cottage, which was something of a misnomer considering that it was three stories high and dominated the country for miles around. It was not intended for cowboys and ordinary trail hands.

On his way to Springfield in December, he stopped over in St. Louis and induced John Gore, the steward of the St. Nicholas Hotel, and his wife Louisa to take charge of the Drover's Cottage. He couldn't have made a better choice. Lou Gore and the Drover's Cottage became almost synomomous and equally famous.

When it opened its doors for business in June, 1868, resplendent in its fresh white paint, thousands of Longhorns were descending on Abilene. Reluctantly the Kansas Pacific put in two miles of siding. It was not to be too much. In another month Abilene was, as the *Weekly Chronicle* aptly put it, "an island in a sea of cattle."

The town had grown some in 1867, and at the turn of the year there may have been a population of as many as two hundred local or "native" residents. But as the weather moderated, carloads of lumber arrived daily. Outsiders flocked in and buildings were slapped together, one after another, seven days a week. The saw and the hammer were never silent. As spring advanced, every train from the east disgorged a dozen or more hard-faced men and women. These newcomers were the offscourings of the dives and underworld of Kansas City, St. Louis, Memphis and other Mississippi River towns. The word had spread that there was to be cash money, the prime requisite of their various professions, at Abilene that summer, and they were there to get their share of it —gamblers, saloonkeepers, sharpsters, pimps and prostitutes.

The Abilene *Chronicle* estimated that on June 1, counting the transients, the town had an over-all population of seven hundred. By midsummer, an army of a thousand to fifteen hundred cowboys was converging on the surrounding prairies. What followed was easy to predict. Abilene was helpless. The only check on lawlessness was the edicts enforced in self-protection by the saloonkeepers. There was no hour of the day or night that was not punctuated by the racketing blast of a six-gun, whether fired in fun or in earnest. Good women and children were afraid to venture on some streets. Painted bawds in their white kid half-boots and gaudy finery had the run of the town. A visiting correspondent of the *New York Tribune* wrote: "Gathered together in Abilene and its environs is the greatest collection of Texas cowboys, rascals, desperados and adventuresses the United States has ever known. There is no law, no restraint in this seething cauldron of vice and depravity."

In thirty days the demand for cars rose to over a thousand. The Kansas Pacific was caught short. Their bridge across the Missouri was still uncompleted, making it difficult for them to lease cars from other lines. To meet the unexpected demand, flat cars were transformed into stock cars by building makeshift frameworks on them.

For the first time ranchmen who were interested in stocking the empty ranges of Nebraska, Wyoming and Montana appeared in Abilene. Heretofore, there had been so little demand for stock cattle that the price had sagged to twelve and fifteen dollars. Now suddenly they were as ready sale as beeves. In fact the competition for them became so keen that buyers were riding south to intercept the herds before they reached Abilene. The Nimmo report estimates that no less than forty thousand head were trailed north out of Kansas that year.

This business naturally increased possibilities of the Abilene market and seemed to guarantee its permanence. The traffic on the Chisholm Trail became so heavy that some drovers were going back to Colbert's Ferry and Rock Bluff Crossing and trailing up the old Texas Road (Shawnee Trail, if you prefer) as far as Fort Gibson; here they turned northwest over what had once been designated the Chisholm Cattle Trail, but which Mark Withers and some others dubbed the West Shawnee Trail, and cut the Chisholm Trail at Round Pond Creek or the mouth of the Little Arkansas.

The future had never looked brighter to McCoy, when, without warning, calamity struck. It was the great outbreak of Texas fever in central Illinois. In Dickinson County, of which Abilene was the county seat, a number of native cattle sickened and died. To still the clamor so near at home, McCoy reimbursed the farmers for their losses. As the furor in Illinois increased, the Abilene market collapsed. The demand for stock cattle continued, but there was no sale for beeves. With his fortune at stake (his brothers had withdrawn from the enterprise) and twenty-five thousand Longhorns being held on the prairie, and other thousands coming up the trail, he knew he had to do something. The epidemic in Illinois had been traced to diseased Texas cattle that had been brought up the Mississippi by steamboat from the mouth of Red River, many of which died as they were being unloaded at Cairo. They weren't Abilene cattle. That was the reed on which he based his case when he hired a number of young men and sent them into

Iowa and Illinois, armed with circulars, to contact cattle buyers and feed lot men.

With cooler weather, the epidemic subsided. McCoy spent five thousand dollars in a newspaper advertising campaign. (In 1868, five thousand dollars went a long way.) He staged sales and auctions. Slowly the market revived. To give it momentum, he hit on the idea of shipping a carload of wild buffaloes into the feed lot country. Capturing wild buffaloes with the lariat was something of an undertaking, but the men he hired (the well-known Mark Withers was one of them) were successful. The animals were placed in a heavily reinforced cattle car, and "after hanging on each side of the car a large canvas upon which a flaming advertisement was painted in striking colors of the cattle at or near Abilene, it was sent through to Chicago via St. Louis, eliciting a great amount of attention and newspaper comment."

There was more to it than that. With the three buffaloes went three wild horses and two elk. A buffalo gored one of the elk before reaching St. Louis. Withers and his companions gave exhibitions of riding and roping. McCoy either forgets or chooses to ignore the fact that he was on hand to manage the exhibitions.

He followed this bit of showmanship by arranging a free excursion of Illinois cattlemen to western Kansas to shoot buffaloes. "On returning to Abilene," he says, "they were shown the fine herds of Longhorns being held on the prairies. Several excursionists were induced to invest. In a few days the market assumed its wonted life and activity. Indeed it seemed to rebound from the depressing effects of the Spanish fever excitement, and long before cold weather set in, the last bullock was sold." [4]

Over the Chisholm Trail, seventy-five thousand Longhorns reached Abilene that year. McCoy places the number shipped out by rail at fifty thousand. The rest were trailed north to Nebraska and beyond.

"With the close of the cattle season the exodus from Abilene began. In a few days the town was deserted. The saloons were closed and padlocked, the gamblers and the crooks were gone; so were the prostitutes and their fancy men. Jake Karatofsky and others had closed their stores. . . . Nobody was through with Abilene; the pickings had been too good. They would be back, with reinforcements, before the following June rolled around. The tumult of their leaving died away and native Abilene gratefully settled down to a long, dull winter. Those who had made money out of the Texans busied themselves with erecting new buildings; others, knowing what '69 would bring, wondered if they could survive it." [5]

The sordid saga of the Kansas cow towns was just beginning. There was nothing noble, glorious, good about them, even using the terms in their broadest sense. Their peace officers, with one or two exceptions, notably Marshal Tom Smith of Abilene, bore no resemblance to the caricatures that masquerade as the Earps, the Mastersons and the Wild Bills today. The trail-end towns that fattened on the cattle traffic—Abilene, Ellsworth, Newton, Wichita, Caldwell, Dodge City, and the smaller fry like Baxter Springs, Ellis, Great Bend and Wakeeney—were all alike. What could be said of one could be said of the others. In turn, each flourished briefly, and as the trade shifted, it was left to wither on the vine, with its empty stockyards whitening in the sun like the bones of a forgotten carcass.

If they had any glory it was the tarnished glory of the saloon, the dance hall and the cribs in which "the fair Cyprians," as Kansas newspapers were prone to call them, held forth. Elsewhere I have told that story in detail and I will not repeat myself. If Abilene and the others are prosperous, substantial cities today, it was wheat, not Texas cattle, that made them so. As someone said a long time ago, "The millions of Longhorns that crossed Kansas built no roads, no schools, no churches; it was the despised granger, the dirt farmer, who made it great." [6]

It is only in Joseph McCoy's connection with the Chisholm Trail and the part he played in making it the most important of all American cattle trails that this narrative is concerned. Of his feud with his old friend turned enemy, Theodore C. Henry, the so-called Wheat King of Kansas, it will only be necessary to explain how it led to his eventual defeat and the eclipse of Abilene.

Over $1,500,000 had changed hands there the past season, 95 per cent of which had found its way back to Texas. It seemed to guarantee that 1869 would be even better. Though the future appeared bright, McCoy found himself facing several unexpected problems almost at once. The Kansas Pacific Railroad refused to honor its commitment to pay him five dollars a car for shipments from Abilene. They offered him two dollars and a half on a take it or leave it basis, threatening, in case he refused, to pull up its switches and siding at Abilene and remove them to Ellsworth, which was hungry for the trail business. If that became necessary, they pointed out regretfully, the money he had invested in the Drover's Cottage would be a total loss. McCoy gave in, but instead of another promise, he got a written contract. (It was to become a matter that was in the courts for years.)

In January, he had a far more grievous battle on his hands. In Illinois the Texas fever outbreak of the previous summer had not been forgotten. The legislature had before it a bill prohibiting the entry into or passage through the state by trail or any other means of Longhorn cattle. It was so widely supported that there was little doubt but what it would quickly be enacted into law. If that happened, it meant the end of the Texas cattle trade. With Illinois extending from the Great Lakes to the Ohio River, every practical means of shipping cattle east by rail would be closed.

Singlehanded, McCoy fought a losing battle against the bill for nineteen days. The Western railroads that had a stake in the outcome failed to rally to his support. Through sheer tenacity he managed to get an amendment attached to the bill that saved the day. This was the famous provision exempting wintered cattle. There is no reason to believe that McCoy realized it was a loophole that would be flagrantly abused. Though he was a showman and crassly commercial in much that he did, there was something above self-interest in the fight he had waged.

Trouble always dogged him, and he no sooner overcame one difficulty than he was faced by another. Usually he was ready for it; however, he seems not to have found anything disturbing in the opposition the residents of Abilene and the farmers of Dickinson County were voicing against the Texas cattle trade. The town was growing and the farm population had doubled in the past two years. When a petition was circulated praying for the incorporation of Abilene as a city of the third class, he signed it. When it bore the required number of signatures, Probate Court

Judge Cyrus Kilgore granted the request and named five men to act as trustees until an election could be held. He was one of them. His friend T. C. Henry was named chairman, which in effect made him acting mayor.

Henry came out openly against what he called "the iniquities and excesses" of the cattle trade, and published articles in the *Weekly Chronicle,* saying that Dickinson County's future prosperity was dependent on agriculture, not on the cattle herds from Texas. Kansas had passed a new herd law, which gave the farmer redress against trespassing. Henry advised his readers to have offenders arrested and demand damages for fences knocked down and fields invaded by Texas cattle.

These were still small voices. But McCoy should have listened to them for they were to swell into a chorus that would not be denied.

10

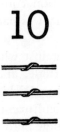

Three Hundred Thousand on the Hoof

CORONADO HAD FAILED TO FIND the Eldorado for which he was searching, but the trail drivers of Texas had found theirs. The 1869 season opened auspiciously; the weather was favorable and the grass came green early. By the middle of April, many herds were across Red River and plodding up the trail to Kansas. They never stopped coming until November was gone. Abilene received 150,000 Longhorns that year, twice the number for 1868. "Prices were good. Second-class beef steers brought $22.50 to $25.00 a head. Extra fine ones brought $26 or more, sometimes as much as $32. Stock cattle often went for $12 to $12.50. Calves were sold for trifling sums or given away." [1]

Indians were a greater nuisance than ever, not only in their demands for beef; given half a chance, they would stampede a herd and in the confusion make off with an outfit's horses and then demand to be paid for helping to round them up the next day. Usually a trail boss found it expedient to give them a few beeves and continue on his way.

A beef herd of fifteen hundred head of threes and fours ran into trouble at the Washita. The river was running bank full. It was narrow but deep. After waiting a day for the flood to drop, the cattle were put into the water. Most of the herd was across when the bank caved in. Several hundred frightened steers went plung-

Colonel Auguste Pierre Chouteau, 1786–1838. From an old print by
V. Lackey

Jesse Chisholm, the Scotch-Indian trader whose wagon road became
the famous Chisholm Trail

Benjamin Franklin Colbert, the Chickasaw Indian whose Red River ferry and subsequent bridge made him rich

The Colbert home at Colbert's Ferry

Joseph G. McCoy, who conceived the idea of a Northern market for
Texas cattle

Abilene, Kansas, 1875, first of the wild and woolly cow towns

Tom Smith, the town marshal who brought law and order to Abilene

English-born Ben Thompson, the Texas gunman and gambler

William Barclay (Bat) Masterson, buffalo hunter, peace officer, head of the Masterson clan, who wrote a large page in cow-town history

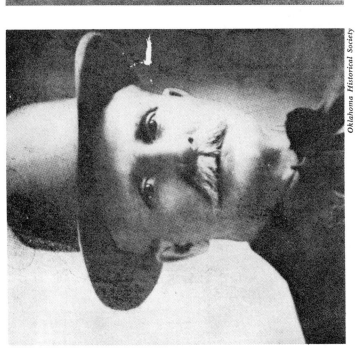

Marshal Bill Tilghman, for twenty-two years a frontier peace officer

Montana Historical Society

John Bozeman, who, with his partner John M. Jacobs, opened the trail from the Montana gold diggings to old Fort Laramie that found its place in history as the famous Bozeman Road.

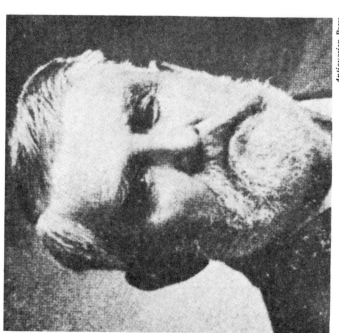

Antiquarian Press

Charles Goodnight, plainsman, trail blazer and cowman second to none

Ellsworth in cow-town days. The famous Drovers' Cottage was brought across the prairies from Abilene in sections and was equally popular in Ellsworth.

Newton in its brief heyday as a cow town won the sobriquet of "Bloody Newton, the toughest town in Kansas."

Wichita in 1875, when it was the "cow capital" of Kansas

Marshal Henry Brown, Assistant Marshal Wheeler, of Caldwell, with the two Cherokee Strip cowboys, Wesley and Smith, following their capture after attempting to rob the Medicine Valley bank at Medicine Lodge. Brown is the second from the left. He was shot and killed when he made a break for liberty; the others were hanged by an infuriated mob.

Front Street, Dodge City, in the mid-seventies

Power dams, power lines and irrigation projects have changed the face of Bighorn Basin. Pictured here is the Boysen Dam and reservoir, south of Thermopolis, Wyoming.

Conrad Kohrs, associated with Granville Stuart, was a great figure in the "free range" era in Montana.

Granville Stuart, properly regarded as the "father" of the range cattle business in Montana

Antiquarian Press

John Clay, one of the giants of the range cattle business

Western Research Center, University of Wyoming

Moreton Frewen, the wealthy and capable Britisher, became a noted figure in the days of the Beef Bonanza.

ing into the river and began milling. A hundred and eighteen head were drowned.

L. D. Taylor, one of the real pioneers of the Chisholm Trail, has left a colorful account of the first drive in which he took part:

"In the spring of 1869 my two brothers, Dan and George Taylor, with Monte Harrell, rounded up a thousand Longhorn beeves, four to twelve years old, and started them to Kansas [he is confused about the year. It had to be 1868]. I had never been out of our home neighborhood before, so I went along to get some experience on the trail. The herd was rounded up in Gonzales County, about where the town of Waelder is now located.

"When we reached Waco the Brazos River was level with its banks, and we had to swim the herd across. It is a wonderful sight to see a thousand steers swimming all at one time. All you see was the tips of their horns and the ends of their noses as they went through the water.

"Near Waco I learned some law, by taking two rails off a fence for firewood with which to cook supper. Was glad to get off by paying two dollars for those rails.

"We swam the Trinity at Dallas, where our herd stampeded and ran through town, creating quite a commotion. The damage they did cost us about two hundred dollars. We proceeded on to Red River, which we crossed and travelled several days in the friendly [sic] Indian Nation. The first night there we rounded up the herd, but next morning they were gone, for they had been stampeded by Indians shooting arrows into them, and it required several days to get them all together again. The Indians resorted to that kind of trick to get pay for helping to get the cattle back again. When we left this section of the Indian Territory we turned our backs to civilization, for the remainder of the trip was to be made through a wild, unsettled, hostile country. After a few days' travel we struck the Chisholm Trail, the only thoroughfare through the Indian Territory to Kansas, and about this time two other herds fell in with us, and, not knowing the country we were going through, the three outfits agreed to stick together. . . . Ours was the third herd that ever travelled that trail."

He was looking back over approximately fifty years when he

made this statement. The Taylor herd may have been the third to reach Abilene that year, but it can hardly have been the third to go up the famous trail. To continue:

"We had plenty of stampedes. . . . One night the herd was rounded up about a half mile from camp, and during the night I was awakened by the shaking of the earth and an awful noise, and found the whole herd coming down upon us in a furious run. I was bunking with Monte Harrell, and when I jumped up Harrell tried to hold me, but I jerked loose and ran around to the other side of the wagon. I soon had Mr. Harrell for company. I think every beef must have jumped over the wagon tongue, at least it seemed to me that every steer was jumping it.

"From here on we had considerable trouble crossing the creeks and rivers, having to float our wagons across. When we reached one of these streams that was on a rise three or four men would swing on behind each wagon to hold it down until we got into the water, then the men would swim alongside the oxen and guide them across."

He recalls an encounter they had with Indians.

"As we were traveling along we saw ahead of us something that looked like a ridge of timber, but which proved to be about four hundred Comanches who were coming our way. When they came up to our herd they began killing our beeves without asking permission or paying any attention to us. Some of the boys of our herd went out to meet them, but the boys of the other herds hid out in the grass. They [the Indians] killed twenty-five of our beeves and skinned them right there, eating the flesh raw and with blood running down their faces, reminding me of a lot of hungry dogs. We were powerless to help ourselves. Every time we would try to start the herd the Indians would surround it and hold it back. Finally they permitted us to move on, and we were not slow in moving, either. These Indians had 'talked peace' with Uncle Sam, that is all that saved us. We heard a few days afterwards that they had engaged in battle with their foes after leaving us, and had been severely whipped, losing about half their warriors."

Where they crossed the Arkansas they saw a couple of cabins on the Kansas side of the river. Bill Grieffenstein and Jim Meade, Jesse Chisholm's old friends, were doing some trading there.

"We began to rejoice that we were once more getting within the boundaries of civilization," says Taylor. "After leaving that wayside oasis we did not see another house until we were within ten miles of Abilene.

"One evening Monte Harrell said the prospects were good for a storm that night, and sure enough we had a regular Kansas twister. We had prepared for it by driving a long stake pin into the ground, to which I chained the wagon, and making everything as safe as possible. At midnight the storm was on, and within a moment everything was gone except the wagon and myself. The cattle stampeded, horses got loose, and oxen and all went. The storm soon spent its fury and our men managed to hold the cattle until daylight and got them all back the next morning." [2]

It didn't take a twister, lightning, thunder or a slashing hailstorm in the middle of the night to start a run. Anything could do it; any unusual or unexpected sound—the slapping of a wet slicker worn by a man on night guard, the banging of a tin pan dropped accidentally at the wagon—was enough to make cattle get up and run. And then there was what Frank Dobie calls an "agitator" in a herd, always an old mossy-horn troublemaker. When he got down in the evening, he never let the air out of him as a range critter does that means to stay down for the night. There were devils in his eyes and he looked around, waiting. Suddenly he would heave himself to his feet with an angry snort. In a flash the herd would be off.

When an "agitator" was the cause and a herd was running night after night, short runs that wore a trail crew down, his days were numbered if the outfit had a boss who knew his business.

There is the classic story of John Chism (not to be confused with Jesse Chisholm, to whom he was not related, stories to that effect to the contrary), who "knew cow" if any man ever did. The owner of a herd that had been getting up night after night, appealed to Chism to find the culprit. Chism rode through the herd after it had bedded down, looking the brutes over individually. Finally he pointed out a lanky, one-eyed paint steer "about as narrow between the eyes as a razorback hog. 'Cut that steer out, drive him down to river and kill him, and your troubles will be over.' "

That proved to be the case. "That one-eyed steer had been setting the whole three thousand off every night until a real cow-man spotted him." [3]

In the mass of what loosely may be called Wild West fiction, the cattle stampede, supercharged with drama and excitement, and often with tragedy, occurs times without number. It lends itself to exaggeration, especially when it is employed as a device to enthrall the reader. You will read about runs of forty to fifty miles in a night. I do not know what the record is, but three to four miles was the average. But there were exceptions. A herd going to North Platte, Nebraska, is said to have run a hundred miles from the point where they got up. Some men were killed. Far fewer, however, than you might suppose from listening to such lugubrious cowboy ballads as "Little Joe the Wrangler" and "Utah Carroll." Usually a stampede hurt only the cattle. They were easily exhausted, lost weight and after two or three nights of running were difficult to drive.

The tales of a stampeding herd plunging over a cliff and being killed by the hundreds undoubtedly originated with the loss of two thousand steers, all fives and sixes belonging to the well-known firm of Wilson Brothers of Kansas City. The herd was bedded down beyond the breaks west of the Brazos River. There had been a severe electrical storm that afternoon. They appeared to have overcome their nervousness when they got down. Then as one, they jumped about ten o'clock and were off, heading for the Brazos. There was a deep gully in their path. Before they could be headed, they were plunging into it, the onrushing mass trampling and killing those that had gone over ahead of them. In the morning when the Wilson crew rounded up what was left, the count tallied over two thousand steers dead and missing. Packs of wolves feasted there for weeks. Appropriately, the place was named Stampede Gully, and the name survived.

Charles M. Russell, the great cowboy artist, sculptor and story-teller, in his *Trails Plowed Under*, puts the stampede in its proper perspective:

"I've read of stampedes that were sure dangerous an' scary, where a herd would run through a camp, unsettin' wagons an' trompin' sleepin' cowpunchers to death. When day broke they'd be fifty or a hundred miles from where they started, leavin' a trail strewn with blood, dead cowpunchers an' hosses, that looked like the work of a Kansas cyclone. This is all right in books, but the feller that writes 'em is romancin' an' don't savvy the cow. Most stampedes is noisy, but harmless to anybody but the cattle. A herd in a bad storm might drift thirty miles in a night, but the worst run I ever see, we ain't four miles from the bed-ground when day broke."

The trail drivers found a new experience awaiting them when they neared Abilene that year. Every hillside seemed to be marked with a dugout and occupied by a farmer armed with a shotgun. Timber not being available, they had fenced themselves in with brush. Most of them had part of their 160 acres under cultivation, corn for the hogs, vegetables and pumpkins for the family. Cattle knocked down fences and ran over the crops, sometimes because they couldn't be held, oftener because there was little disposition on the part of the drovers to respect the settlers' rights. The farmers—they preferred to be called grangers—had the votes to control the legal machinery of the county. Naturally, they elected justices of the peace who favored them. Though a bewhiskered judge might hold court in a dugout or soddy, he had the new herd law penalizing trespassing to guide him in assessing damages. The Texans ranted and railed against "this damned Yankee justice," but they paid their fines. On Walnut Creek, a herd intent on reaching a bed-ground that the boss had selected, started to cut across a homestead only to be confronted by a group of armed men. The grangers fired into the cattle, killing several. A showdown was averted when the cattle turned back. When redress was sought for the slain cattle, Judge Renner found the homesteader within his rights in protecting his fields against destruction.[4]

Theodore Henry was now the elected mayor of Abilene. Under his direction a small jail and a schoolhouse built of native limestone, readily obtainable along the Smoky Hill River, were built, the only stone buildings in the town. The little jail was built on Cedar Street, around the corner from "Texas Street" (First Street) where it would be handy to the nightly rioting. Had it been placed elsewhere it might have survived undamaged, but the trail crews took exception to having it rammed down their throats, so to speak. One midnight they ripped off its wooden roof, freed a Negro prisoner and shot out its two small windows and riddled the wooden door with their six-guns.

Mayor Henry had a new roof put on the calaboose and had it bolted down. At his urging the office of town marshal was created and some new ordinances passed, one of which forbade the carrying of a deadly weapon within the town limits. Tom Sheran, the prosperous grocer, was induced to see what he could do about giving Abilene some semblance of law and order. The task he had set himself was comparable to trying to push back the ocean from the shore. He collected the license fees from the saloons, gambling joints and cribs and let it go at that.

Early one morning, a group of young Texans, twenty strong, came racing up North Cedar Street on their way to the stockyards. They shattered the morning stillness with a wild Rebel yell as they bore down on the little cottage in which Henry conducted his real estate business, and as they swept past, they peppered the building with a fusillade of shots. Inside, the mayor had to hug the floor. They raced away, laughing and shouting. It was just their way of letting him know that they didn't intend to take any more nonsense from him.

Sheran turned in his badge, and a man named Jim McDonald took his place. He didn't last the season out. By the middle of October the annual exodus of the undesirables got under way and Abilene grew quiet again. But not for long. The outcry against the cattle trade was raised once more. The *Chronicle* attacked McCoy. He replied to his critics by pointing out that everyone connected with the Texas cattle business had made money out of it. The rift between Henry and him had widened into an open break.

McCoy had spent money with a lavish hand since opening his Great Western Stockyards in Abilene. He had made fortunes for others, but not for himself. He was a notoriously poor businessman, which is so often the case with visionaries. When he had sold the Drover's Cottage to his friend Major M. B. George in July of that year for a reported eight thousand dollars, a third of what it cost, it was believed to be just a move on his part to relieve himself of a white elephant in his dealings with the Kansas Pacific, and not a bona fide sale. Major George leased the cottage to the Gores and it continued to do a thriving business. By December it became apparent that McCoy was in debt and being pressed by his creditors. Late in the season he had purchased a herd of nine hundred mature Longhorns, with the intention of wintering them on the Abilene prairies, feeding them on hay and selling them at a fancy price after the grass came green in the spring. It tied up at least $25,000. Needing money, he hurried to St. Louis to demand a settlement of his account from the railroad company.

The Kansas Pacific had paid him approximately $6,000 for yarding and loading charges, but nothing had been done about the bonus of $2.50 a car which his contract called for. He quickly learned that the company didn't intend to do anything about it, claiming a clause in the contract rendered it invalid. After months of wrangling, McCoy turned to the courts. The case was settled in his favor, but not until it had gone to the Supreme Court of Kansas, some years later. On May 28, 1870, he was forced to sell the stockyards to Edward H. Osborne, of Quincy, Illinois. The new owner took over operation of the yards as the season opened. It was a blow from which Joe McCoy never recovered.

The Longhorns came north in incredible numbers in 1870. The total was put at 300,000, four times as many as arrived in 1868. The fear was expressed in some quarters that the market would be glutted and prices would tumble. Just when those fears appeared about to be realized, the principal railroads east of the Mississippi engaged in a rate-cutting war that put a new face on the situation. The war became so bitter that freight rates were cut in two. It was reported that the Erie Railroad, in its fight with the New York Central, transported a trainload of cattle from Dunkirk to New York City free of charge to keep the rival road from getting the business.

This was an unexpected windfall for feed-lot operators. Taking advantage of it, shipments of livestock out of Illinois shot upward. What the pessimists failed to realize was that in fifteen years following the Civil War beef had supplanted pork as the mainstay of the American dinner table. Sold over the counter, beef was relatively cheap. The demand for American beef in England and on the Continent was increasing; from Boston and New York, Texas cattle were being exported. Nearer to home, the first packing plant was being operated in Wyandotte (Armourdale), Kansas, across the Missouri from Kansas City.[5] It was a market that was to grow until it was second only to Chicago.

In the meantime, McCoy had been reduced to buying scrub cattle and contracting them to various Indian reservations. In Abilene itself changes were taking place. It was growing. The *Chronicle* boasted that its permanent residents numbered over five hundred. Dickinson County was erecting a two-story brick courthouse. Even more important was naming Thomas J. Smith marshal of the town.

That spring two local men had applied for the job, but they had no sooner been appointed than they resigned. With the beginning of the cattle season at hand, Abilene was without a marshal. The story has been told a hundred times that, becoming desperate, Mayor Henry wrote the police chief of St. Louis to recommend three men who could enforce the law in Abilene. In due time three former policemen arrived. After looking the town over, they shook their heads and took the next train back to St. Louis.

Out in Kit Carson, Colorado, where he was living at the time, Tom Smith heard that Abilene was in need of a marshal. Aboard his gray horse Silverheels, he came across the prairies to apply for the job. Though he was only five feet eleven, weighing a hundred and seventy-five pounds, he was burly. But he was so mild-mannered, so soft-spoken, that he didn't appear formidable enough to the mayor to warrant any serious consideration. He took his name and address and dismissed him.

Smith looked the town over, found it about as he expected, and headed back for Colorado. Two nights later a fight that began in the Old Fruit Saloon boiled out into Texas Street. One of the participants was killed and another mortally wounded. On the theory that anything was better than nothing, Mayor Henry telegraphed the man from Kit Carson and caught him at Ellis, a small settlement a few miles west of Hays City, and offered him the job.

"Bear River" Tom Smith wasn't the unknown individual that the mayor, in his ignorance, took him to be. The Bear River,

Wyoming, riot was almost as celebrated as the Wild Bill—Mc-Canles affair at Rock Creek. In 1867, while the Union Pacific was being built, Smith was employed by one of the construction companies. Construction workers were fair game for the jackals who were slapping up little towns as the rails advanced. A young friend of Smith's was thrown into jail with three vicious murderers on a trumped-charge of having disturbed the peace. After failing to get the boy released, Smith and his fellow workers descended on the town, fought a gang of bogus vigilantes to a standstill and freed the youngster. Badly wounded, Smith had been forced to remain behind as the construction advanced. When he recovered, the conduct he had exhibited in the Bear River riot had been such that he was chosen marshal of the next town, and the next, as the railhead moved westward and old towns were abandoned for new ones along the right of way.[6,7]

He was to do the well-nigh impossible—give the town law and order. Don't be misled by the myth that Wild Bill Hickok tamed Abilene, that it was "his town." An unprejudiced study of the records completely refutes that story. Tom Smith tamed Abilene, and he did it without killing. When Wild Bill, who succeeded him after he had been foully murdered by homesteaders in a dugout on Chapman Creek, several miles from town, took over, the backbone of lawlessness had been broken.[8]

Tom Smith was not a "gun" marshal; he patrolled the street on horseback. He went armed but his gun was hidden in a shoulder holster. When he had to make an arrest, he slid to the ground and used his iron fists. His method of enforcing the peace bewildered young Texans. No matter what you may have read or seen to the contrary, cowboys were not fistfighters. In their code, it was permissible to buffalo a man with a pistol barrel or break a chair over his head; but they did not fight with their fists. They needed good hands in their work, and they wore gloves to protect them. A bruised hand incapacitated a man more than a bruised leg or ribs.

The Texans pulled down or shot full of holes the signs the marshal put up prohibiting the carrying of guns. He put up new ones, and he continued to put them up. In the end, they stayed put. When a man rode into town, he deposited his hardware at his favorite saloon.

You will not find Tom Smith's equal among frontier peace officers. For courage, bravery and iron will he stands unmatched and practically unknown. This is an opinion I voiced some years ago. The story of Thomas James Smith has yet to be written. His beginnings are shrouded in mystery. He was of Irish descent, a devout Catholic. It has been said by some that he was a former New York City policeman. I have never seen any documentation for it. Though he and the young Texans, who regarded Abilene as a playground in which they could satisfy pent-up hungers and raise a certain amount of hell, remained on opposite sides of the fence, he won their respect. They denounced such Kansas marshals as Wild Bill, the Earps and the Mastersons as the "fighting pimps," but they did not include Tom Smith in that category.

It is worthy of note that the "no gun law," as the ordinance making it a crime to carry a gun within the town limits was commonly called, that Tom Smith enforced in Abilene was adopted by other Kansas cow towns as the trade shifted from one to the other. Only in Dodge City was a serious effort made to enforce it. Ellsworth and Wichita had it on the books, but it was never strictly observed.

An event took place in Abilene in October that to the observing eye cast a long shadow ahead of it. It was the First Annual Dickinson County Fair. Farmers exhibited their produce. The variety and quality of the vegetables and hard grains on display were telling evidence of the progress the plow was making. At the dinner, Mayor Henry was the principal speaker. Winter wheat was his subject. It would be the salvation of this land with its scanty rainfall, he told his listeners. Planted in the fall, it could be harvested before the seering hot winds of dry summer withered it as it did spring wheat.[9] He had an announcement to make before he sat down: he had signed a contract with the Kansas Pacific Railroad to farm its right-of-way from the outskirts of Abilene to Detroit (five miles east of Abilene), thousands of acres that he would plant to winter wheat! It was breathtaking. Regretfully, he added, the demands on his time would be such that he would not be a candidate for re-election in the spring.

This unusual farm, five miles long and a mile wide, was to receive nation-wide publicity. Newspaper correspondents named it the "Golden Belt" and grew lyrical about riding through miles of waving, golden grain. They fastened the title of "Wheat King of Kansas" on Theodore Henry. It induced scores of settlers to take up land in Geary, Dickinson and Saline counties, which was what he and the Kansas Pacific Railroad wanted. Both had land for sale.

Henry was a land speculator rather than an experienced agriculturist, but with the prominence that had come his way, he moved about the state expounding his theories of farm management. Of those who put their faith in him many prospered; others lost everything.

Wherever he spoke, he continued to attack the Texas cattle trade, demanding its abolishment. A surprisingly large number of Abilene's influential citizens did not share his views. They were making money out of the cattle business, and they did not want anything to interfere with it. Casting about for a man they could support for mayor, they settled on Joe McCoy. He was little more than a figurehead now, but he was a stockman and if elected could be depended on to favor the Texas trade.

Far to the south, at the confluence of the little Arkansas and the Arkansas, where Jesse Chisholm had had his ranch, trouble of another sort was brewing. Bill Greiffenstein and Jim Meade had platted a townsite that they named Wichita. Some lots had been sold and it claimed a modest population of twenty. It lay astride the great trail. Past it had streamed over half a million Longhorns in four years. If it could entice a railroad, it would save the drovers four to five days' driving, and the farmers could do what they pleased with Abilene. After three or four false starts the Atchison, Topeka and Santa Fe was making the dirt fly at last as it built across Kansas. It was nearing Emporia already. Nobody knew where it was going. If it missed Wichita, it wouldn't be by much.

11

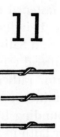

They Called Him Wild Bill

IN THE OLD DAYS when the Chisholm Trail was new, it was the custom of some trail bosses to point the wagon pole at the North Star in the evening so that in the morning they had only to glance at it to know which direction to take. Those days were gone; after crossing Red River, a child could have found its way to Abilene without going astray.

Soon after the season of 1871 got into full swing, so many herds were moving toward Kansas that it was often difficult to keep them from treading on one another's heels. By midsummer overgrazing made it necessary to detour from the trail for a mile or two to find grass. At the Arkansas River Crossing where, the previous July there had been nothing but Greiffenstein and Meade's trading posts, they found a growing town of a hundred people.

Agents from Ellsworth were on hand to try to induce them to drive there instead of to Abilene. This effort to divert the Longhorns from the old trail met with some success, car loadings at Ellsworth for 1871 accounting for 64,000 head shipped.

As they moved into Dickinson County the drovers were harassed by fences and the organized resistance of the farmers. Still another herd law had been enacted, and this one had teeth in it. In some places the old brush fences had been replaced by a new invention just being put on the market and named, appropriately, barbed wire. It was cheap and it was deadly enough to turn back any critter that tried to break through it. The Texans shook their heads when they saw it for the first time. They couldn't have surmised that in a few years it would be adopted by cattlemen north and south, and in time become the great safeguard for the orderly functioning of the livestock industry.

Though Theodore Henry had campaigned against him, McCoy had squeaked through and was elected mayor on April 3. In a few days, the undesirables were flocking back to Abilene; saloons were being refurbished and new ones made ready for business. The pace of the town quickened. In another month the Longhorn carnival would engulf Abilene again. It confronted the mayor and the town council with the necessity of finding someone to replace the slain Tom Smith. James Butler Hickok was available. They were familiar with his record as the late marshal of Hays City. In his brief tenure there he had killed Jack Strawhan (the name is spelled several different ways) and two troopers of the 7th Cavalry. Prior to that he was alleged to have downed a score of men—the number depended on who was doing the talking—not including Indians. As Wild Bill, the Prince of Pistoleers, he had a fearsome reputation. Did Abilene want to take a backward step and be ruled by the kind of gun law he represented?

The mayor and the town council stood divided. McCoy says he was at first opposed to hiring Hickok. He doesn't say what made him change his mind, but on April 15, all were in agreement and "Hickok was sent for and hired at $150 a month, plus a percentage of the fines levied."

Here I must part company with those writers who have Charles F. Gross going to Fort Harker (Ellsworth) to inform Hickok of his appointment. Gross, you will remember, was the man that McCoy brought out from Sprinfield to act as his bookkeeper and later as clerk of the Drover's Cottage. The tale of Gross having gone to Fort Harker for Hickok is based solely on a letter he wrote J. B. Edwards, Abilene's most trustworthy local historian, years later.

When Hickok beat a hasty retreat from Hays City following the killing of the two troopers, he spent some time in Topeka but was in Abilene early in April. When asked why he had fled Hays City, he replied laconically: "I couldn't fight the whole 7th Cavalry."

Under those circumstances he would hardly have found a welcome at Fort Harker. Stuart Henry says: "Hickok was in Abilene for ten days preceding his appointment as town marshal, spending his time in the Alamo Saloon, gambling." [1] In view of corroborating evidence, I accept this statement as true. In this instance, as well as others, Gross proves himself unreliable. He was the author of the fantastic tale that Frank and Jesse James and Cole Younger were "smuggled into Abilene and put up at Drover's Cottage." According to his story they registered under aliases, but he recognized them and they admitted their identity. He gives his alleged talk with them, in which he asked if they weren't afraid Wild Bill would try to put them under arrest. According to him, Cole said: "We got too many friends here among the Texans. All we want to do is rest up a bit and give our horses time to do the same. We won't bother Wild Bill and he won't bother us." [2]

All of this is sheer nonsense. Frank and Jesse James and Cole Younger were never in Abilene. The three of them never rode anywhere together after 1869; Frank and Cole, yes, but never with Jesse. Cole didn't like Jesse, and he didn't trust him. Anyone familiar with the history of the James-Younger Gang will recall that on June 3, 1871 (a few weeks prior to their alleged appearance in Abilene), they looted the Ocobock Brothers Bank at Corydon, Iowa, and made off with $45,000—one of their biggest hauls. They dropped from sight thereafter and were not heard from again until they cracked the bank at Columbia, Kentucky, April 29, 1872. Frank and Jesse spent those eleven months hiding out near Nashville, Tennessee, with relatives.

Edwards, taken into camp by Gross' tales, has a gunfight between the famous outlaws and Wild Bill when the former tried to make off with the cashbox at the Dickinson County Fair. The James-Younger Gang, in a hair-raising exploit, made off with the receipts of the Kansas City Fair as they were being taken to the bank, on September 26, 1872, the proceeds of the robbery amounting to $10,000. Very likely that affair provided the inspiration for Gross' story about a similar job having occurred in Abilene. Fifty-one years passed before he got around to putting his "recollections" down on paper. As with so many old-timers, his imagination was keener than his memory.

Hickok put aside his fringed buckskins and blossomed forth in Prince Albert, a red sash and ruffled shirt. With his shoulder-length brown hair and drooping mustache he was a handsome figure. He didn't patrol the streets as Tom Smith had done. His address was the Alamo Saloon. Through the glass triple doors passersby could see him seated at a table, playing poker, his back to the wall. Sometime during the afternoon he would take a turn up and down Texas Street, and again in the evening, a brace of pistols at his waist, his stony blue eyes roving from right to left. On his walks, he kept to the middle of the street, speaking to no one. It heightened the effect of his deadly reputation. It was the image of the peerless gunfighter, nerveless, quick to kill, he brought to Abilene that was his best weapon. The town rocked along, and though the ever changing army of cowboys, some just coming off the trail and others getting ready to head back to Texas, reviled him and talked about a showdown, they weren't rash enough to try it.

Hickok must have doubted his ability to hold the town in check as the big herds began to reach Abilene in an almost continuous stream and the cowboy population mounted to over three thousand. He asked for assistance, and on June 16, James Gainsford, Tom Carson (Kit Carson's nephew) and Jim McDonald, the former deputy sheriff whose cowardice was said to have been responsible for Marshal Smith's murder, were appointed policemen. Between them they kept the town reasonably quiet. The law against carrying firearms had become a dead letter. New signs forbidding the carrying of guns or other weapons were put up by Hickok. They were disregarded, and he made no effort to enforce the ordinance.

As the Chisholm Trail continued to disgorge its thousands of Longhorns, comely Susanna Moore arrived in Abilene. She was an old flame of Wild Bill's. Over her he had killed Dave Tutt, her paramour, in the town square at Springfield, Missouri, in 1865. He established Susanna in a cottage in back of the Alamo and resumed relations with her. Apparently the old spark was dead, for he soon sent her packing. Business of a more serious nature now claimed his attention in the person of John Wesley Hardin, only eighteen at the time and already a killer, who was able to boast, before he was shot down in an El Paso saloon, that he had put away forty men.

Hardin had come up the trail with a herd belonging to Colonel O. W. Wheeler. There were warrants out on him, a fact certainly known to Hickok; but the latter never tried to serve them. He did, however, demand that Wes hand over the guns he was wearing when he encountered him on Texas Street. This sets the stage for one of the hoariest of all myths, and you will not be able to read about the Chisholm Trail and Abilene without encountering it. According to Hardin, and we have only his word for it, when Wild Bill asked him for his guns, he presented them butts first and then, keeping his fingers in the trigger guards, brought them up sharply enough to flip them over and put the butts back in his own hands. This was the old "road agent's spin." Don't be taken in by it. You can be sure that Hickok was as well-acquainted with the "road agent's spin" as a fresh young punk of eighteen.

And that brings us to the redoubtable Ben Thompson, Texas gambler and gunfighter, who never took a backward step for any man. Eugene Cunningham has described him as ". . . that square-jawed Wizard of the Pistol; that black-haired, blue-eyed Typical Gunman of the great inky-black mustache—Confederate soldier, professional gambler, peace officer, and a gunslinger second to none that Texas ever produced." [3] When he was in his cups, which was oftener and oftener as he grew older, he was as dangerous as a diamondback rattler. Of him no less an authority than Bat Masterson wrote: "Ben was the most dangerous killer in the Old West. The very name of Ben Thompson was enough to cause the general run of 'man-killers,' even those who had never seen him, to seek safety in flight." [4]

Thompson was almost broke when he arrived in Abilene, but a miraculous run of luck at poker put him back on top. His friend and fellow Texas gambler, big, handsome, blond Phil Coe, was there. They pooled their resources and opened the Bull's Head Saloon, which soon shared the spotlight with the more elegant Alamo. Over the front of the establishment, which made it appear to be two stories high, they placed a large painted picture of an old mossy horn bull with its masculine appurtenances boldly depicted.

The good people of Abilene called the painting obscene and were enraged that children on their way to school had to pass it. The mayor and council ordered Marshal Hickok to see that it was taken down. When the ultimatum was delivered to Ben, he swore that he'd be damned if he'd take it down.

What followed is told several ways. Some say that the offending picture was removed, others that Hickok had it taken down and repainted. On the best evidence available what the marshal did was to send a man up a ladder with a bucket of paint and blot out certain parts of the bull's anatomy. When the fresh paint dried, the old came through, and the original, somewhat murky, stood revealed in ghastly clarity. Naturally the painting drew more attention than ever. The ribald art lovers of Texas Street embarrassed Wild Bill with their tittering. He didn't appreciate being made a laughingstock. There is some evidence that this was the incident that turned him against Thompson. Certainly Ben felt that Hickok had stepped on his toes, and he was not one to forget an indignity of that sort.

The Bull's Head was said to be a gold mine for the proprietors. Rumors started circulating that the games in the back room were rigged. It could hardly have come from the Texans, for in Abilene, or wherever Ben appeared in Yankee-land, they regarded him as their spokesman and rallied around him. It could have, as some hinted, originated with Hickok. However it was, Ben and his partner were forced to move their games into the main barroom.

Men who were acquainted with Ben Thompson agreed that it was the prelude to trouble; his integrity had been questioned, and sooner or later he would do something about it. To their surprise, he did nothing at all. Wes Hardin was still in town. He made capital out of Thompson's failure to go gunning for Hickok. In his book, published twenty-five years later, he claimed that Ben had been afraid of Wild Bill and tried to hire him to do away with the long-haired marshal. Of course, Ben had been dead for fifteen years, and Wes, always a plausible and sometimes humorous liar, could safely spin the tale.

The business of the Bull's Head did not suffer under the new arrangement. It wasn't only the cowboys, with three or four months' wages to squander who crowded about the tables; many owners bucked the games, and they played for big stakes. They liked Ben and his partner, handsome Phil Coe. Though the two of them were making money hand over fist, they sold their license to Tom Sheran, the grocer and ex-marshal, but continued to operate the Bull's Head. Very likely the purpose of this stratagem was to make it difficult for Hickok to close the place, which he had threatened to do.

Lake's Olympiad and Mammoth Circus reached Abilene on July 13. Agnes Thatcher Lake, a widow of two years, was the owner and star performer. She was a skilled equestrienne, lion tamer and high-wire artist. It is not necessary to go into her history other than to say that in her world she was a person of some consequence. For many seasons she and her late husband, Bill Lake, had toured the country with the famous John Robinson Shows, the best of their era.[5]

If figures do not lie, Agnes Lake was a well-preserved handsome forty-five when she met Hickok. He was thirty-four. Despite the difference in their ages, the one thing on which all commentators agree is that she was smitten with him on sight. "She fell for him hook, line and sinker, all the way to the basement," says the unreliable Charles Gross, "and wanted to marry him and make him manager of her circus."

Hickok was on hand at the performances, ostensibly to maintain order. Whether she saw in him a lover or a stellar box-office attraction, no one can say. He did not follow her to Topeka and other Kansas towns, as some have it. According to the record, they next met three years later in Rochester, New York, where her circus was exhibiting and he was appearing (or had been) in a Wild West stage show.

They did not meet again until February, 1876, in Cheyenne. The gold rush to the Black Hills was in full swing. Cheyenne was a favorite jumping-off place for Deadwood. Hickok had guided several large parties to the diggings the previous fall, and he was back in Cheyenne, waiting for spring to reopen the trails. He and his friend Colorado Charlie Utter, an experienced frontiersman, let it be known that they were organizing a sizable party that would take off for the north as soon as the weather warranted, and that it was their intention to remain in the Black Hills this time and try their luck at prospecting.

It could hardly have been by accident or coincidence that Agnes Thatcher Lake arrived in Cheyenne to spend several weeks with her friends S. L. Moyer and wife. That Mrs. Moyer had written Agnes that Bill was in Cheyenne for the winter seems a justifiable speculation. The Hickok name had lost some of its glamour, and Agnes had grown plump and fiftyish. They met and renewed their old acquaintanceship with obviously mutual satisfaction, for on March 5, 1876, they were married. A brief honeymoon with her relatives in Cincinnati followed. Spring came on, and Hickok left her there, never to see her again, and returned to Cheyenne, where Charlie Utter had everything in readiness to leave for Deadwood. What followed scarcely needs repeating. About four o'clock in the afternoon of August 2, Jack McCall, a two-bit gambler, strolled into Carl Mann's Number Ten saloon, in Deadwood, where Hickok sat playing poker, and shot him dead.

Turn back the clock to July, 1871, and Abilene, where the season was so far advanced that it was freely predicted the figure for cattle received in 1871 would double that of the previous year. It would reach half a million head, no less, men said. As the exodus from Texas continued, it seemed to many that the Lone Star State was being swept clean of all its cattle.

The upstart Atchison, Topeka and Santa Fe put its rails into what had been known as the Newton Prairie in July, 1871, and stuck up a signpost reading NEWTON. After pausing to catch its breath it headed west for Great Bend and Dodge City. A tent and shack town grew up almost overnight when the Santa Fe announced that Newton was to be a railroad division point and market for shipping Texas cattle. It hired Joe McCoy to come down from Abilene and superintend the building of a six-chute stockyard. McCoy was still mayor of Abilene. At the time he had no reason to believe that its days as a cattle market were about ended. What impelled him to stab it in the back, so to speak, can only be explained by a pressing need for money.

It passes belief that Abilene was unaware of the activity at Newton and the threat it posed, and yet no commentator on the Kansas scene of the period has had anything to say about it. One

or two merely mention that McCoy went to Newton in July, 1871,
but they do not say why nor offer any comment on how Abilene
felt about it.

Work on the yards was pushed forward with great energy, and
on August 15, the first trainload of cattle pulled out of Newton,
bound for Kansas City. In some ways Newton was an ideal site for
a cattle market. It was almost astride the old Chisholm Trail to
Abilene and sixty-five miles shorter than the drive to Ellsworth;
the surrounding prairies were well-grassed. The only drawbacks
were a short supply of water and no buyers. The Santa Fe hired
McCoy to hurry to Illinois and contact the scores of traders and
feed lot operators with whom he was acquainted and get them to
come to Newton. He must have done fairly well, for although the
season was half gone, Newton shipped better than 30,000 head
that year.

Floyd B. Streeter, who was never given to exaggeration, says:
"The Texas cattle trade in Abilene reached its height in 1871. It
is estimated that 600,000 cattle arrived in western Kansas during
the season. For miles north, south and west of Abilene one was
scarcely out of sight of a herd." [6] The Kansas City stockyards reported receiving over 100,000 Longhorns by rail from Abilene.
Several hundred thousand head of stock cattle were sold as they
came off the Chisholm Trail and were driven on into Nebraska
and the Northwest.

The Reverend George Webb Slaughter, head of the famous
Slaughter family of Texas cowmen and a hero of the Texan Revolution, was one of the few who ever revealed any figures regarding
his trail-driving operations. This is his accounting:

1868—	800 head,	$ 32,000
1869—	2,000 head,	$ 90,000
1870—	3,000 head,	$105,000
1871—	2,000 head,	$ 66,000
1873—	2,000 head,	$ 66,000
1874—	2,000 head,	$ 60,000
1875—	1,000 head,	$ 45,000

He gives no figures for 1872, possibly because he was in partnership with his son, C. C. Slaughter, that season. But the sums received total almost half a million dollars. It becomes really

impressive when you consider that the big outfits, like the Ellisons, the Dewees brothers, the Blockers and a score more, pointed
three, four, even five times as many Longhorns north, year after
year, beginning in 1869, as the Reverend Slaughter.

12

Farewell to Abilene

In the summer of 1871 Mrs. Lake had not been gone from Abilene for more than a week when Hickok became enamored of one of Mattie Silks' new "boarders," a girl named Jessie Hazel. The irrepressible Mattie could rightly claim to have been the town's first "madam." Until she came, prostitution in Abilene had been a sordid, ugly business. In her old age—she lived to be eighty-one —Mattie was fond of recalling her days in Abilene, Dodge City, Denver and the Yukon, but she never disclosed who built for her the elegant (elegant for Abilene) square, two-story house on Cedar Street, around the corner from Texas Street (and across from the schoolhouse, of all places), the backyard screened from public view by a high board fence. In its yellow paint, curtained windows and expensive furnishings, it was, with some justice, dubbed "the mansion."

Her "boarders" were young, pretty, and a far cry from the hay bags and worn-out whores who had left their good years behind them in the dives of St. Louis and other Mississippi River towns, to which Abilene was accustomed. If the folklore of the day can be believed, Jessie Hazel was the fairest of the fair. She was flattered at first by Hickok's attentions, and he believed he was riding high with her. And then she met bearded, handsome Phil Coe. Her ardor for the marshal began to cool. He was quick to discover why. That she preferred Coe to himself was bitter medicine for a man of his ego.

From here on you can chart your own course in pursuing the Coe-Hickok feud, and no matter what direction you take you will find some recognized writer agreeing with you and a dozen others violently disagreeing. According to the Hickok adherents Phil Coe was a loud-mouthed, arrogant, overbearing coward, particularly troublesome when he was drinking, who depended on the menace of his partner Ben Thompson's guns to see him through. The Texans said he was a pleasant, well-mannered man whose intentions were so peaceful that he never went armed.

The trouble between the two gladiators began one afternoon in September. The season was so nearly over that the town council had dismissed the last of Hickok's deputies. He was standing at the bar of Billy Mitchell's Novelty Theatre having a drink with Mike Williams, the theatre's private policeman (Hickok had got him the job), when he was informed that the fair Jessie was in Coe's room at the Gulf House, indulging in some extracurricular romancing. Some accounts have it that they were downstairs, drinking wine in the "wine room." Wherever they were, Hickok rushed in on them, slapped Jessie around and knocked her to the floor as he stormed out—all this without Coe raising a hand. The Texans said no, that Coe leaped at Hickok as the later reviled the "lady" with the vilest names he could lay tongue to, and would have strangled him if she had not intervened.

One version is as unbelievable as the other. But there was a meeting at the Gulf House, and the two men never spoke again until the night of October 5, when gunfire closed the lips of one forever. The tragedy that occurred that evening is not important in itself, but its repercussions on the cattle trade and the great trail were tremendous.

Dismissing the conflicting and strictly partisan accounts of what happened, these facts emerge: the season was over; some of the saloons were closed already; most of the floating population had left town. During the afternoon as many as half a hundred cowboys, who were pulling out for Texas in the morning, had been marching up and down Texas Street in a body in a riotous but good-natured final celebration. Phil Coe was one of the celebrants.

He was going down the trail with them. Ben Thompson had been gone for weeks and was on his way to Texas with his wife.[1] The Bull's Head was closed. Hickok confronted the crowd. Realizing that it was all in fun, he was willing to go along with the merry-makers, warning them, however, to leave their guns at camp when they came in that evening. The tale that they lifted him to their shoulders and carried him into the Applejack Saloon and made him stand treat need not be taken seriously.

The hilarity continued. Theophilus Little, by his own admission a prejudiced witness, says, "I saw this band of crazy men. They went up and down the street with a wild swish and rush and roar, totally oblivious to anything in their path. It was a drunken mob." [2]

Shortly after nine o'clock that evening, Wild Bill was standing at the bar in the Novelty Theatre, talking to his friend Mike Williams, when a shot sounded. Running up the alley, he entered the Alamo from the rear and ran through to the front of the saloon. The glass doors stood open. He confronted the rioters, demanding to know who had fired the shot. Phil Coe readily admitted he had. His gun was in his hand. He had fired at a mad dog, he said. His friends snickered; they had not seen any "mad dog"; the shot had been fired in the air, in drunken exuberance.

Beyond doubt Hickok realized that this was the long-put-off showdown between Coe and himself. You will read that he drew a pair of Derringers and fired, which is fiction; the guns he used were his favorite .44 six-shooters. The Texans have it that Hickok fired first; that Coe had received "two balls in the abdomen" before he shot, one slug piercing Hickok's coat and a second missing him completely and lodging in the door frame at his back.

Wild Bill's story was that he saw Coe lower his arm as though to return his pistol to the holster, then stop suddenly and point it at him. His version makes it a justifiable killing; according to the Texans it was murder.

There is no question about what followed a few seconds later. A man ran up the sidewalk. Hickok whirled on him and put two balls into his head, killing him instantly. The dead man was Hickok's friend Mike Williams, killed as he was rushing to his assistance.

Coe died two days later and his friend Bud Cotton took the body back to Austin, Texas, for burial.

When Hickok felled Williams, he must have fired a number of times, for two other men were slightly wounded. Elsewhere I have said: "What actually happened in that blazing minute or two will never be known. The truth is lost in controversy. But whichever version you accept—you search in vain for the image of the great scout, the coolheaded, steely-eyed killer with ice water in his veins, and find only a suddenly panic-stricken Hickok. The illusion of greatness grows even dimmer when you learn that the following morning he bought a shotgun, and had the barrels sawed off, and that he kept it at his elbow day and night for the rest of his stay in Abilene." [3]

The double killing aroused the town against the cattle trade as never before. Crowds of irate citizens stormed the council meeting, demanding that the trade be banned. McCoy tried to stem the rising tide. He praised Marshal Hickok. "Talk about a rule of iron!" he exclaimed. "We had it." And yet on December 12, he affixed his signature to a council resolution discharging Wild Bill "for the reason that the city is no longer in need of his services." It went into effect the following day. There was no word of commendation, no thanks expressed.

Hickok served eight months less two days. Instead of the dozen or more with which legend credits him, he had killed only two men—one of them by mistake.

Bypassing Mayor McCoy and the town council, Theodore Henry organized what he called the Dickinson County Farmers' Protective Association. You didn't have to be a farmer to be eligible for membership; all that was required was that you were opposed to the cattle trade. Mass meetings were held in December and January, and the attendance they attracted warned McCoy and his followers that they had a real fight on their hands. McCoy accused the *Chronicle*, which devoted a great deal of space to the doings of the new organization, of being T. C. Henry's paid tool. Doubtless this was true, for Henry had bought control of the paper.

Early in February, the following circular, written by Henry and bearing his signature and several hundred others, was first printed in the *Chronicle* and then copies were broadcast over Texas:

> We the undersigned, members of the Farmers' Protective Association, and officers and citizens of Dickinson County, Kansas, most respectfully request all who have contemplated driving Texas cattle to Abilene the coming season to seek some other point for shipment, as the inhabitants of Dickinson will no longer submit to the evils of the trade.

The circular was sent out over the angry protests of McCoy and his associates. They began an organized letter campaign begging Texas drovers to ignore the Henry broadside and return to Abilene in the spring. Had they known what was afoot, both sides could have spared themselves weeks of anxious waiting to see what was going to happen.

The Kansas Pacific had never done anything for Abilene. It couldn't do enough for Ellsworth, and for the best of reasons— namely, the progress its rival, the Santa Fe, was making. Through its subsidiary, the Wichita and Southwestern, it would soon be in Wichita and turn it into a great cattle market. That was not all; its rails were now west of Great Bend (which was in an excellent position to capture the herds coming up from the Texas Panhandle) and lining out for Dodge City with its thousands of dried buffalo hides to be shipped. If the Santa Fe was to be kept from taking over the entire Texas cattle and hide business, the Kansas Pacific had to establish a market second to none along its main line that the drovers could reach without being subjected to the harassment they had encountered in Dickinson County; a market that would be convenient for buyers of both beef and stock cattle. Ellsworth was the answer.

They hired Shanghai Pierce and Colonel W. D. Hunter to superintend the building of a stockyard with seven chutes, capable of loading two thousand cattle a day. William M. Cox, its general livestock agent, and a party of engineers were dispatched to Indian Territory to survey a trail to Ellsworth. This new trail, breaking away from the old Chisholm Trail at Pond Creek Ranch, halfway between the Salt Fork of the Arkansas and Pond Creek, was to come north to the west of Kingman, Kansas, cross the Arkansas at Ellinwood and shoot straight for Ellsworth, with a net saving of thirty-five miles over the old route.

In passing, it is worth noting that while various other extensions of the original trail (of which the Abilene Trail was one) took the name of the parent trail, it was never used to designate the route William Cox opened. Invariably it was called the Cox Trail.

The Kansas Pacific's next move was to send the popular and colorful Shanghai Pierce into Texas to drum up business for the Ellsworth market. He didn't disappoint his employers. When he returned to Ellsworth it was with commitments from Mabry, Perryman, Print Olive and others that they would point their herds for Ellsworth.

It spelled the demise of Abilene as a shipping point for cattle. The circulars and letters had had little to do with it. Ironically, it was the trail drivers who had got through with the town; not the other way around. Texas Street stood deserted. Rents fell to a pittance, with no takers. Jake Karatofsky, the enterprising young Russian immigrant, moved his stock of goods to booming Ellsworth. Others did the same. Part of the Drover's Cottage was taken down and moved in sections to Ellsworth, where it functioned until it was destroyed by fire.

Thirty years later, T. C. Henry, made comfortably rich by his farm and irrigation schemes, said, in recalling the former great cow town as it was in 1872: "Abilene became quiet—painfully quiet. Its mortuary fame was nearly as celebrated as its 'live' infamy had been before." Of course, Abilene survived and became the thriving farming and industrial city it is today. But it has not forgotten its glamorous past; a handsome stone marker proudly proclaims it "Abilene—The End of the Chisholm Trail," which, to be generous, it was.

As Ellsworth was ready to emerge as an important trail town, Newton, which had been left to wither on the vine as a cattle market by the Santa Fe, retreated into semiobscurity as the trading center of a prosperous farming community, which was the best thing that could have happened to it. It was soon to have the payroll of the Santa Fe shops to bolster its economy, but better still the almost two thousand Mennonite farmers put on the land by the railroad's colonization department. The Mennonites were a religious sect that had left their native Germany to escape religious persecution and migrated to the Volga Basin of Russia in the time of Catherine the Great. Oppression there had turned them to America.

They were, without exception, men of the soil. Each family brought with it a bag of hard Turkey Red wheat, which was to prove perfectly adapted to the semiarid prairies and largely impervious to the extremes of heat and cold. It was the greatest gift Kansas ever received and made it what it is today, one of the great grain-producing states of the Union.

Though Newton's days as a cow town were brief, they were violent. At one time or another at least half a dozen towns won the sobriquet of "the toughest town in Kansas"—or in the United States. If toughness was to be measured by the number of killings that occurred, Newton outdid them all. Deservedly, it became known as "Bloody Newton." One night in Perry Tuttle's dance hall in "Hide Park," the town's Red Light district, policeman Mike McCluskie, Pat Lee, a freight-train brakeman and three Texans, Jim Martin, Bill Garrett and Jim Wilkerson, were killed. At least two other participants and several nonparticipants were wounded—an event referred to ever afterward as the "Newton Massacre."

This riot grew out of the killing of a cowboy named Bill Bailey by night policeman McCluskie—by all accounts a justifiable killing. Hugh Anderson, Bailey's friend, had sworn to avenge the latter's death. Anderson was the ringleader of the dance hall battle, and though he came out of it seriously wounded, he was charged with killing McCluskie. Though his condition was desperate, his friends smuggled him aboard a waiting train, with the connivance of the train crew, and got him to Kansas City. Ten weeks later, he was back in Bell County, Texas, but he never fully recovered and died a year or two later.

Newton at the time had no town government. Tom Carson, who had served under Hickok at Abilene, was in town. The saloonkeepers and gamblers hired him, as they had hired McCluskie, to take over. He restored a semblance of order but there was little he could do. The killings continued. In afteryears some wild statements were made that as many as fifty men met a violent death in Newton between August 15, 1871, and the following June. According to my research the number was twelve.

The township in which Newton was located was one of the six northern townships of Sedgwick County, all practically unorganized. When a number of leading citizens appealed to the county for help in maintaining law and order, a constable and deputy sheriff were assigned to Newton, along with two justices of the peace.[4] Their presence had some effect. A form of town government was established. The cattle season came to an end. A large amount of money had changed hands. The town began to quiet down, but on November 7, Justice of the Peace Halliday stopped in at the Gold Room, Harry Lovett's popular saloon, for a toddy before going to his office. Pat Fitzpatrick, who had been employed at the stockyards, came in and demanded that Halliday set up the drinks. When the latter angrily refused, Fitzpatrick drew a pistol and shot him dead.

It had a sobering effect and a town board was named and application made for incorporating Newton as a city of the third class. The request was granted on February 3, 1872; and on the last day of the month the six northern townships separated from Sedgwick County, and Harvey County was organized. This was accomplished only by Harvey County agreeing to underwrite $70,000 of the $200,000 bond issue that had been voted for the construction of the Wichita and Southwestern Railroad, which was to connect Newton and Wichita by rail. This needs a bit of explaining.

On August 15, a few weeks after the first herd of Longhorns reached Newton, the new cow town had been asked to vote on the railroad bond issue. Realizing that once Wichita had a railroad it would take over the cattle business that otherwise would come to Newton, the town voted solidly against it. But the majority of votes were in the southern part of Sedgwick County. Now, less than six months later, Newton was being asked to cut its own throat for the second time. The measure carried by a scant margin. Unquestionably the Santa Fe had a finger in the outcome, for it was vitally interested in having the Wichita and Southwestern built. Jim Meade and Bill Grieffenstein were the incorporators, but they were believed to be only figureheads and would bow out soon after the road was in operation. The little Wichita and Southwestern would then become a part of the Santa Fe system. To no one's surprise, that was what happened.

After some delays due to the nonarrival of material, grading began in March. Two months later, May 16, 1872, the rails were laid and Wichita saw its first locomotive. It spelled the total eclipse of Newton as a cattle market, and for several years it was as moribund as Abilene.

To return to Abilene briefly. An incredible number of Longhorns had been trailed into Kansas in 1871. Late arrivals found prices taking a downward turn. As a consequence, thousands of cattle were driven west of Ellsworth and turned out on the short, succulent buffalo grass to be wintered. Save for the fringe of scrub timber along the Smoky Hill River and the creeks, it was open, rolling country, exposed to every wintry blast that blew.

Of the total number being held, 30 per cent or more were stock cattle. Late as the season was, some were sold, but for the rest there would be no demand until the following spring. To make matters worse, the price of beeves fell so low that owners decided to risk wintering their herds on the prairies. They might better have taken whatever they were offered and written 1871 off as just a bad year, for ahead of them they had such a winter as did not come again until the great die-up of 1885–86, when upward of a million cattle, horses, mules and sheep died on the western plains from Montana to the Texas Panhandle. Snow, freezing blizzards and icy rains glazed the plains of western Kansas. Mules and horses could break through the hard crust to grass; the helpless cattle starved and froze where they stood.

A few found shelter in the wooded creek bottoms and managed to survive. There was nothing men could do to help them. It was sometimes as much as life was worth for men to stir out of the dugouts in which they had holed up. Horses subsisted on the bark of trees and what grass they could find; cattle could only turn their rumps to the icy blasts and stare blindly through the icicles that fringed their eyes. When the weather moderated, few were left alive. For miles around, the prairies were strewn with the carcasses of dead Longhorns. All the owners could salvage from them were the hides.

Estimates of the number of cattle that perished on the prairies of Ellsworth County that winter run as high as 150,000, along with hundreds of horses. That figure does not seem extravagant when measured against the following item in the *Ellsworth Reporter* the following June: "We are informed that about 30,000 head of mixed cattle, the surviving remnants of the many herds that faced the terrible winter just passed on the Ellsworth prairies, have fully recuperated and are now being offered for sale." Further confirmation is found in the number of cowhides that were shipped from Ellsworth that spring.

It was a loss from which, in any other occupation, few men could have recovered financially. It was different with the Texas cattle trade; you might be on the verge of bankruptcy one season, due to circumstances beyond your control, without any damage to your integrity, and be back on your feet the next. It may, in a way, explain why the business failed to produce a man of national reputation, comparable to the giants of petroleum, steel, railroads and automobiles. In his old age Joe McCoy, who had had his share of ups and downs, when asked why this was, said facetiously: "They don't last long enough. The rich retire early and the rest go broke."

Of course, historians and Western buffs are acquainted with the great trails and the men who made trail driving a multimillion dollar business, but the only name the average American schoolboy knows is Jesse Chisholm.

13

North to Ellsworth

ELLSWORTH WAS AN ORGANIZED TOWN with a population of twelve hundred, chartered as a city of the third class, when it proudly proclaimed itself the leading cattle market of Kansas.

The season started with the proverbial bang. Late in May the first herd came up the new Cox Trail. Three more followed a few days later. On June 15, as many as thirty herds, averaging 2,500 head, blackened the surrounding prairies. Counting the 30,000 wintered cattle, now salable, no less than 100,000 Longhorns were gathered at the Ellsworth market. Half of them were young stock cattle, for which there had been no demand at the end of the previous season. Buyers were on hand now and they were ready sale, and at favorable prices.

Ellsworth boomed. The weather was dry and clouds of dust drifted over the town from the stockyards to the west. The saloons did a land-office business, and the old Drover's Cottage, renamed The Cottage, now reduced to eighty rooms, served as many as a hundred and fifty dinners a day. Ellsworth had done its best to capture the cattle trade, and now that it had, it took steps to curb the evils that had plagued Abilene. It had a police force of four men, supplemented by a sheriff and deputy sheriff who could be called on for assistance when needed. To keep the prostitutes out of the business section it established a district for them in the Smoky Hill bottoms, half a mile away, which promptly was dubbed Nauchville. No attempt was made to police its bordellos, saloons and gambling joints, the town fathers theorizing that whoever visited the district knew why he was there and what he came for.

Ellsworth soon discovered that the measures it had taken to brace itself against the onslaught of the cattle trade were inadequate. It wasn't Abilene all over again, but it was wild and tough. Thirteen persons were licensed to carry on the business of saloon and dramshop keepers. An English visitor wrote: "Ellsworth reminds me of a town in California in its early days, when gambling flourished, and vice was at a premium. Here you see in the streets men from every state, and I might say from almost every nation—the tall, long-haired Texas herder, with his heavy jingling spurs and pair of six-shooters; the dirty greasy Mexicans, with their unintelligible jargon; the gamblers from all parts of the country, looking for unsuspecting prey; the honest emigrant in search of a homestead in the great free west; the keen stock buyers; the wealthy Texas drovers; dead beats; 'cappers'; pickpockets; horse thieves; a cavalry of Texas ponies; and scores of demi-monde.

"Gambling of every description is carried on without any attempt at privacy. I am told there are some 75 professional gamblers in town; and every day we hear of some of their sharp tricks. Whisky-selling seems to be the most profitable business. But there are many honorable business men here, who are doing a heavy business." [1]

John Montgomery, the fiery, hard-hitting editor-publisher of the Ellsworth *Reporter* and brother-in-law of Sheriff Cap Whitney, was even more critical. He knew that the police force, the "four Jacks"—Brocky Jack Norton, a transfer from Abilene, Jack DeLong, Jack Morco and Jack Branham—were corrupt, that young Texans were being fleeced right and left and that the officers were enriching thmselves from the fines they collected from the alleged drunk and disorderly arrests they made. For personal gain the ordinance against carrying firearms was enforced so rigidly that a man who rode into town with the intention of hanging his guns on one of the racks with which all saloons were provided was likely to be arrested before he had time to get out of the saddle.

Editor Montgomery feared that the mounting resentment of the Texans would result in an explosion of bloody violence. "The blackleg element is becoming entrenched and the police do nothing about it," he wrote. "Like the ostrich, the City Council keeps its head buried in the sand and sees no evil. Let some house-cleaning be its first order of business."

When he complained that the council was doing nothing about keeping the three blocks of the business district on North Main Street and South Main Street (the Kansas Pacific had cut the town in two, hence the two main streets, with a wide space, sometimes called a plaza, in between them) sprinkled to lay the clouds of dust that blew in all day from the stockyards, he was curtly informed that the expenses of running the town already exceeded its receipts.

All right, Montgomery responded in effect, if it's money Ellsworth needs to conduct the town, let it license the several hundred prostitutes in Nauchville, which was inside the town limits. "If it can't be rooted out, the vicious vocation should be made to contribute to the expense of maintaining law and order." The suggestion shocked the good people of Ellsworth, but the council voted it into law. Criticism of the measure subsided to a muted whisper when it became apparent that this licensing alone would more than defray the expenses of the municipality.

Ellsworth's reign as the Cow Capital of Kansas was to be brief, but as long as it could lay claim to the title, the license money collected from Nauchville was the town's major source of revenue, which led the Topeka *Commonwealth* to comment sarcastically in a story appropriately entitled "The Wages of Sin": "The city of Ellsworth realizes $300 per month from prostitution fines alone. . . . The city authorities consider that as long as mankind is depraved and Texas cattle herders exist, there will be a demand and necessity for prostitutes, and that as long as prostitutes are bound to dwell in Ellsworth it is better for the respectable portion of society to hold prostitutes under restraint of law."

It wasn't something peculiar to Ellsworth. It began in Abilene and became the practice of every Kansas cow town. As has been indicated, Ellsworth had some substance apart from the cattle trade. It had nearby Fort Harker to depend on for business. Fort

Harker was the forwarding depot for army supplies to a number of military posts. It gave Ellsworth merchants a wide market for their goods. Arthur Larkin's drygoods and clothing business had made him a wealthy man. His new three-story brick hotel, the Grand Central (the first one of that name had been destroyed by fire), was the most imposing structure in town. Jerome Beebe's general store had branches at Wilson and Brookville. Whitney and Kendall had a prosperous furniture business in which the sheriff was a silent partner. Seitz' Drug Store, conducted by George Seitz, a German-born apothecary whose professional reputation was to become state-wide, was reputed to carry the widest selection of drugs in Kansas, Topeka included. While this evidence of permanence had no direct bearing on the cattle trade, it impressed the trail men, as did the twelve-foot-wide magnesia limestone sidewalk, said to be the finest in the state, that Arthur Larkin put down in front of his Grand Hotel. It wasn't a little thing to men who had never seen anything but a plank sidewalk.

When the season of 1872 was over it was estimated that not more than 350,000 Longhorns had been trailed north that year, which was far below the record set in 1871. Of the total that reached Kansas, Ellsworth did not receive more than 150,000 head. Of that number, the car loadings show that no more than 40,000 were shipped out by rail; stock cattle that were sold to Northern ranchmen accounting for the rest.[2] That Ellsworth did as well as it did was due in part to the efficient manner in which its stockyards were managed by Colonel R. D. Hunter, who was well-acquainted with and admired by the big drovers, but mainly because of the shortage of stock cars at the Wichita yards. Faced with long delays, many owners had driven on north to the Kansas Pacific.

Though Salina, Junction City, Brookville, even Abilene, shipped some cattle in 1872, Ellsworth had had a big year. With season's end, the exodus of parasites occurred as it had annually in Abilene. Miraculously, the town had escaped without a killing. Cantankerous, hotheaded Print Olive, one of the Big Ten of all trail drivers, had been seriously wounded in the Billiard Saloon in an argument arising out of a card game. Though he stopped three slugs, he was tough enough to recover and be able to spend the winter at home in Texas.

By April, 1873, some financial experts were making dire predictions about the state of the country's economy. They said that money was going into hiding and that investment capital was disappearing. They pointed to the strange fluctuations of the New York Stock Market as evidence.

Ellsworth and Wichita paid little attention to such pessimistic talk; they had heard it before and nothing had come of it. They were far more concerned with what was going to happen now that the Katy Railroad was in Texas and completing a stockyard at Denison that would compare favorably with anything to be found in Kansas. Did it mean the end of trail driving to a Northern market? No one could say. Thousands of Longhorns had been shipped over the Missouri, Kansas and Texas long before it reached Red River. Herds had been driven up to the end of track, loaded, and sent steaming off to Kansas City and St. Louis.

The Kansas Pacific and Santa Fe were interested observers of what transpired at Denison. Early figures seemed to indicate that it would handle no more than 35,000 to 40,000 head for the year. The rival railroads, with their stake in the Kansas market, were further relieved to learn that the great majority of Longhorns being trailed to the Katy terminal were either from immediately surrounding country or east Texas.

Shipping by rail direct to a packing plant was a great work-and-time saver. You could count on getting four dollars more a head than if you sold at one of the Kansas markets to a cattle dealer. Subtracting the four dollars from the freight charges of $6.25 a head, your net marketing cost was $2.25 as against the $1.50 that was accepted as the cost of driving a critter to Kansas. That difference of seventy-five cents amounted to something if you were putting five to ten thousand head over the trail in a season. It sufficed to keep the big herds coming to Ellsworth and Wichita.

By early June a dozen of the most important men in the Texas cattle trade were in Ellsworth with their herds, or waiting for them to arrive. Colonel John Myers was there, and Seth Mabry,

William Pennyman, Jesse Driskill, Gene Millett, John Blocker, Dick Withers, among others. Print Olive was back with his brother Marion and a herd of 3,000 straight stock cattle that they were taking through to their pens at Ogallala, Nebraska.

The familiar face and loud voice of Abel Shanghai Pierce were missing. Why he severed his connection with Ellsworth has never been explained. Whether, flushed with success, the town decided it no longer needed his services is a likely surmise, but no more so than that Wichita lured him away by offering him a proposition more in keeping with what he thought he was worth. He was never accused of being a shrinking violet. By midsummer he and Colonel Hitt, McCoy's old friend, were down in Indian Territory intercepting the northbound outfits and inducing many of them to ship from Wichita.[3]

Among the notables who arrived in town early that year was Ben Thompson. He was joined by his younger brother Billy a few days later, Billy having come up the trail with cattle. It was Ben's intention to open a saloon. Finding Ellsworth already over-supplied, he took charge of the games in Joe Brennan's place. As in Abilene, he quickly became the spokesman for the Texans. Mayor Miller, Police Court Judge Osborne and Sheriff Cap Whitney became very friendly with him. Only once during the summer—that is prior to Friday, August 15—was he in any difficulty with the law, and on that occasion it was a minor infraction. Learning that policeman "Happy Jack" Morco, the illiterate pet hate of the Texans, had filed a charge against him of being drunk and disorderly, he surrendered himself to Judge Osborne, pleaded guilty and paid his fine of twenty-five dollars. This radical departure from his usual behavior in such instances must be taken as evidence that he wanted to keep his slate clean in Ellsworth. His brother Billy was often in trouble, a chronic condition with him. Ben spent a good part of his life getting him out of one scrape after another. Whatever Ben Thompson's transgressions were, and they were many, he never wavered in his loyalty to Billy. It was put to its greatest test on the afternoon of August 15, in Ellsworth, and in the events that day set in motion.

Among the Texans, the feeling against Happy Jack Morco and Brocky Jack Norton (the latter now marshal of the town) had

been rising to the breaking point. It exploded this August afternoon, the trouble beginning in Joe Brennan's soloon, where a
monte game for high stakes was in progress. Ben was looking on.
Billy, who had been drinking heavily, was also among those
present, as was John Sterling, a professional gambler. Neil Cain
was dealing and Cad Pierce was doing the betting. Both were
popular Texans. Cad wanted to play for higher stakes than Neil
was willing to take. Ben asked Sterling to sit in and take the over-
bets, which he did, telling Ben he would split his winnings with
him.

Sterling was drunk and abusive. When he had won a thousand
dollars, he quit and walked out. Ben accosted him later in the
afternoon and demanded his share of the winnings. Morco was
with Sterling. He drew his pistol and ordered Ben to go on about
his business. Sterling, whisky brave, slapped Thompson's face.
Ordinarily that would have been equivalent to signing his death
warrant, had Ben been armed. That he would get his pistols and
go gunning for Sterling seemed inevitable. But that was not the
direction the trouble was to take.

Returning to Brennan's, Ben was trying to borrow a gun when
Sterling and Happy Jack came to the door and yelled, "Get your
guns you damned Texas sons of bitches and fight!"

The Thompsons ran out the back way and up the alley to Jake
New's saloon, where Ben armed himself with a pistol and a six-
teen-shot Winchester rifle; Billy grabbed his brother's double-
barreled breech-loading shotgun.[4] They then ran out the front
door to the railroad tracks and made their stand at the end of the
combination freight and passenger depot. Billy reloaded the shotgun as they waited. On running out of New's saloon he had
stumbled and one barrel had gone off, the shot plowing into the
plank sidewalk near where Major Seth Mabry and Captain Gene
Millett were standing.

Sheriff Whitney had heard the shot. He ran down from home
in shirtsleeves to discover what it meant. He saw the Thompsons
at the depot. A group of Texans were gathered in front of Brennan's saloon. Otherwise the two Main Streets were suddenly
deserted. Brocky Jack Norton, the marshal, stepped out of a convenient doorway and is alleged to have offered to go out and

arrest Ben and his brother, which seems improbable. Witnesses swore later that they heard Whitney say, "They will shoot you. I will go; they will not harm me." [5]

Whitney, unarmed, walked out to the tracks and up to the west end of the depot. According to Ben's sworn testimony, the sheriff said, " 'Boys, let's not have any fuss or difficulty.' I told him we didn't want any trouble but would defend ourselves if they wanted to fight.

" 'Put up your guns and I will see that you are protected,' he promised. 'I am satisfied you will,' I told him. 'We will go to the saloon [Brennan's] and take a drink and get Billy to put his gun away.' "

They started for Brennan's, the sheriff walking between the brothers. When they reached the saloon Billy went in, followed by Whitney, with Ben bringing up the rear. As he stepped into the doorway W. A. Langford, a Texan, called, "Look out, Ben; here they come with guns!"

Ben whirled around and saw Happy Jack coming on the run, armed with a pair of six-guns. There was an alley between the saloon and Beebe's General Store. Ben darted into it and flung his rifle to his shoulder.

Whitney and Billy had heard Langford's warning cry. They came out only a few steps behind Ben. The sheriff stopped a few feet from the alley. Morco, seeing the rifle trained on him, darted across the porch into Beebe's store. Ben fired but missed, the slug splintering one of the columns that supported the second-floor veranda. At the moment, said witnesses, Billy came staggering out of the saloon, half-raised the shotgun, loaded with buck, and fired. The blast tore into the sheriff's right arm, shoulder and breast, inflicting a mortal wound.

"Look, Billy!" Ben cried. "My God, you've killed our best friend!"

Whitney was still alive. Friends carried him to his home, two blocks away, where Dr. Fox and Dr. Gregg, the town's best, fought to save his life. Dr. Finlaw, the post surgeon at Fort Riley, hurried to Ellsworth but there was nothing he could do; the lung had been pierced, producing internal hemorrhaging. The end came early Monday morning.

Ben realized a moment after the shooting that if Billy was to escape the consequences of what he had done, he had to get away from Ellsworth at once. "For God's sake leave town," he told him, "or you will be murdered in cold blood."

He exchanged his rifle for the shotgun Billy was carrying, and after asking Neil Cain to get his brother's horse from Sam John's livery stable in back of the Grand Union and bring it around in front, he walked across the street and went to his room to get shells for the shotgun. When he came down, Cain was helping Billy to get into the saddle. Cad Pierce shoved a roll of bills into Billy's hand, saying, "Billy, you'll need this."

Montgomery, the editor of the *Reporter*, who was there, says Billy rode away cursing and that he was so little impressed by his danger that he stopped in Nauchville to spend a few minutes with his current light of love, one Molly Brennan, Joe Brennan's ex-wife.

Up and down North Main Street men had gathered in groups and began finding their tongues as they overcame the shock of what had happened. Deliberate murder they called it. For half an hour Ben walked back and forth in front of the hotel, holding the town at bay. Mayor Miller, enraged at the failure of the police to arrest him, discharged them on the spot, leaving only Deputy Sheriff Hogue to make an arrest. Hogue was reluctant to face Thompson. Finally, the mayor confronted him. Ben agreed to hand over his guns if Happy Jack, Sterling and Brocky Norton were disarmed. Miller agreed to it. Ben appeared before Judge Osborne to answer any charges that might be brought against him. He was charged with shooting at Happy Jack Morco but was released on bond posted by Millett and Mabry. In the morning, Morco declined to press the charge and the matter was dropped.

Billy had made good his escape, but a warrant charging him with murder was out and it was kept alive, together with a reward of five hundred dollars for his capture. He was a fugitive from justice for three years but was captured in Texas and returned to Kansas and lodged in jail at Salina, Ellsworth not being deemed safe. Fear that his friends (Ben's friends) would try to arrange his escape led to his being taken to the state penitentiary to await trial. Between the money he had spent fighting his brother's extradition and supplying him with expensive counsel, Ben was broke.

The trial, once it got under way, did not take long. Billy's defense was that he was drunk and the shooting of Whitney accidental. To the dismay of Ellsworth, that was the verdict the jury returned.

Following the killing of Cap Whitney, rumors started flying that several hundred Texas cowboys were organizing to charge into Ellsworth and leave it in ashes. They proved to be not only exaggerated but completely without substance. The controversy as to whether the slaying of Cap Whitney was accidental or malicious murder did not end with the acquittal of Billy Thompson. Obviously it was a question that could never be resolved. The interest that the death of Sheriff Whitney had aroused throughout the state began to wane, and eventually, even in Ellsworth, it was forgotten, which is understandable, for it had been ballooned out of all relation to its importance. Forgotten it remained until the appearance of the spurious biography *Wyatt Earp, Frontier Marshal*, published in 1931, which not only resuscitated it but made that afternoon of August 15, the most sensational and controversial in Western history.[6]

Granting that Chauncy B. (Cap) Whitney was a good man, a Civil War veteran who had distinguished himself later as an Indian fighter in the Battle of the Arickaree, as a peace officer he did nothing to mark him as outstanding. He was killed in the line of duty as many sheriffs and marshals were. His assassin was a drunken young punk who by no stretch of the imagination could be called a gunfighter. As for Ellsworth, there is no evidence that it was aroused to a fighting pitch that afternoon. Billy Thompson had been gone for an hour before a posse went in pursuit, being careful, it was said, not to overtake him.

Those are the facts—but not as Wyatt Earp in his old age, with Dodge City and Tombstone behind him, says they were. With the aid of his brilliant biographer, the late Stuart N. Lake, he makes that afternoon of Friday, August 15, 1873, one of the most exciting and memorable in the annals of the West.

He says it was August 18, an excusable error. The following is not excusable:

"At the roar of gunfire, saloon, hotels and stores spouted five hundred men into the Ellsworth plaza, nine tenths of them Texas gun-toters, an unarmed minority, local citizens." He goes on to tell how he told Mayor Miller that if he were a member of the police force, he would walk over, disarm and arrest Ben Thompson. Miller tears off the badge from Marshal Brocky Jack Norton's shirt and pins it on Earp. With the whole town holding its breath, Earp walks across the plaza and faces "the deadliest killer in all the West," orders him to drop his shotgun and then herds him to court.

"Wyatt Earp's short journey across the Ellsworth plaza under the muzzle of Ben Thompson's shotgun established for all time his preeminence among gunfighters of the West, but the episode has been ignored in written tales." And for the excellent reason that it never happened. Wyatt Earp was not within a hundred miles of Ellsworth that afternoon.

But for ten years and more this fantastic account was accepted as factual, those who believed it forgetting that at the time it was supposed to have occurred Earp was an unknown ex-buffalo hunter. The tremendous success of *Wyatt Earp, Frontier Marshal,* both as a *Saturday Evening Post* serial and in book form, did more to distort and confuse Western history than any book published before or since. Today, it is recognized as a colossal fake, its pretensions and conceits demolished by such writers as Eugene Cunningham, William McLeod Raine, Floyd B. Streeter and—humbly, I may add—by myself.

On September 18, two New York banks closed their doors. A wave of selling swept the New York Stock Exchange. In Philadelphia, Jay Cooke and Company, the most important house in America, suspended payment. By September 20, the worst financial panic in the history of the country (prior to the 1930's) was widespread. Cattle prices began to go down and down. It was so late in the season that men with cattle left for sale let them go for whatever was offered. Ellsworth was soon deserted. The market situation was the same down in Wichita.

Including the thousands that had gone to Ellsworth, an estimated 400,000 Longhorns had come up the Chisholm Trail and entered Sedgwick County that year. Thousands had gone to nearby Indian reservations. But when all the subtractions had been made, the figures showed that Wichita had taken over first place among the cow towns.

There were plenty of cattle left on the Wichita market. They were going at bargain prices. A man with money and the requisite amount of nerve might do well by buying now and wintering his herd in the wooded bottoms of Cowskin Creek, the Ninnescah, or one of the other creeks. Shanghai Pierce was one of the dozen or more men who took a chance. Wintering cattle in Sedgwick County was vastly different from holding them on the open prairies around Abilene and Ellsworth. An estimated 75,000 Longhorns grazed on the network of creeks near Wichita that winter, with only minimum losses.

It meant employment for several hundred cowboys. They spent their wages in Wichita, which helped to keep the wheels turning. Dutch Bill Greiffenstein, riding a wave of prosperity, was building a row of two-story brick business buildings next door to his three-story Douglas Avenue Hotel, the finest in Wichita. Despite the slowness with which the country was recovering from the financial crisis that had swept it, his confidence in the future of the town that he and his partner Jim Meade had built out of nothing did not waver. No one could say what 1874 would bring, but Shanghai Pierce had a number of commitments from his Texas friends. If any herds came up the trail, Wichita would get them; Ellsworth was finished. By midsummer it would be as dead as Abilene and Newton.

14

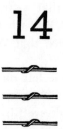

Beef Bonanza

FOR MANY YEARS, I have been acquainted with the Amanda Burks story. She was the first woman of record to go up the Chisholm Trail. When Emerson Hough, the Western historical novelist, famous for his *Mississippi Bubble, Oregon Trail, Fifty-Four Forty or Fight,* etc., wrote *North of Thirty Six,* there can be little doubt that Tazie Lockhart, his young and beautiful heroine, was a romantically fictionalized Amanda Burks. Although the book became a popular best-seller, it was savagely attacked for its inaccuracies by Stuart Henry, the author of *Conquering Our Great American Plains* and the brother of T. C. Henry, the "Wheat King." It precipitated an acrimonious literary hassle in which several prominent writers and the *Saturday Evening Post* and the then-powerful *Literary Digest* became involved. Henry scoffed at the idea that a young woman would have been permitted to accompany a trail drive. He was mistaken.

Mrs. Burks and her husband, W. F. Burks, lived on a ranch at Banquette, down in Nueces County, Texas. To quote her:

"In the early spring of 1871 Mr. Burks rounded up his cattle and topped out a thousand head of the best to take to market. Jasper Clark (better known as 'Jap') was getting ready to take the Clark herd also, so they planned to keep the two herds not far apart.

"They started in April with about ten cowboys each, mostly

Mexicans, and the cooks. The cattle were road-branded at Pinitas and started on the familiar trail. They were only a day out when Marcus Banks, my brother-in-law, came back with a note to me from Mr. Burks asking me to get ready as soon as possible and catch up with the bunch. He also said to bring either Eliza or Nick (black girl and boy who worked for us) to look out for my comfort, and suggested that Nick would be of more help than the girl.

"So Nick and I started in my little buggy drawn by two good brown ponies and overtook the herd in a day's time. Nick, being more skilled than the camp cook, prepared my meals. He also put up my tent evenings, and took it down when we broke up camp. It was intended that he should drive my horses when I was tired, but that was not necessary, for the horses often had no need of anyone driving them. They would follow the slow-moving herd unguided, and I would find a comfortable position, fasten the lines and take a little nap.

"The cattle were driven only about ten miles a day, or less, so that they would have plenty of time to graze and fatten along the way. They were in good condition when they reached Kansas.

"The night before our herd reached Beeville the Clark herd stampeded and never caught sight of us until we were 'way up-state. . . . All went pretty well with us till we reached Lockhart, and here we lost thirty cows in the timber. They were never recovered. Whenever we came to timber we had to rush the cattle through, sometimes driving all day without stopping, for if they were scattered it was almost impossible to gather them again in the thick undergrowth.

"Being springtime, the weather was delightful until we reached Central Texas. Some of the worst electrical and hailstorms I have ever witnessed were in this part and also in North Texas. The lightning seemed to settle on the ground and creep along like something alive."

Amanda Burks must have been a rather remarkable young woman, who was devoted to her husband. She says that being near him was compensation for all the hardships and dangers she experienced. She gives a picture of trail life that has a freshness and air of reality about it that is not found in masculine accounts.

The little pleasures, day-to-day annoyances, that she mentions, which veterans of the trail ignored, perhaps did not even remember, form an important part of her narrative.

"Over in Bosque County late one evening a storm overtook us, and Mr. Burks drove me off into a more sheltered part of the timber. He unfastened the traces from the buggy and gave me the lines, but he told me if the horses tried to run to let them go. Hail had begun to fall by this time and he had to hurry back to help the men hold the frightened cattle. Harder and heavier fell the hail, and rain was pouring down in torrents. The horses worked their way to one side of the buggy, seeking protection, and it seemed it would be only a few seconds before they pulled away from me entirely. Determined not to let the horses go, I left the shelter of my buggy top and tied the horses with a rope I always carried with me. I got back in the buggy and sat there cold and wet and hungry and all alone in the dark. Homesick! This is the only time of all the months of my trip that I wished I was back on the old ranch at Banquette.

"After what seemed ages to me I could hear the rumble of wagon wheels on the trail, and later still the sound of the beat of a horse's hoofs going the same way; but no one seemed to pay me any mind.

"Later I learned that it was the cook driving the wagon, not knowing which way to go after being lost in the dark woods; and that Mr. Burks rode after him to bring him back to cook supper for the hungry men who had had nothing to eat since morning.

"After I heard the return of the wagon the woods rang with the sound of Mr. Burks' voice calling me, and I lost no time in answering. It was one o'clock in the morning when I reached camp."

They had very little trouble with Indians, but they were beset with a number of prairie fires, one of them ignited inadvertently by Mrs. Burks. The crew controlled it on the flanks; straight ahead, it burned a swath for miles. It has been said often enough to become axiomatic that a cowboy would run from a woman in camp as from the devil. That wasn't Amanda Burks' experience. She says the men rivaled each other in their attentiveness to her. "They were always on the lookout for something to please me, a

surprise of some delicacy of wild fruit, prairie chicken, or antelope tongue."

Burks took his cattle to Ellsworth. When prices began dropping
at season's end, he was tempted to winter his herd on the prairies.
Fortunately for him, he changed his mind and sold. "So in December we left Kansas, dressed as if we were Eskimaux," Mrs. Burks
recalled. "Our homeward journey was made by rail to New
Orleans via St. Louis, and by water from New Orleans to Corpus
Christi." [1]

By 1874 rustlers, white renegades from the Cherokee and Creek
reservations to the east, were more troublesome than Indians.
Fort Sill had become a major military post and was able to exer-
cise a measure of control over the Kiowas and Comanches. The
spirit of the wild Plains Indians had not been broken, however,
and raiding parties were continually slipping away from their
reservations and roaming at will over the vast region between
the upper Cimarron, the Canadian and North Fork and Prairie
Dog Town Forks of the Red River, country that was practically
uninhabited save for the scores of buffalo hunters working out
of Dodge City.

Under the treaty negotiated with the Plains Tribes at Medicine
Lodge, Kansas, in 1867, the government agreed to prohibit the
hunting of buffalo below the southern boundary of Kansas. An
experienced hide hunter could earn up to a hundred dollars a
day. For that kind of money no law could keep them out. They
were willing to risk arrest and their lives as well. The wanton
slaughter not only continued but grew until the plains were
white with bleaching bones.

Even an "ignorant" Indian could understand that he had been
betrayed and that with the disappearance of the buffalo herds his
last hope of ever regaining the free nomadic life he had once
known would be gone forever. The buffalo supplied him with
food, shelter, clothing, and was entwined in the mysticism of his
religion. The best the Indian could do to stop the slaughter was
to dodge the troops who were chasing him, swoop down on the
hide hunters and their skinners, kill them and leave the mutilated
bodies as an object lesson for others. It wasn't enough. It seemed

that for every man they killed, there were always two to take his place.

April of 1874 saw the herds from Texas going up the trail again as they had been doing for six years. A feeling of optimism had returned. Wichita was ready. The town had voted $15,000 to increase the size of its stockyards. Joe McCoy had supervised the work. The new Douglas Avenue toll bridge, the first to span the Arkansas, was finished. As evidence of how far Wichita was prepared to go in its welcome to the Texans, an ordinance was passed designating Douglas Avenue, its main street, the thoroughfare that cattle coming off the bridge from the west (as all did) were to use on their way to the stockyards in the southeastern section of town. Large signboards posted at the four entrances to town read:

> Everything goes in Wichita. Leave your revolvers at police headquarters and get a check. Carrying concealed weapons strictly forbidden.

Due to police laxness the carrying of firearms was overlooked. Wichita was noisy, violent and prosperous. It was already twice the size of Abilene and Ellsworth, and growing rapidly. A tough district, known as Delano, sprang up across the river. With its dance halls, saloons and prostitutes it achieved fame of a sort. Rowdy Joe Lowe and his wife Kate, dance hall proprietors, were said to run "the swiftest joint in Kansas." Most of Wichita's violence occurred in Delano. Shooting scrapes and killings happened so frequently that Marsh Murdock, the ambitious editor of the *Eagle,* reduced his coverage of them to a few inches of type.

Vice was not confined to Delano. The center of town was where Main Street crossed Douglas Avenue. Within two blocks of that intersection were the city hall, police station, the principal hotels, stores, saloons, Whitey Rupp's Keno Hall, Emil Warner's beer garden and a dozen brothels. One of the popular establishments in that category was Bessie Earp's house. She was Wyatt Earp's sister-in-law, the wife of Jim Earp, the eldest of the four Earp brothers. Jim Earp was tending bar in Pryor's Saloon, next door to Keno Hall. If Wyatt Earp was in Wichita during 1874, as he claims, it was not as a member of the police. The first mention of

him in the Wichita newspapers came on October 29, in the *Eagle*.
The gist of the incident was that patrolman John Behrens had
got a leave of absence from the city and with Earp had gone in
pursuit of some men who were fleeing the country without paying for a wagon and harness. They had overtaken the men near
the border of Indian Territory and compelled them to make
good.[2]

It was not until April 21, 1875, that Earp became a member
of the Wichita police force, on which he served until May 10,
1876, the new city council voting on that date on nominations
for the ensuing year. According to the minutes of that meeting,
Earp was dismissed, the vote against him being six to two.[3]

The Report of the Police Committee to the council as of May
22 recommended that "the scrip of W. Earp and John Behrens
be withheld until all moneys collected by them for the City be
turned over to the City Treasurer. The report was sanctioned
and accepted." As part of their official duties Earp and Behrens
had been collecting the license money from the saloons, gambling
rooms and sporting houses. Apparently they had not been report-
ing all of it. Earp lost no time in getting out of Wichita, for on
May 24 the Wichita *Beacon* reported that "Wyatt Erp [sic] has
been put on the police force at Dodge City."

That is not the way Earp tells it. He says he left Wichita in
response to an urgent telegram from George Hoover, the newly
elected mayor of Dodge, saying: "You have cleaned up Wichita.
Come over and clean up Dodge." Of course, he had done nothing
of the sort. Credit for whatever "cleaning up" had been done
belonged to Mike Meagher, four times marshal of Wichita. Earp
received sixty dollars a month for his services, which could not
have been notable, judging by the rare occasions when the *Eagle*
or *Weekly Beacon* mentioned his name.

There was a carnival air about Wichita that no other cow
town ever presented. Rupp's Keno Hall, at the northwest corner
of Main Street and Douglas Avenue, provided music by a small
brass band that he imported from Kansas City. During the late
afternoon and evening, he kept it perched on the second-floor
balcony, blaring forth by the hour. "The band helps to keep
things lively," he explained. Keno was the featured game but far

more money was wagered at faro. Ben Thompson, still deeply concerned about the safety of his brother Billy, spent some time in Wichita that season and got a job running a faro bank for Rupp. He must have behaved himself, for there is no record of his being in trouble with the police.

Shanghai Pierce gave them more trouble. He was making so much money as a cattle trader that his periodic celebrations edged on the cyclonic. One occasion skirted between tragedy and comic opera. Hilariously drunk, he sat on the bench in front of Jim Collins' North Main Street saloon, a gun in his hand, taking pot shots at the wooden eagle that ornamented the roof of the store across the way. Assistant Marshal Parks and policeman Cairns were stumped about what to do. They appealed to Mike Meagher, the former marshal of the town. (After serving for three years, Meagher had been defeated by William Smith in the spring election. He was re-elected in 1875.)

Meagher sat down with Shang—they were old friends—and soon they were laughing together. He got the big man inside a few minutes later and they began drinking. Before long he had so much whisky in Shang that he was helpless and could be handled. A hack was brought to the rear entrance, and he was bundled into it and put to bed at the Texas House. The following morning Shang appeared before Police Court Judge Ed Jewett and good-naturedly paid his fine of twenty-five dollars for being drunk and disorderly. Mike had slipped him a check for his gun. Shang recovered the pistol from the police rack, and to prove that there were no hard feelings, the two of them stepped into Pryor's bar for an eye-opener.

A man named Saunders got a permit from the council to conduct what he called a "variety" theatre. The flimsy building on Water Street was put together quickly. The theatre was thronged from the opening performance. The comedians were lewd and the girls stripped down to the bare essentials. Women were admitted. Presumably they were having a night off from their professional chores.

Jake Karatofsky, who knew when to desert a sinking ship, left Ellsworth and arrived with a trainload of merchandise and opened the finest store on Douglas Avenue. The *Weekly Beacon* commented on the size and elegance of his store windows.

Wichita now had a population of over twenty-five hundred. Among the hundreds of unknowns were two young men who were to distinguish themselves in the years to come, though not in Wichita. One was a dishwasher and part-time bootblack at the Texas House, by the name of Edward L. Doheny, the future multimillionaire oilman. The other, James Beauchamp Clark, was to have a far more illustrious career. He was a lawyer, a graduate of the University of Kentucky and Bethany College, West Virginia. He found clients so hard to come by that he was reduced to doing odd jobs to support himself.

He dropped the James Beauchamp from his name, and Wichita knew him as plain Champ Clark. When a minor opening in Missouri presented itself, it took him weeks to put together enough money for his railroad fare. Missouri took notice of him and soon hailed him as one of the great political orators of the day. He was sent to the Congress, where he distinguished himself by besting the veteran "Uncle Joe" Cannon and becoming Speaker of the House. At the Democratic National Convention in Baltimore, in 1912, he missed being nominated for President of the United States only when William Jennings Bryan deserted him for Woodrow Wilson.[4,5]

Wichita was so engrossed with the cattle trade that it gave the cold shoulder to the land speculators who were setting up shop in town and to the farmers they were attracting from the Midwest, many of them foreign-born with unpronounceable names. But they kept on coming in growing number. When they inspected the soil and drainage of Sedgwick County, they knew no finer wheat land existed anywhere. Their descendants are there today, so prosperous that after the harvest it is not unusual to find some of them taking off for a long vacation in their ancestral homelands.

Hurricane Bill Martin, a noted horse thief, who was reputed to have killed half a dozen men, was the badman of Wichita. He and his roughs, known as the Texas Gang, became bolder as summer approached. Mike Meagher had held them in check, but the weak-kneed policy Marshal Bill Smith pursued had given them the run of the town. The trouble that led to the showdown with the gang, and gave Wichita a taste of vigilante law, began with a fight between a member of the gang named Ramsey and Charley Saunders, a Negro hod carrier, who was working on the Miller Building that was being built on South Main Street. Saunders took Ramsey's abuse for a time and then, forgetting that he was a Negro, gave him a licking. Both were arrested, but got off without being fined. Having one of their number hauled up before a judge for mistreating a "nigger" was too much for the Texas Gang. Seeking revenge, Ramsey caught Saunders two afternoons later as he was climbing a ladder with a hod of bricks and fired two shots into him—one slug hitting him in the ear and the second piercing his lungs. The giant Negro came crashing down in a shower of bricks.

The Texas Gang, a dozen strong, rushed out of a saloon across the street, their pistols drawn as City Marshal Smith reached the scene. He did nothing. He defended his conduct later by saying, "There was nothing I could do with all those guns leveled at me." In the confusion, Ramsey mounted a horse and fled across the Douglas Avenue bridge and made good his escape.

This brazen killing—Saunders died two days later—was closely followed by the killing of one soldier and the wounding of another and a dance hall girl in Delano. Overnight, a Vigilance Committee of a hundred, recruited from the town's most substantial citizens was organized and armed. A giant iron triangle hung in front of the police station. It could be heard all over town when struck. When it sounded it was to be the signal for the vigilantes to rush there at once.

The vigilantes were called out twice on what proved to be false alarms. At suppertime, July 6, the triangle rang out again, and this time it was for real. Policeman Botts, recently appointed to the force, came face to face with an armed member of the Texas Gang as the latter stepped out of a North Main Street saloon. As Botts was ordering the man to hand over his gun, Hurricane Bill Martin and his followers pushed out through the swinging saloon door, pistols drawn. There seems little doubt that the incident was prearranged by Hurricane Bill as part of a showdown with the police and the so-called vigilantes.

Botts said no more and hurried off to ring for help. In no time at all, no fewer than forty men, armed with shotguns and Henry rifles, were assembled at the police station. Among the first to arrive were Sim Tucker, the lawyer, one of the organizers of the Vigilance Committee and a bitter critic of Marshal Smith. Tucker took command as the vigilantes gathered on the sidewalk across the street from Hurricane Bill and his gang. When the latter started moving toward Douglas Avenue, Tucker gave the word to follow them. The opposing forces came abreast of each other at Horsethief Corner, a vacant lot high in weeds.

Horsethief Corner was a Wichita landmark, so named because in the past horses had been traded there, some of which were believed to have been stolen.

Marshal Smith arrived on the scene and pleaded with Tucker to disperse his following and let the police handle the situation as the only way that a lot of shooting could be prevented. Otherwise, innocent citizens might be struck.

"This is the third time we've been called out without an arrest being made," Tucker told him. "We're not afraid of trouble. You walk over there and arrest Hurricane Bill or we will."

This was the first time that Smith's hand had been called openly. He glanced at his men—the whole police force was there by then—but they made no move to come to his rescue. Desperate, he said, "All right, Tucker, you arrest him."

Silence descended as the lawyer cocked both barrels of his shotgun and stepped into the street, the gun raised. "Bill, you're under arrest," he called out.

The outlaw leveled his pistols.

"Drop those guns," Tucker said with quiet determination.

After a moment that seemed an hour long, Hurricane Bill said with a sullen grin, "You can take me," and tossed his revolvers in the road.

His stunned blacklegs hesitated momentarily and then flung their pistols into the weeds behind them. The vigilantes marched Hurricane Bill and his men to the police court, where they drew fines amounting to six hundred dollars. It broke the reign of the Texas Gang. Convinced that the vigilantes could and would act, Martin and his thugs soon shook the dust of Wichita off their heels.[6]

By the middle of August it was apparent that the number of cattle to come up the trail that year would fall far short of the figures set the past two seasons. Fortunately for Wichita, it was getting most of them. With McCoy directing operations, Great Bend had built an excellent stockyard and engaged him to drum up business. It shipped some 16,000 head. A few thousand stock cattle were sold at Ellsworth and trailed north from there. Wichita shipped 49,720. Perhaps half as many more were sold to military supply and the Indian reservations. But it wasn't to the cattle trade that Kansans were referring when, looking back, they spoke of "the terrible year of '74"—1874 was the year of the grasshoppers. For days, beginning in the first week of August, hordes of what were erroneously called "Rocky Mountain locusts" blackened the skies. "For three days the flight of the insects was so great as to spread a haze over the sun. When they landed they began to eat. They ate the crops, they ate the leaves off the trees, they invaded homes and went to work on everything therein. So thick were the hoppers that for several days neither horse nor man could stand up to them and work. Trains on the A&T (the Santa Fe) were slowed, then stalled where they stood by the thick slimy pulp of crushed bodies on the rails." [7]

Virtually all business had to be suspended. In central Kansas where farms were just coming into production, families were left destitute. Governor Osborn appealed to the federal government for aid. Hard-boiled Wichitans, whose livelihood depended on the cattle trade and who regarded all farmers as a menace, raised several thousand dollars for the relief of the sufferers in Sedgwick County. "The saloonkeepers, gamblers and madames were among the biggest contributors—sinners all," the *Eagle* commented, "but they can always be depended on in an emergency."

15

Caldwell, the "Border Queen," Takes Over

SEVERAL THINGS WERE HAPPENING IN KANSAS, as yet unrelated but which were to merge and become one in the next few years, their joint purpose being the abolition of the Texas cattle trade. If they were impelled by different reasons, their goal was the same.

In 1874 the first State Temperance Convention was held in Topeka. It revealed the great strength of the Prohibitionists in the eastern counties. In convention assembled they took dead aim on the "riotous, lawless and immoral cow towns." They were "a blot on the fair name of Kansas." It was agreed that the only way to control them and restore decency was to close the saloons.

The Shorthorn Breeders' Association began to clamor for a state-wide ban on all Texas cattle. The Longhorns were a menace to domestic stock. Down in Sumner County, which lay between Sedgwick and the Kansas–Indian Territory line, hundreds of farmers had taken up land. Wellington, the county seat, had become a prosperous farming community. The embattled tillers of the soil had been fighting the trespassing herds individually for years, but now they had the united voice of the Grange to speak for them. Chartered units of the Grange, the Patrons of Husbandry, were sprinkled all over Kansas and far beyond its borders. Each of these three groups, for reasons of its own and for some overlapping reasons, began to merge. What one wanted was what all wanted: the closing of the door on the Texans and Texas cattle.

The Santa Fe had reached Dodge City in September, 1872, and hurried on to Colorado to claim its land grants. Dodge City (five miles west of Fort Dodge, so placed as to be free of army regulations concerning the sale of intoxicating beverages) made no effort to attract the cattle trade. It was *the* buffalo hunters' town. Fort Griffin, Texas, the settlement that had grown up around the fort of that name on the Clear Fork of the Brazos, its only rival for the honor, was a bad second. Dodge wanted to keep things that way. Robert M. Wright, the town's leading outfitter to the trade and its most important citizen, estimated that 25,000,000 buffalo remained within hunting range of Dodge. That the tremendous herds could be decimated, killed off, was beyond his comprehension, as it was with others.

When a German tanner in Philadelphia discovered a process by which the heretofore worthless buffalo hide could be made into good-grade boot and shoe leather, he presented the former robe hunters of the plains with a bonanza; overnight they became hide hunters. A flint hide delivered in Dodge City was worth two, three, even four dollars. The number of animals an experienced hunter could kill in a day was limited only by the ability of his skinners to keep up with him. News of the fabulous money they were making could not be kept a secret. Every train that rolled into Dodge City from the east brought its quota of would-be hunters—many of whom had never fired a rifle—all anxious to get in on the easy pickings.

And now the real slaughter began. Besides the Santa Fe tracks for half a mile, dried hides were stacked up in piles twenty feet high, awaiting shipment. Greed led men deeper and deeper into the forbidden Texas panhandle and many to their death.

A Bent's Fort party of hunters established themselves on the South Canadian at the ruins of Bent's abandoned fort, which was thereafter to be known to history as Adobe Walls. There, at dawn Sunday, June 28, 1874, they were attacked by an estimated five hundred Comanches, Kiowas and Cheyennes. The defenders numbered twenty-eight. With them there was one woman, Mrs. Bill Olds, the wife of a hunter. Repeatedly the Indians were driven back. They killed three men and some fifty horses and oxen. No count of the Indians' casualties could be made, for as usual they swept in and carried off most of their dead and wounded.

The besieged got word through to Dodge City, and Tom Nixon, the veteran hunter, hurriedly organized a relief party. Though the Battle of Adobe Walls is famous for the brave de-defense that was put up, it was not decisive in itself. It was responsible, however, for the military action that followed. Colonel Nelson A. Miles divided his force into three columns on setting out from Fort Dodge and drove the hostiles out of the northern Panhandle. Colonel Ranald Mackenzie left Fort Richardson, Texas, with seven troops of the 4th Cavalry and five companies of the 10th Infantry and blocked escape to the south. The purpose of the campaign was not to see how many Indians could be killed, but to put them afoot. In Palo Duro Canyon, Mackenzie, by an adroit maneuver, captured a herd of fifteen hundred Comanche ponies, which he destroyed, along with caches of dried meat. It broke the back of Comanche resistance. Coupled with Colonel Miles' defeat of the Kiowas at McClellan's Creek it swept the hostiles out of northwest Texas.

Long before there was a Dodge City, thousands of Longhorns had crossed the Arkansas River four miles west of where the town was subsequently located. They were cattle that had come up the Texas Road to the Three Forks and were driven through Indian Territory and across No Man's Land (the Oklahoma Panhandle) on their way to the Colorado mining camps. The trail the military used between Fort Dodge, Kansas, and Camp Supply (or Fort Supply) in Indian Territory closely followed the route taken by those early herds.

Dodge City's indifference to the cattle trade continued until the spring of 1879, when the hide hunters of Dodge and Fort Griffin waited in vain for the return of the great herds of shaggies from the southern plains. It was incredible but true; the millions of buffalo that had once blackened the landscape had been all but exterminated. "From the Texas buffalo ranges the smoke had cleared. By the spring of 1879 the last of the hunters had to look elsewhere for a living," says Wayne Gard in his *The Great Buffalo Hunt.* "The herds that had darkened the southern plains were almost gone. The small, scattered bunches that remained were not enough to make the taking of hides worthwhile." [1]

There is no evidence that Wichita regarded Dodge City as a possible rival for its cattle trade. As long as Texas cattle came up the Chisholm Trail, they would come to Wichita, not to a town a hundred and fifty miles to the west. The first flaw in this reasoning appeared in May of 1877 when "Maxwell and Morris, with a big herd of stock cattle from South Texas, bound for Ogallala, Nebraska, left the Chisholm Trail at Belton and, striking northwest, followed the Leon River through what are today Coryell, Hamilton, Comanche, Eastland and Stephens counties. They had no trail to follow, and as the old saying had it, they were just following their noses, with the North Star their only compass. Another forty miles brought them to Fort Griffin." [2]

Fort Griffin was still a booming buffalo hunter's town. Frank Conrad, the resourceful trader and former post sutler, had three acres of flint hides piled up, waiting to be hauled off by his ox-teams to Fort Worth and the new railhead of the Texas and Pacific. Getting what direction they could at Fort Griffin, Maxwell and Morris headed directly north through Throckmorton and Baylor counties and on through unorganized Wilbarger County to Red River. There was just a brush-covered wilderness where they crossed. It had no name but time was to give it one. Along with Colbert's Ferry, Red River Station, it was to become one of the three great cattle crossings, named for the man who built a crude trading post there—Jonathan Doan.

After leaving Red River, Maxwell and Morris drove up the North Fork and keeping slightly to the west of the Wichita Mountains reached Elm Creek. Pointing north again, they crossed Sweetwater Creek a few miles east of Old Mobeetie and continued on to the Washita, the Canadian, the North Canadian and finally the Cimarron. They were so far upstream in each instance that the herd could be walked across. Following the Fort Dodge–Camp Supply Road, they reached the Arkansas River crossing west of

Dodge City without difficulty. Ahead of them they had the Jones and Plummer Trail to take them to Ogallala.

The route Maxwell and his partner had blazed was, almost without change, to become the famous Western Trail over which several million Longhorns and mustangs would travel in the years to come. For livestock going to western Nebraska and Wyoming it was the shortest trail yet opened. It was true that Dodge City was a hundred and fifty miles west of Wichita, but for the herds coming up from south Texas, the westward angling of the new trail saved most of those miles. It ran through open country, which was a big advantage, and the easy stream crossings were another. There was very little timber to add to the difficulty of controlling a herd that was off and running. And there wasn't a fence between Red River and Dodge.

Santa Fe car loadings show that Dodge City shipped some cattle in 1876 and 1877. A generous estimate would be 10,000 in 1876 and about twice that number the following year. They came from the plains of Colorado and up the so-called Dodge Trail from west Texas.

It took time for news of the new route Maxwell and Morris had blazed to circulate through south Texas. The talk was so favorable that when the 1878 season opened, many herds that ordinarily would have gone up the Chisholm Trail turned west at Belton and reached the new crossing of Red River via Fort Griffin and on past Mobeetie, Longhorn Roundup and eventually Dodge City, which for the great majority was only a stopping place on their way to Nebraska and the Northwest. For the others, the wide bottomland of the Arkansas, across the river from town, provided an excellent holding ground until sales could be made.

No effort was made to improve Dodge City's primitive and already inadequate shipping facilities, which would indicate that it was not reaching out for the business nor dreaming of becoming a great cattle market. On the face of it, there seemed to be little reason to believe that with the longer haul and higher freight rates it could compete with Wichita.

There was no Interstate Commerce Commission or other governmental authority regulating the conduct of railroads. As

Stewart Holbrook has said: "They ran their trains when and where they pleased and raised and lowered passenger fares and freight rates as they pleased." [3]

The Santa Fe took a good look around and decided that Wichita and Dodge City freight rates should be equalized. This move by the company was not prompted by a fondness for Dodge City. It was done to serve its own ends, its purpose being to put a check on the increasing number of Longhorns that the Kansas Pacific was shipping from Ellis and Wakeeny and, hopefully, to have the same effect on the Union Pacific's growing business at Ogallala. For five years and more it had handled the bulk of the rail shipment of Texas cattle; with Wichita in the east, Dodge City in the west and Great Bend in between, it was reasonable to believe that it could retain its stranglehold on the trade. If Dodge City was to amount to anything as a shipping point, it needed modern stockyards and proper facilities. The Santa Fe saw to it that they were provided.

No one can say with any authority how many Longhorns were pointed north in 1877. The total may have been as high as 250,000, not more. Such figures as are available indicate that not more than half of them reached Kansas. Many got no further north than the Texas Pacific at Fort Worth. Joseph McCoy was now scouting cattle for Denison and the Katy Railroad. Denison had a slaughtering plant and was shipping dressed beef in its new refrigerator cars.[4] Dallas, which now had two railroads, the Texas and Pacific and the Houston and Texas Central, shipped thousands of Longhorns. Fort Worth bested its rival by averaging about ten carloads a day, which amounted to better than 50,000 head for the season. This competition resulted in car loadings at Wichita shrinking to 4,102. Very likely that figure does not represent more than 35 to 40 per cent of the cattle marketed there that season.

With Fort Worth, Dallas and other Texas shipping points making inroads on the Northern market, it was obvious that the Chisholm Trail, north of Red River Station, would never again see the four to five hundred thousand Longhorns a season it had known in the days when Abilene got them all. The Cox Trail was dead, but a new diversion now occurred where the Chisholm

Trail crossed Turkey Creek, Indian Territory, thirty miles above the North Canadian. Striking off to the northwest, it reached the Cimarron and then followed that stream for a hundred miles to Longhorn Roundup, where it intersected the new Western Trail. This diversion, which drained more business away from Wichita, was promptly named the Cut-Off Trail.

Wichita seethed with indignation, charging that the Cut-Off Trail was the work of Dodge City interests. Dodge City retorted just as angrily that it had had nothing to do with it. No evidence to the contrary was ever produced. Red Clark, who had put up a log roadhouse at Longhorn Roundup and stood to profit from the herds passing his door, likewise denied knowing anything about it. But the fact remained that the Cut-Off was marked every half-mile with a bleached buffalo skull. Someone had placed them there. Whoever he was, he kept his secret and it remained an unsolved mystery.

Mark Withers, the veteran trail driver of Lockhart, Texas, was the first man to put a herd over the Cut-Off. He had 3,500 head of mixed cattle, the beeves contracted to Day Brothers, Dodge City delivery. Yearlings and cows were sold to John R. Blocker when they reached the Smoky Hill River and were driven to Ogallala. Coming up through Texas, Mark Withers says, "The herd was strung out for four miles." It was really two herds, with two crews, two wagons and two cooks, one section following the other, the only practical way of handling an outfit of that size. He led the way with his capable brother Dick Withers. Gus Withers bossed the second section.

I do not believe that Mark Withers' decision to leave the old trail and risk his immense herd on the unproven Cut-Off Trail was taken on the spur of the moment when he reached Turkey Creek. Certainly tales of the difficulties drovers had with barbed wire and armed grangers in Sumner County the previous fall had had a wide circulation in Texas that winter. The Cut-Off offered a way of avoiding those troubles. Very likely Withers' decision to take it was made weeks before he reached Turkey Creek. It came as a surprise to his crew, however. "We were twenty-five miles above the North Canadian when the word was passed that we were going to turn off the old trail and head for

Longhorn Roundup," wrote George Mills. "It was well marked with buffalo skulls, about half a mile apart." [5]

Other herds followed the Cut-Off, draining away business from Wichita. It helped to explain why car loadings at Dodge City for the year were double those at Wichita.

If Longhorn Roundup, situated out on the open plains, was to be distinguished for anything, it was for the violence and frequency of the lightning storms that plagued an area a hundred miles wide of which it was the center. Though the electrical disturbances were always accompanied by rain, the annual rainfall was normal for a semiarid country. No accounting of the number of men, cattle and horses struck down by lightning has ever been attempted, but the recorded history of trail driving reveals that instances of men and beasts being electrocuted occurred too frequently to be regarded as exceptional.

You will recall Amanda Burks saying that in a bad storm the lightning seemed to run along the ground like a living thing. George Mills says: "I saw unbelievable doings of the lightning; it beat anything I ever saw. The lightning would hit the side of those hills and gouge out great holes in the earth like a bomb had struck them, and it killed seven or eight head of cattle in the herd back of us and two horses out of the remuda." Ben Borroum, of Del Rio, Texas, on his way to Dodge City with a herd owned by himself and Monroe Choate, remembered "balls of lightning bouncing along the ground. The grass would be set afire and be put out by the driving rain. There was so much lightning all around us that the air smelled like sulphur. The horns of the cattle seemed to be tipped with fire. The tips of the horses' ears were touched by it. The herd wanted to run, but they didn't seem to know which way to go; the lightning was all around them. We counted the damage in the morning. We lost twenty-seven head. I figured we'd got off lucky." [6]

Dick Withers often recalled how Otis Ivey, of Caldwell County, Texas, was killed by lightning on Bluff Creek. The cattle had been watered for the evening and were grazing before bedding down, when the wind stiffened and rain began to fall. By the time the remuda had been driven into a rope corral, the rain had become a downpour, with thunder rolling and jagged flashes of forked lightning splitting the sky. Ivey was walking to his horse to go on night guard when he was struck. The bolt that killed him and a score of cattle melted his gold watch. Withers called it the worst night he ever spent on the trail.[7]

His brother Mark Withers had a similar experience between Longhorn Roundup and Dodge City several years later.

"In 1882, while I was delivering cattle to Gus Johnson, he was killed by lightning," he said in recalling his years on the trail. "G. B. Withers, Johnson and I were riding together when the lightning struck. It set Johnson's undershirt on fire and his gold shirt stud, which was set with a diamond was melted and the diamond was never found. His hat was torn to pieces and mine had all the plush burned off the top. I wasn't seriously hurt, but G. B. Withers lost one eye by the same stroke that killed Johnson." [8]

Men who were with him said he was stunned and knocked off his horse.

Cato Thompson, as trail-wise as any Texan, was struck dead by lightning on the Smoky Hill River, a few miles from Hays City, in August, 1873—despite more precautions than trail men were in the habit of taking. He and his three-man crew were on their way to Ogallala with three hundred mustangs. This was tornado country and the tornado season. A peculiar stillness in the air warned him that while they might not be caught in the path of a twister, they were in for a violent storm—wind, rain and lightning—before evening. Accordingly, he made camp early and had the wagon roped down to prevent its being turned over. A firm believer in the old adage that steel attracts lightning, he removed his pistol and spurs and ordered his men to do the same.

Supper was over and the cook had put his pots away when they saw a funnel-shaped black cloud rushing toward them at express-train speed. It was still a few miles away when it changed course and swept past to the north of them. But the heavens opened then and rain fell in torrents. Chain lightning was a continuous flash along the northern horizon; chain lightning split the heavens above. A bolt struck the steel shoe of the wagon pole and ricocheted. Cato Thompson was standing twenty feet away. It struck him and killed him instantly.[9]

Such incidents occurred again and again. But it is death in a stampede, not by lightning, that has been successfully dramatized into the thrilling tragedy of cowboy life. It has given us such lugubrious ballads as "Little Joe, the Wrangler" and others of the same vintage. The facts indicate, however, that fewer men met death in stampedes than were killed by lightning.

By the spring of 1879 it was obvious to anyone who had the courage to look the facts in the face that Wichita's importance as a cattle market was gone, or almost gone. Not only were the new Western Trail and the Cut-Off Trail threatening its existence as a cow town; a more potent cause for anxiety was the growing town of Caldwell, "The Border Queen," fifty-two miles to the south.

Ever since the first herds of Longhorns had gone up the Chisholm Trail to Abilene, in 1867, Caldwell had been wallowing in the dust of the passing Longhorn millions. It no longer sat astride the line between Indian Territory and Kansas as it once had, the U. S. resurvey of the boundary in 1872 having given Kansas an additional 2.47 miles of the so-called Cherokee Strip.

It was both a tough little town and a substantial one: tough because being no more than a long hop-skip-and-jump from the state line made it attractive to men who were on the "scout" and who could quickly put themselves beyond the reach of the law, when necessity demanded; substantial because there was more land under cultivation in Sumner County than in all of the surrounding area. By 1875, the business district had shifted from the wooden shacks on Chisholm Street to Main Street, up the hill. It is still Caldwell's main street, and the brick buildings put up in the late seventies are still there, along with the Leland, then as now Caldwell's best hotel.

Its geographic position and many natural advantages made it a matter of simple logistics that once Caldwell had a railroad it would capture the cattle trade of the Chisholm Trail. It seemed that its hopes were destined to be realized when the Cowley, Sumner and Fort Smith Railroad was granted a charter. The road was to run northwest across the Cherokee Nation to Arkansas City, Kansas, and then west through Hunnewell to Caldwell, then north to Wichita. It proved to be just a paper railroad, not a foot of it being built. Two years back, the Santa Fe had acquired the charter of the defunct Cowley, Sumner and Fort Smith. Now, Caldwell dared to hope, construction would begin. But a year passed before the Cowley, Sumner and Fort Smith, under its original corporate name, timidly began to lay tracks between Wichita and Wellington, the Sumner County seat, about halfway to Caldwell.

In view of the favorable terrain over which it was to run, the twenty-five miles to Wellington could have been built in a month, had the Santa Fe so desired. But it was in no hurry; it was well-satisfied with its business in Wichita. Construction came to a halt every few days and every imaginable excuse was offered for the numerous delays.

Eventually, the Cowley, Sumner and Fort Smith reached Wellington and announced that it did not plan to proceed any further for the present. Then, suddenly, in the spring of 1880, it was in a lather to reach Caldwell and the border. On June 13, with appropriate ceremonies, the first train steamed into the Border Queen. The Santa Fe now dropped all pretense and revealed that the line to Caldwell had been incorporated into the Santa Fe system—which surprised no one.

It was taken for granted that in building down to Caldwell the railroad company was in effect acknowledging that Wichita was finished as a market for Texas cattle. Undoubtedly that was true, but it had nothing to do with the end result that the Santa Fe foresaw.

I think it is fair to say that the Santa Fe, through its officials and its lobbyists in Topeka, the state capital, was able to keep abreast, or even ahead, of the trends of public opinion in Kansas. While the coalition of Grangers, Prohibitionists and Shorthorn Breeders had as yet made no attempt to jam through the legislature a strong state-wide embargo against the entry of Texas cattle into Kansas, there can be little doubt that the railroad company's political advisers warned that it was only a matter of months when such a law would be enacted, with safeguards to guarantee its enforcement. It best explains why the Santa Fe, when it reached Caldwell, did not stop but built down to the border and erected its stockyards there, which would permit it to load and ship Texas cattle without coming into conflict with the provisions of any future ban.

The agitation against the entry of the Longhorns increased throughout the eastern half of Kansas, and nowhere was it more intense than in Sumner County. But Caldwell, due to the foresight of the Santa Fe, offered the trail drivers a shipping point that could be reached without bringing them into contact with barbed wire and hostile farmers. Before the season was over, it was second only to Dodge City as the leading cattle market of Kansas.

After five years of bitter fighting, led by Dodge City, the Quarantine Law of the State of Kansas Against Texas Cattle was finally approved on March 7, 1885. It put other towns, including Dodge City, out of the cattle business, but Caldwell continued to ship until the Chisholm Trail was abandoned.

Due to its favorable location, a far greater percentage of the thousands of Longhorns reaching Caldwell were shipped out by rail than had been shipped from the other major cow towns of Kansas. At the close of the 1880 season, car loadings at Caldwell totaled 25,531 head; while at Dodge City the figure was only 17,957.[10] But Dodge saw a grand total of not less than 275,000 head that year, most of them stock cattle that were trailed on north to Ogallala and the Northwest.

Over the years, the figures given concerning the northward movement of Texas cattle are so astronomical as to make them suspect, and justifiably so. The only authentic figures are the car loadings, which are a matter of record; all other figures are of necessity only estimates. Such estimates, when made by men who were in a position to know what they were talking about, must be regarded as reasonably accurate. For instance, George B. Loving, the son of the famous Oliver Loving and founder of the Texas Cattle Raisers' Association, in statements made to Joseph Nimmo, Jr., Chief of Bureau of Statistics, Washington, D.C., declares:

"The assessment rolls of the State of Texas, according to the Comptroller's report, shows that there are at least 7,000,000 cattle in the State. . . . The actual number is about 9,000,000, the discrepancy in the report arising from the fact that few, if any, of our largest ranchmen render the full number of cattle owned by them for taxation.

"Texas has for several years disposed of fully 500,000 head of cattle, which have been used to stock northern and western ranges. Last year Texas sent up the trail 450,000 young cattle. These cattle consisted of one and two-year old steers and heifers. . . . The number of beef cattle marketed was excessive and the low average in price is due to the marketing of immature cattle and dry cows." [11]

In confirmation of the above is this extract from a statement to Mr. Nimmo made by W. H. Miller, Secretary of the Kansas City Board of Trade:

"My information is that the drive of 1880 included but 300,000 head of cattle, 150,000 less than the statement made to you by Mr. Loving, of Fort Worth, Texas. I include, however, only cattle that crossed the State lines into Kansas, Colorado and New Mexico, while his, most likely, included all that passed Fort Worth, many of which stopped in the pan handle of Texas and in Indian Territory. This probably accounts for the difference in his estimate and mine, and, if I am correct in this surmise, about that difference ought to exist."

Speaking of 1884, he continues:

"No cattle now come to this market direct from Texas. Our receipts are all of native and range cattle; but the range cattle are mostly all of Texas origin, having been driven from that State in previous years as stock cattle. The number shipped eastward (from Kansas City) during 1884 was 411,706. The total number shipped was 463,001, besides which there were 90,991 driven out of the yard for local consumption and packing purposes." [12]

The figures we have been dealing with ever since the first herd of Longhorns was driven into the shipping pens at Abilene have often seemed incredible, but the foregoing would indicate that they were not just numbers drawn out of a hat.

16

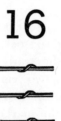

The Chisholm Trail Fades into the Past

IN 1870, Captain C. H. Stone, J. H. Dagner and several others had formed what was then known as a "town company," platted a townsite and named it Caldwell, in honor of U. S. Senator Alexander T. Caldwell. The first building or two had no sooner been erected than the lawlessness that was to distinguish it for years began. But it was not the typical lawlessness of other cow towns. In fact, it was not connected with the cattle trade until the railroad arrived in 1880, and had very little to do with the cattle trade thereafter.

Once it had become a shipping point for Longhorns, Caldwell was treated to the usual cowboy rowdiness. That was quite apart from the depredations of several organized horse-thief rings and the numerous lynchings that resulted. Lynchings were rare in Kansas, but no fewer than eight men were strung up in and around Caldwell, all horse thieves. One of them, as the *Caldwell Press* put it tersely, "was found idling his time away under a cottonwood tree on Falls Creek."

Caldwell, hog-wild and overrun with blacklegs and cutthroats, was hard on its marshals and peace officers. In a period of four months four men were killed in the line of duty. Some quit after a few weeks, and others were fired for incompetence. Prostitutes solicited business openly on Main Street. Cowboys were slugged and rolled for whatever they had on them.

The toughest joint in town was the notorious Red Light, a combination saloon and dance hall, with rooms on the second floor for its resident whores, conducted by George Woods and his wife, Mag. Criminals who were on the dodge from the law made it their headquarters. There was a saying in Caldwell that if you saw a dozen men lined up at the Red Light bar, you could be sure half of them were wanted somewhere in the Midwest.

In one way or another, it figured in a number of killings. Ex-Marshal George Flat, dismissed for drunkenness, was ambushed as he was staggering home from the Red Light. Deputy Marshal Frank Hunt was shot down by parties unknown as he stood at one of its windows, peering in at the dancers. Marshal George S. Brown walked into the Red Light one morning to arrest two cowboys who had been shooting up the town in drunken exuberance. They killed him as he came up the stairs to the second floor. George Flat, when he was city marshal, and John Wilson, a constable, tried to take George Wood and Jake Adams, Texas cowboys, into custody following a spree that started at the Red Light. They cornered the two men in Jim Moreland's saloon and killed both. Flat's subsequent murder was put down as a revenge slaying by friends of the two Texans. No evidence to that effect was ever produced.

On the afternoon of August 18, 1881, a young Texan named Charlie Davis quarreled with one of the female inmates of the Red Light. George Woods, the nominal proprietor (Mag Woods was the real boss), took the woman's part. Davis shoved his pistol in Woods' face and killed him instantly. Reaching his horse, he raced out of town and was never apprehended.[1]

Mike Meagher, four times city marshal of Wichita, and its all-time best, was among the hundreds who moved down to Caldwell when it became certain that the town was going to boom, and engaged in the saloon business. Popular and widely known, he was elected mayor in the spring of 1880. Twelve days after the ambush slaying of George Flat, Mayor Meagher and his entire city government, consisting of Marshall William Horseman, policemen Frank Hunt, James Johnson, Constable Dan Jones, and town clerk George W. McFarland and town treasurer R. H.

Collins were arrested by Sumner County Sheriff Thralls, charged with complicity in the killing of Flat.[2]

They were taken to Wellington, the county seat, where a number of witnesses, friends of Flat, testified that ex-Marshal Flat had been silenced because he threatened to expose the grafting of Caldwell city officials. No evidence against Meagher was presented, and the farcical proceeding against him was dropped. The others were bound over for the next term of the district court, but they were never brought to trial. According to the Caldwell *Commercial*, "The whole thing was a money-making scheme by Wellington officials to bring business to that town and cast odium on the city of Caldwell." [3]

Meagher refused to stand for re-election in 1881. He did serve as city marshal for a week that summer. His days were numbered, and on December 17 he was cut down by an assassin's bullet in a gun battle in which at least twenty men participated and in which a hundred shots were fired.

Jim Talbot, a well-known Texas desperado, had come up the Chisholm Trail with a late herd belonging to Gene Millett. He had a wife and two young children living in a house on Chisholm Street. He moved in with them and in a week or more was joined by six members of his gang, by name: Doug Hill, Dick Edelman, Bob Munson, Jim Martin, Tom Love and Bob Bigtree. They had been around town for a month or more, drinking, gambling and making themselves obnoxious.

George Speers, who had been with George Flat on the night the latter was killed, threw in with them. When he was in his cups, Talbot boasted that he had come to Caldwell to kill Meagher to avenge the slaying of a half-brother by Mike when the latter was marshal of Wichita.

The record says that Mike killed only two men during the course of the four terms he served in Wichita. One of them might have been the mysterious "half-brother" that Talbot meant to avenge. There is no way of knowing, since men of that caliber always hid their identity with an alias even as Jim Talbot was doing. His real name was Sherman. It satisfies me to believe that Talbot's purpose in wanting to gun down Meagher was to win the distinction of having killed a famous marshal. Evidently Mike did not regard Talbot's threats as so much idle talk, for at his urging Mayor Hubbell added five policemen to the force on a temporary basis.

After an all-night drinking spree the Talbot Gang stepped out into Main Street and began firing their pistols. It sent the few people on the street at that early hour scurrying to cover. Marshal Wilson arrested Tom Love, but the gang freed him. Meagher went to the marshal's assistance. The sporadic shooting grew hotter as the special police and a number of armed citizens rallied to the support of the marshal and his assistants. The outlaws began to drop back. Concerning this phase of the battle, Sheriff Wilson testified at the coroner's hearing: "I started to take Tom Love to the calaboose, when he resisted. I called Mike Meagher to assist me, when the party made a rush for us and made an attack upon Meagher. Meagher went up the Opera House stairway, and I stood at the bottom. Jim Talbot and Tom Love were loudest in their threats against his life. I stopped at the entrance of the stairs, and told them I would shoot the first man making the attempt. . . . The party then dispersed."

It was no later than eleven o'clock by then. The gang went down to Talbot's house on Chisholm Street and secured their Winchesters. They spent an hour or more there, drinking. On their way back uptown, they stopped at Kalbflesch's stable and had their horses saddled for a quick getaway, after which they walked on to Main Street.

"About one o'clock I arrested Jim Martin," Marshal Wilson testified, "who was still armed; took him before Judge Kelly, who fined him. Started him to York & Co.'s with Assistant [marshal] Fosset to get money [for his fine]. He passed down the street, where Love, Talbot, Munson and Edelman took the prisoner away from Fosset. Talbot started to run south, turned around and fired two shots at me. I followed down sidewalk on east side, passed through alleyway south of Pulaski's store. Mike Meagher with me. Stopped in alley back of store. Jim Talbot commenced firing at us from north of Opera House on sidewalk with Winchester rifle. No one was with him. Saw Talbot take aim in the direction we were in. I took hold of Meager and warned him to look out. I heard the report of the gun, and Meagher said 'I am hit, and hit hard.' Took hold of him and helped him to a box. Then left him and went with Hubbell [the mayor] to laundry back of Hubbell's, and began firing at Talbot, Bob Bigtree and three others who were firing at citizens." [4]

Special officer Ed F. Rathbun saw it somewhat differently. "I was with Meagher and Wilson at the rear of Pulaski's store," he testified. "We were firing at Bob Bigtree near the Chinese laundry, they returning our fire. I looked north toward the M. & D. Bank building. Saw Talbot standing with a Winchester rifle aimed at Meagher or myself. Saw the smoke issue from the gun, heard the report and saw Meagher begin to sink down. Said, 'Good God, Mike, are you hit?' 'Yes, tell my wife I have got it at last.' "

The outlaws reached the stable and mounted. George Speers was there. He was saddling one of Talbot's horses, obviously intent on fleeing with them, when he was killed by an unknown marksman who fired from the direction of the Chinese laundry.

The outlaws raced down the slope, crossed the railroad tracks and struck off to the east. They were hotly pursued and overtaken in a canyon on Deutcher Brothers horse ranch, twelve miles from town, where they forted up and held the posse at bay until night fell. After Sheriff Thralls arrived with reinforcements, W. E. Campbell, whose wrist had been shattered by a rifle slug, was taken to town. The sheriff took what measures he could to prevent the escape of the wanted men, but with the coming of daylight it was discovered that Talbot and his men had got away.

Of the Talbot Gang, several were arrested and got off with light sentences. Talbot himself was not captured until 1895. He was brought back from Ukiah, in northern California, and tried for murder in the first degree. His first trial ended in a deadlocked jury, and in the second he was acquitted. Returning to California, he was shot to death by an unknown assassin as he drove up to his ranch several miles from the village of Covelo.[5]

Rumors persisted in Wichita and Caldwell that John Meagher, Mike's brother, had followed Talbot to California and blasted the life out of him. This was only wishful thinking on the part of Mike's old friends; Talbot had killed a neighbor in Mendocino County, and the retribution he suffered was of local origin.

The frequent killings and the vicious character of the Red Light brought a demand by the responsible citizens of Caldwell that it be closed. Mag Woods defied city officials to board up her place. The clamor soon died down and nothing was done, primarily because B. O. (Bat) Carr, the new marshal, was both weak and corrupt. Early in July, Hendry N. Brown, a soft-spoken, colorless, stony-faced gunfighter, arrived in Caldwell and applied for the vacant position of assistant marshal. His appointment followed.

Hendry Brown's credentials for the job were excellent. He had served as marshal of Tascosa, out in the Texas Panhandle, and survived, which was no mean accomplishment. Prior to that he had been a deputy sheriff of Oldham County, Texas. As further proof that policing Caldwell was not too tough a nut for him to crack, he had run with Billy the Kid's gang in the Lincoln County War in New Mexico. Along with other members of the gang he had been granted amnesty by the territorial government after the death of the Kid.

Beyond doubt Brown wanted Bat Carr's job and took dead aim on him almost as soon as he was appointed. Marshal Carr took a long leave of absence, and Hendry Brown was named acting marshal. When Carr returned from his exile, he was quickly dismissed and Brown took over. Several weeks later, Ben Wheeler (an alias; his honest name was Burton) reached Caldwell. Brown had him appointed assistant marshal, a job that was almost permanently open.

Between them, Brown and Wheeler proceeded to give the town a taste of law and order that won its shocked approval. At the marshal's urging several new ordinances were passed. They gave him the authority to remove lewd women from the streets and to prohibit entertainment in the saloons. Caldwell was being policed as it never had been before. Brown and Wheeler hauled Mag Woods and almost a score of the habitues of the Red Light before Police Judge Reilley. Despite Mag's virulent protests, he fined them twenty-five dollars each. The good people of Caldwell responded so enthusiastically that the mayor, A. M. Colson, and the city council found the courage to declare the Red Light a public nuisance and order it closed.

Mag hired lawyers and put up a fight to have the two policemen removed from her premises. It was a losing battle. Under the
terms of the ordinance defining a public nuisance, she and her
bawds could be deported. "Mag Woods Must Go," proclaimed
the Caldwell *Post*. Not waiting to be run out of town, she sold her
fixtures and stock of liquors and marched her retinue down to
the depot and boarded the morning train for Wichita. But she
was to have the last word. Before leaving the Red Light she had
set it afire, and as the train pulled out for the north she watched
it burn.

There were no more killings, fewer saloon fights, no more
buffaloing of the town by drunken cowboys. Several robberies
occurred, in two of which prominent Texan owners were relieved
of the money they had just received from the sale of their herds.
One of these robberies occurred in town, at the Southwestern
Hotel; the other just across the line in Indian Territory. No one
in Caldwell was further removed from suspicion than Marshal
Hendry Brown and his partner Ben Wheeler. In view of what
was to happen a year and a half later, it seems more than likely
that they were guilty of both robberies.

Some idea of the high esteem in which Hendry Brown was
held by the leading businessmen of Caldwell is to be gained from
the fact that on New Year's Day, 1883, he was called into the
York, Parker and Draper store and presented with a gold-
mounted, highly engraved Winchester rifle, bearing on the stock
an engraved silver plate, inscribed: "Presented to City Marshal
H. N. Brown for valuable services rendered the citizens of Caldwell, Kansas. A. M. Colson, Mayor, Jan. 1, A.D. 1883." [6]

Few, very few, frontier peace officers were accepted socially by
the leading families of the towns they policed. Hendry Brown was
one of the rare exceptions. By the time he began his third term
as marshal of Caldwell, no door was closed to him. He was often
a prominent figure at church socials and picnics. This could have
been only a role he was playing, founded on deceit and treachery,
or the direction in which he honestly wanted to go. No one can
say. The kindest explanation is that a cross-pull went on in him,
bending him first one way and then the opposite.

On March 25, 1884, he married Maude Levagood, the daughter

of a prominent Caldwell family. A month later he came to a shocking and ignoble end.

On Saturday, April 26, Brown and Wheeler (it was discovered subsequently that Ben Wheeler was in fact Ben Robertson of Rackdale, Milam County, Texas) asked Mayor Colson for a brief leave of absence, stating that they knew where a murderer, with rewards on him totaling twelve hundred dollars, was camped across the line in the Cherokee Strip. They could claim the reward if they took him into custody. Colson granted their request, and on Sunday afternoon, their horses freshly shod and armed with .44-caliber pistols and Winchester rifles, they rode west out of town.

Somewhere in the Strip, and obviously by appointment, they met Bill Smith, who worked on the T 5 Range, and a cowboy calling himself Wesley, who was employed on the Treadwell and Clark ranch. Both bore the reputation of being hard cases. It is presumed that this meeting occurred sometime on Monday. With their plans perfected, the four of them headed west for Medicine Lodge, Kansas, the county seat of Barber County, still without a railroad but a prosperous farming town nevertheless and the home of the Medicine Valley Bank. It was the bank in which they were interested.

In a driving rain they rode into Medicine Lodge on Wednesday morning, a few minutes after nine o'clock. Leaving their horses behind the shed in which the bank kept its coal, they walked around to the front door. Wesley stopped there and Brown, Wheeler and Smith hurried inside.

George Geppert, the cashier, was behind the banking counter. When he refused to open the safe as demanded, Ben Wheeler shot him dead. Wylie Payne, the president, seated at his desk a few feet away, reached for a gun. Brown shot him, inflicting a mortal wound that resulted in his death twenty-four hours later.

The Reverend George Friedly heard the shots as he was passing the bank and ran to Marshal Denn, who was standing in front of the livery stable a few yards away. Denn began shooting at the heavily armed man at the bank door, who returned his fire. The town was quickly aroused. Inside the bank, Brown and his companions, evidently realizing that the game was up, broke for their horses without even pausing to scoop up what money was in sight and raced out of town, heading south for the Gyp Hills.

Usually at such times precious minutes were lost before pursuit could be organized. Not this morning. Led by Barney O'Connor, a local cattleman, a party of nine men, the Reverend Friedly among them, took off after the fleeing bandits and cornered them in a small canyon in the gypsum hills. Though reinforcements soon arrived, the bandits held them off for two hours before they threw away their guns and marched out with hands raised. It was only then, and to its utter amazement, that the posse discovered that two of the would-be bank robbers were Hendry Brown, the popular marshal of Caldwell, and Assistant Marshal Ben Wheeler.

Sheriff C. F. Riggs arrived in time to take charge of the prisoners and place them in the town's one-room log jail, amid cries of "Lynch them!" As the day wore on and it became obvious that Wylie Payne, the bank president, was dying, threats of mob violence grew louder. Sheriff Riggs swore in four men to help guard the prisoners. "About nine o'clock the stillness of the night was broken by three shots fired in rapid succession," the semiweekly Medicine Lodge *Cresset* reported the following day, "and at the signal a crowd of armed men advanced toward the jail and demanded the prisoners. This was refused, but, not withstanding their spirited resistance, the sheriff and his posse were overpowered and the doors of the jail opened, when the prisoners who were in the cell unshackled made a sudden dash for liberty. . . . Of the robbers, Wheeler, Smith and Wesley were captured, Wheeler badly wounded. Brown ran a few rods from the jail and fell dead, riddled with a charge of buckshot, besides having a few stray Winchester balls in various parts of his body.

"Wheeler, Smith and Wesley were taken by the crowd to an elm tree in the bottom east of town." [7]

After being given a chance to speak if they had anything to say, the ropes were adjusted, and they were left dangling in the air.

Caldwell did not hang its head in shamed silence for long. It could not afford to, not with the 1884 shipping season opening so inauspiciously that the future prosperity of the town seemed to be threatened. In some quarters the fear was expressed that the Texas cattle trade had collapsed and that few herds would be pointed up the Chisholm Trail in the future. In proof of it, they pointed to the fact that car loadings the previous year had dropped to slightly more than 28,000 head.

There was little reason for such pessimism. The year 1880 had been a good one, and 1881 even better. In 1882 the town had shipped a record-breaking 64,000 head, its all-time peak year. That figure was due in part to the thousands of mature cattle that the Cherokee Strip Livestock Association loaded at Caldwell. The association was running upward of a 100,000 head of cattle on range leased from individual Cherokees when the federal government attacked the legality of the leases and declared them null and void.

If 1883 had been a poor year it was largely due to the prolonged drouth that struck most of Texas. The grass failed, and thousands of Longhorns died from starvation or for lack of water. The big owners had strung miles of barbed wire, enclosing much public land as well as their own, making it impossible for the small outfits to drive their herds to water they had been accustomed to using. It led to what came to be known as the "fence-cutting war." Fence-cutting became so widespread and accompanied by so much violence that a special session of the Texas Legislature was called to deal with the problem. It resulted in fences being removed from public lands.

After a mild winter and an early spring, cattle began to put on fat again. Though some Texas owners were of the opinion that trail driving had about run its course, others began to shape up herds again. Though the drives were late in getting started, before the season was over not less than 300,000 head were pointed north, and with them went thousands of mustangs. The majority went up the Western Trail, but Caldwell and the Chisholm Trail got over 57,000 head.

It was Caldwell's last big year. It had always had the disadvantage of not being a good market for stock cattle. Dodge City, on the other hand, was ideally situated to receive cattle that were going on to Nebraska and the Northwest, and it firmly established its right to the title of the Cowboy Capital, queen of the cow towns.

Herds continued to come up the Chisholm Trail, but in steadidly dwindling numbers. After the quarantine law of 1885 went into effect, Caldwell's shipping increased temporarily. Barbed wire was beginning to appear in Indian Territory, blocking the old trail in places. It was the beginning of the end; the big drives from Texas were a thing of the past.

Caldwell, no longer a cow town or cattle market, was to make the headlines again when the federal government threw open the Unassigned Lands in Indian Territory to white settlement on April 22, 1889. Thousands of land-hungry "boomers" gathered along the Kansas line to make the "run." Old Oklahoma (to distinguish it from the present state of Oklahoma) was settled overnight. This was only the prelude to the Cherokee Strip Opening on September 16, 1893. It was really the opening to white settlement of the great Cherokee Outlet, but it is idle to debate that point; to the forty thousand men and women who gathered on the Kansas line to await the bugle that would send them rushing across the border to claim free land, it was the Cherokee Strip Opening. Ten thousand people crowded into Caldwell to make the "run." Food became almost unobtainable. Wells ran dry and water had to be brought down from Wellington.

Optimistically, in its edition of September 21, the *Caldwell Weekly News* said that: "It [Caldwell] is already a busy commercial center, has a splendid trade but will double it . . . by the opening of the territory below us. There will be no rival town nearer than 17 miles [Hunnewell] and a vast trade territory is ours to reap." But Perry and half a dozen other towns sprang up in the so-called Strip almost at once, and Caldwell was fortunate to have its farm population to support it. By then, the Chisholm Trail was fading into memory, and grass was beginning to blot out the scars its millions of Longhorns had cut in the prairie sod.

17

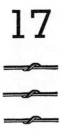

The Western Trail to Dodge

LONG AFTER THE CHISHOLM TRAIL from Red River Station to
Kansas was virtually abandoned, it retained its identity from
Belton, Texas, to the Gulf Coast. Thumbing through the two
precious volumes of reminiscences contained in *The Trail Drivers of Texas,* you will find many of the old-timers recalling how
they went up the Chisholm Trail to Belton and then turned off
on the Western Trail for Dodge City and the Northwest, via
Fort Griffin, Doan's Store, the North Fork of Red River and
past Elm Creek, Mobeetie, the upper Washita, the Canadian,
North Canadian, the Cimarron, and on to their destination.

If the importance of a cattle trail is to be measured by the number of animals passing over it on their way to market, then the
Western Trail was second only to the Chisholm as the greatest of
all American cattle trails. To me, there is more of the story of the
Western Trail to be found in Doan's Store than in Dodge, itself.
Perhaps this is because so much has been told about Dodge City
and so little about Doan's Store. As a "store"—the last place where
supplies could be had for the long drive ahead—it was, in the days
of the great cattle and mustang drives, the most famous store west
of the Mississippi River. But it was more than that. It was a landmark, a post office, the last contact the Texans were to have with
civilization for many weeks, and it was the place to which owners

came for a final look at their herds before meeting them several months later at Dodge City.

With the prominence it achieved and the tremendous amount of business that was transacted there, it might have been presumed that a town would take root. That never happened; from the first it remained just Doan's Store—the third and the last of great cattle crossings of the Red. Twenty-five miles to the south, the squalid collection of picket and adobe houses known as Eagle Flat became the county seat when Wilbarger County was organized and grew into the thriving and pleasant town of Vernon, then as now the gateway to Doan's Store. And it is as Doan's Store, not Doan's Crossing, that it has taken its place in history.

You will recall that up and down the river for miles there was nothing but an endless stretch of lonely, brush-covered wilderness when Maxwell and Morris, the trailblazers, put their herd across the Red in 1877. Before the season closed, other herds were crossing there. Indians carried word of this activity to Jonathan Doan and his cousins, Corwin F. and Robert E., who were trading with the Comanches and Kiowas at their post on Cache Creek, two miles from Fort Sill. Jonathan Doan visited the crossing that fall and was so impressed by the commercial possibilities of locating a store on the Texas side that during the winter he and Corwin Doan decided to open a trading post there and arranged to have supplies freighted in from Gainesville. The store opened for business in April, 1878, and Bob Lauderdale, a seasoned trail veteran from Atascosa County, was one of the first to see it. "It consisted of three or four buffalo hides and a wagon sheet," he recalled jocularly. Actually it was a building made of pickets with a dirt floor and dirt roof.

"It was primitive," Corwin Doan acknowledged years later. "The first winter we had no door, but a buffalo robe did service against the northers."

Jonathan Doan is credited with having established the store that bore his name, and perhaps rightfully so, for Corwin Doan had suffered a serious illness early that year and had returned to the family home at Wilmington, Ohio. The season of 1878 was over before, fully recovered, he arrived with his family at Doan's Store and took charge of the business. In the following seven years several million Longhorns and mustangs were to pass his door, and the kings and princes of the cattle trade were to enjoy his hospitality.

The original store was replaced with a new and more commodious one, built of adobe. As the business grew, a frame building was erected. Daily, freighting outfits arrived with merchandise from Gainesville and Sherman, and later from Wichita Falls. To quote Corwin Doan; "We thought nothing of selling bacon and flour in carload lots." Old account books show that sales for one day often topped two thousand dollars.

Red River could show its teeth when it was "on a rise," but for most of the summer it became a deceptively placid stream, exposing stretches of quicksand as it contracted. To prevent cattle and horses from getting mired, the Doans built what they called a "straw bridge." Wild hay was piled up to a depth of several feet. As soon as it was chewed down by the passing herds, fresh material was added. It was a continuing process, and gangs of men were soon employed the year around cutting hay for the bridge. In time it rose several feet above the surrounding river bottom. A toll of twenty-five cents a head was charged for using it.

As a post office Doan's Store was unique. There, a cowboy might expect to find a letter awaiting him from a sweetheart he had left behind in south Texas. "It was at this office all mail for the trail herds was directed, as, like canned goods and other commodities, this was the last chance," Corwin Doan recalled. "Many a sweetheart down the trail received her letter bearing the postmark of Doan's Store and many a cowboy asked self-consciously if there was any mail for him while his face turned a beet red when a dainty missive was handed him."

One of the defects in the image we have fashioned of the cowboy of the period is that we have not allowed him any room for romance. Of course he had his softer side; he wasn't always just the brave, tough young rowdy who worked hard and played hard. If some owners were indifferent to how the men they employed deported themselves, that was not true of all. There was D. H. Snyder of the firm of D. H. and J. W. Snyder, one of the giants of trail driving. "We adopted three rules for our cowboys to be governed by on our first drive in 1868, as follows," he said:

"First: You can't drink whisky and work for us.

"Second: You can't play cards and gamble and work for us.

"Third: You can't curse and swear in our camps or in our presence and work for us.

"These rules we kept inviolate as long as we were in the cattle business."

Both the Snyder brothers were often at Doan's Store, many times for as long as a week, waiting for herds they had coming up the trail. Names to be found on the old account books are a veritable Who's Who of the trail-driving era—such names as the Blockers, the Slaughters, George Saunders, the Ellisons, the Dewees brothers, Dillard Fant, Captain Miflin Kenedy, Colonel Ike Pryor, the Driskills. They were all there, and that included Captain John T. Lytle, who must stand as the most successful of all trail drivers. "With his partners John W. Light, T. M. McDaniel and Captain Charles Schreiner, he directed the movement of 450,000 Longhorns and thousands of horses, delivering them in Kansas, Colorado, Montana and other states and territories. During this time he directed investments in livestock aggregating $9,000,000, a record never equalled." [1]

When he retired to his ranch in Medina County, twenty-five miles south of San Antonio, after fifteen years of trail driving, Lytle often said reminiscently that whatever success he had had he owed to the men who worked for him. Like the Snyder brothers, the conduct and comfort of his cowboys were a first consideration with him. No wagon of his ever left Doan's Store until its contents had been checked and rechecked. It paid off; he got the best riders and the best cooks, and they gave him their best— which was not the pattern with some owners who wasted no money on themselves and none on their men. If you want to know how bad a boss could make life for a trail crew, read Teddy Blue Abbott's *We Pointed Them North*, the best of all cowboy accounts of life on the trail. [2]

Red men as well as white visited Doan's Store, chieftains with whom the Doans had become acquainted when they were trading on Cache Creek. Among them were Big Bow, who had succeeded Satanta as principal chief of the Kiowas, and Quanah Parker, chief of the Comanches. In his old age Corwin Doan recalled his friendship with Quanah, who spoke English and dressed like a white man. "After moving to Doan's of course I saw a great deal of Quanah, who at that time had become head chief. He told me he had often been invited to return to his white relations near Weatherford but refused."

The story of how his mother Cynthia Ann Parker had been carried off as a child by the Comanches, following the massacre at Fort Parker, in 1832, and when she reached womanhood became the wife of Chief Peta Nocona, has been told many times. In 1860, in the battle on Pease River, Nocona was killed and his band almost annihilated by Texas state troops led by Captain Sul Ross. Cynthia Ann Parker was captured with a baby daughter. Against her wishes she was returned to her relatives at Weatherford, after an absence of twenty-eight years. But she had been an Indian too long to be able to adjust herself to her new environment. Miserably unhappy, her health failed and she soon passed away.

" 'Corwin,' Quanah said to me," Doan recalled, " 'as far as you see I am chief here and the people look up to me. Down at Weatherford I would be a poor half-breed Indian.' Perhaps he was right."

Corwin Doan arrived at Doan's Store too late to see the herds that crossed the Red in 1868, but he was there to see the last of them that passed in 1885. The Kansas embargo on Longhorn cattle had gone into effect. Early in the season some of the Texans were disposed to believe that they could put their herds through; that the new law would prove as porous as its predecessors. By midseason, they were convinced that the Western Trail had been closed. With its trade gone and the crossing abandoned, the famous store had to close its doors. Though its business had always been seasonal, for seven years it had enjoyed a fabulous prosperity. Presumably, it had netted the Doans a snug fortune.

I have told elsewhere how my curiosity regarding what had become of the fortune took me to Gerald Doan McDonald, a direct descendant of Corwin F. Doan. He greeted my question with a rueful laugh. " 'There wasn't any,' he said. 'The extremely high cost of freighting in everything the store sold meant doing business at a small profit. Bad debts ate up most of what remained. Goods were sold on credit; when a cattleman went broke, and many did, his indebtedness had to be written off as a loss.' " [3]

But Doan's Store has not been forgotten. In nearby Watt's Grove, several thousand people from up and down Red River and North Texas gather annually to celebrate Doan's Picnic. It has been observed for eighty years without a break, a lasting tribute to the man and "handful of women" who originated it in 1884.

It is not only the annual picnic that keeps the memory of Doan's Store green. On October 22, 1933, the Trail Drivers' Association of Texas erected a large granite marker there. The inscription reads:

> IN HONOR OF THE TRAIL DRIVERS WHO FREED TEXAS FROM THE
> YOKE OF DEBT AND DESPAIR BY THEIR TRAILS TO THE CATTLE
> MARKETS OF THE FAR NORTH, WE DEDICATE THIS STONE, A SYM-
> BOL OF THEIR COURAGE AND FORTITUDE AT THE SITE OF THE OLD
> DOAN'S STORE.

The following figures by Colonel Ike T. Pryor provide an informative insight into the arithmetic of trail driving, its expenses and profits. They indicate that the cost of moving a herd from Texas to the Northern markets showed no marked increase between 1870 and 1884.

"Trail driving of cattle from Texas to Northwestern States in the old trail days was reduced to almost a science, and large numbers of cattle were moved at the minimum cost.

"To illustrate, I drove fifteen herds in 1884 from South Texas to the Northwestern States. It required a minimum of 165 men and about 1,000 saddle horses to move this entire drive. . . . These cattle were driven in droves of 3,000 to each herd, with eleven men, including the boss, and each man was furnished with six horses.

"The salaries of these eleven men, including the boss, were $30.00 each for the ten men, including the cook, and $100.00 a month for the boss. This gave an outlay of $400.00 a month, and estimating $100.00 for provisions, there was an expense of $500.00 a month to move a herd of 3,000 cattle 450 to 500 miles. In those days it was possible to drive 3,000 cattle 3,000 miles for $3,000. . . . When I had sold and delivered all of these cattle to Montana,

Dakota and Wyoming ranchmen I had lost 1,500 head, or 3 percent.

"Today [1919] it would cost $25,000 or $30,000, and the only way they could be moved would be by rail. And I daresay the loss would be equal to 3 percent. . . . I paid $12.00 for my yearlings, $16.00 for my two-year olds and $20.00 for my three-year olds, and I had them contracted to the ranchmen of the Northwest at $4.00 a head margin." [4]

A little work with a pencil will show that, counting his expenses and losses, Pryor had a net profit of $127,440 for the year's work.

Unquestionably some Texas cattle were bootlegged into Kansas and shipped from Dodge City after the state-wide embargo became law. But armed border guards began moving into the western counties with orders to confiscate all cattle that had entered the state in defiance of the embargo. Realizing that the door was really closed this time, the Texans turned back when they reached the line and drove west through the Oklahoma Panhandle until they could turn north into Colorado, thereby avoiding Kansas. Some went as far west as the old Goodnight-Loving Trail, about which more later.

That Kansas regarded Dodge City as a liability and a blot on the fair name of the state is reflected in its newspapers of the period. Almost without exception their comments are caustic and unfriendly. These diatribes invariably took pot shots at William Barclay (Bat) Masterson, who at various times had been deputy sheriff, then sheriff of Ford County, Deputy U. S. Marshal, and, toward the end, seemingly deputized a deputy sheriff at will. On July 2, 1885, the Topeka *Capital* described him as being "one of the most disreputable characters in the West. . . . He was at the head of 300 ruffians who were bent on driving Griffin [Albert Griffin, editor of the Manhattan, Kansas, *Nationalist* and president of the State Temperance Union] from the town, or if they failed in that, killing him."

The Topeka *Commonwealth* was equally bitter. "The statutes of Kansas do not apply to Dodge City; it makes its own laws. Maybe ex-Mayor Webster was stretching things a little, a year ago, when he informed the U. S. Attorney General: 'Dodge City ain't in the United States.' He would have been more accurate if he had said, 'Dodge City ain't in Kansas.' "

This dig at Ab Webster was harking back to the "Dodge City Bullfight," which he had staged on July 4, the previous year. The purpose of this extravaganza, the first (and only) of its kind held within the territorial limits of the United States, was to put Dodge City on the front pages of newspapers the country over and pour a golden flood into the town. Matadors and picadors, so called, were imported from Mexico and wild bulls brought in from the surrounding range. It proved to be a shabby performance. But opposition to it had been immediate from the moment it was announced. When the legal machinery of the state for preventing it had been exhausted, Webster received a telegram from the U. S. Attorney General warning him that bullfighting was against the law in the United States. He is alleged to have wired back: "Dodge City ain't in the United States."

The story is perhaps apocryphal. But the bullfight was only one of several grievances Kansas had against Dodge City. It had fought the Texas fever embargo for its own selfish interests and undoubtedly had connived to circumvent it after it became law. Of far greater concern to the Prohibitionist party and the Temperance Union was its utter and continuing defiance of the Prohibition Amendment, banning the sale or possession of intoxicating liquors in Kansas, ratified by the voters in November, 1880.

The trouble broke out into the open on July 2, 1885, when the aforementioned Albert Griffin arrived in Dodge City to lecture on the evils of whisky. He was accompanied by A. B. Jetmore, assistant state's attorney general, who was in Dodge to investigate the saloon business. They were charged by a mob at the Southwestern Hotel. A saloonkeeper named Sheridan, the leader of the rioters, had struck Dr. Galland, the proprietor of the hotel, when Deputy Sheriff Bat Masterson appeared on the scene and ended hostilities.

The incident was over, but it was to have a far-reaching effect. On the following day, back home, Griffin said in the Manhattan *Nationalist:*

"Bat Masterson, the reputed leader of the lawless elements of

Dodge City, voluntarily called on us and stated that neither Colonel Jetmore nor myself should be molested, and when the assault was made on Dr. Galland . . . he went out and ordered the mob to go across the street. . . . Bat Masterson stayed in front of our room for half an hour or more, and sent the men back as they attempted to come and they finally retreated across the railroad. So far as I know, Mr. Masterson steadily did all he could to prevent any attack being made upon us.

"Bat Masterson is a professional gambler who has killed two or three men and shot several others. He is smart and has many elements of a leader, but is unquestionably a vicious man. He did not want Assistant Attorney Jetmore or myself killed, and the reason he is said to have given his associates was that 'they could not afford to bring down upon themselves the vengeance of the State government and the State Temperance Union. . . . The very fact that he has the qualities of 'good fellowship,' 'occasional generosity,' 'steadfastness to friends,' 'fluency of speech' and 'cool courage' make him all the more dangerous a man in such a community." [5]

Newspapers spread Griffin's statement and coupled with it a vitriolic condemnation of the sporting fraternity of Dodge City. Very likely Griffin would have suffered nothing worse than being ignored if he had confined himself to making a speech on his visit to Dodge. But he had no sooner arrived than he attempted to get an injunction against the open saloons. Failing in that he publicly denounced town and county officials, including District Judge J. C. Strang, for their failure to enforce the Prohibition Amendment. Judge Strang added fuel to the fire in a letter to Governor John A. Martin, dated July 5:

"Griffin wants to close them [the saloons] with a proclamation, or with a great hurrah—with the State Temperance Union on the ground, and the Atty-Gen'l, and Judge of the district court present, to do the bidding of the representative of the said Union, so he can send out an Associated Press dispatch to the world saying Albert Griffin, organizer of the State Temperance Union, has closed the Saloons in Dodge.

"Dodge City is in a transition stage and will come all right soon of itself. The quarantine law passed last winter is quietly working out the salvation of Dodge City. The festive cowboy is already becoming conspicuous by his absence in Dodge, and ere long will be seen & heard there, in his glory, no more forever. The cowboy gone, the gamblers and prostitutes will find their occupations gone, and, from necessity, must follow. The bulk of the saloons will then die out because there will be no sufficient support left, and the temperance people can close the rest as easily as they could in any other city in Kansas." [6]

It was to prove to be an accurate prophecy. But Dodge, which had always been slightly incredible, was to be incredible to the very end. Bat, who had been in Colorado for several months, returned to town on March 10, 1886, and literally stood Dodge City on its ear by "inaugurating a determined crusade against the vendors of alcoholic beverages." When he arrived, two men were with him. Whether they were officials of the Kansas State Temperance Union or in the service of Attorney General Bradford's department remains a question. But that they were in Dodge to advise Bat on how to proceed seems certain. Officially, he was still a deputy sheriff of Ford County. Supported by County Attorney Mike Sutton, he filed complaints against all of the saloon men and druggists in the city. Warrants were issued and the offenders arrested and indicted, then freed on bail.

"The saloons are all closed now and the prohibitory law apparently enforced," commented the Dodge City *Democrat*. If this was unbelievable, it was not half as incredible as that Bat Masterson, always a saloon "man," a professional gambler at times, a leading figure in the sporting life of the town, a man whose morals were negative, had switched sides and dried up the fabulous "Bibulous Babylon of the Frontier."

It has never been satisfactorily explained. The Dodge City *Times* sought to give it political implications, suggesting that A. B. Webster, who was running for mayor again, was being secretly knifed by the saloon element that had nominated him and that Masterson, rushing to his friend Webster's support, had turned the tables on them and put them out of business. Ab Webster, himself, was the proprietor of a Front Street saloon at the time. It is not likely that he knowingly would have conspired to put himself out of business.

With trail driving at an end, and with nothing else to take its place, Dodge City's population was shrinking at the very time in which more and more farmers, who were almost solidly anti-saloon, were taking up land in Ford County. In Dodge there had always been a considerable Prohibitionist element, never strong enough to make its voice felt, but now by joining ranks with the farmers it must have been fairly obvious that the saloons could be closed. Undoubtedly Bat was aware of this. It has given rise to the speculation that in taking charge he had his own political advancement in mind. There is nothing in the record to justify it; up to the time he left Dodge the following year he did not seek nomination for any office.

It could have been that he had honestly come to believe that the saloon was an evil and had to go. At least no one has said closing the saloons was a job he had been hired to do.

The courage, bravery and integrity of the man cannot be questioned. If his morals where women were concerned do him no credit, they were typical of his time and environment and make it no less certain that he was the best and best-liked peace officer Dodge City and Ford County ever had.

Bat was the head of the Masterson clan. His eldest brother Ed Masterson was killed while he was marshal of Dodge City. Jim, the youngest of the brothers, was a policeman, assistant marshal and marshal of the town. Bat's connection with the city force was a brief period as a policeman. It was as, first, under sheriff of Ford County, then sheriff, and much later a deputy sheriff, that he became famous. Tom Masterson, a fourth brother, made his home with his parents, near Wichita. Briefly, he was a deputy sheriff under Bat.

Contrary to what fiction and television have led many to believe, Bat was never marshal of the town. But of its many marshals and sheriffs none was to have the impact on Dodge that he did, and that included Bill Tilghman, who later was to win enduring fame in Oklahoma Territory as one of "The Three Guardsmen." Though Dodge City had lost some of its edge, it was still a wild town when he was appointed marshal on April 10, 1884. When he resigned two years later it was no longer a cow town.

In their Dodge City days, Masterson completely overshadowed

Wyatt Earp, who served two separate hitches as assistant marshal.[7]
Separating fact from fiction, Earp was a better than average officer. Police court dockets, newspaper comment and other documentary evidence reveal that the feats he attributes to himself
in his alleged biography, *Wyatt Earp Frontier Marshal,* are complete fabrications and at best are only exciting accounts of events
that never occurred.

That he made very little impression on Dodge can be gathered
from the infrequency with which his name occurs in the local
press. He was never marshal of the town, as he claims. Though
reputed to be a great gunfighter, in his two terms on the force he
killed only one man, a young Texan named George Hoy, who
had been creating a disturbance in the Comique Theatre and was
fleeing in the darkness across the old wooden bridge that spanned
the Arkansas. He was wounded and died a few days later. Some
doubt exists that the shot that killed Hoy came from Earp's gun,
since Tom Nixon, a fellow officer, and he fired at the same time.

The political battles of Dodge City found expression in the
columns of the rival and bitterly partisan Dodge City *Times* and
the Ford County *Globe.* It was continued when the *Globe* became the *Globe Live Stock Journal* and the Dodge City *Democrat*
joined the fray. All featured "Letters to the Editor," and the
"letters" were usually vindictive, accusing and no doubt often
libelous. If you were in politics, and Bat always was, in one way
or another, you were certain to come under attack. Being an
incessant letter writer, his name was always in the papers. If it
wasn't in connection with his activities as sheriff, it was likely to
be a blistering retort to a personal attack that had appeared in
the public prints. On several occasions these charges and counter-
charges threatened to erupt into gunfire, as when Bob Fry, publisher of the Speareville (Ford County) *News,* said editorially:

> We hear that Bat Masterson said he was going to whip every
> S—— of a b—— that worked and voted against him in the county.
> The above was given to us on the best authority and taking
> into considration the source of our information and the fact that
> two or three citizens have been fearfully beaten by himself and
> friends, would give the above statement a credence that but
> few would attempt to deny.

On November 15, a week later, the Dodge City *Times* published Bat's side of it:

In answer to the publication made by Bob Fry of the Speareville News, asserting that I made threats that I would lick any s—— of a b—— that worked or voted against me in the last election, I will say it was as false and flagrant a lie as was ever uttered; but I did say this: that I would lick him, the s—— of a b—— if he made any more dirty talk about me; and the words s—— of a b—— I strictly confined to the Speareville editor, for I don't know of any other in Ford County.

Charles Roden, Fry's source of information, subsequently was forced to admit he had lied. The *News* retracted and the incident was forgotten.

In March of that year Bat had engaged in some extra curricular duties that have puzzled many readers interested in Western history. The Santa Fe and the Denver and Rio Grande railroads were battling for possession of the Grand Canyon of the Arkansas—the Royal Gorge—with both sides importing gunmen. The Santa Fe turned to Masterson and asked him to recruit a force of "reliable" men. Bat opened an office for that purpose and left for Colorado on March 25 with thirty-three armed mercenaries. The editors of *Cowtown Police Officers and Gunfighters* ask, as many others have, how the sheriff of a Kansas county could legally aid a private corporation in another state. Of course, he couldn't—not even in his role of deputy U. S. marshal to which he had received appointment.

Ben Thompson, the Texas gambler and gunfighter, was one of the notables who accompanied him. They engaged in some skirmishing at the Santa Fe roundhouse in Pueblo and took part in the fighting at Canon City in which one, possibly two, D. & R. G. men were killed. They were back in Dodge, none the worse for wear, in time for the 1879 shipping season. The good wages received had made it a profitable adventure. The *Times* and the *Globe* expressed the opinion that a good time had been had by all.

18

Fabulous Dodge

FOR A DECADE, 1875–85, Dodge City's pre-eminence as the greatest of all cow towns could not successfully be challenged. Its longevity was more than double Abilene's and other predecessors'. Farmer oppositiion and fences had shortened their days. If the quarantine law had not rung down the curtain on Dodge, the wave of farmers that was spreading westward across Kansas would have done so in another year or two, perhaps before the railroads that were buiding across Texas made trail driving unnecessary.

It wasn't only the number of car loadings and the tens of thousands of stock cattle that swept past Dodge City on their way to the Northwest that made it—the town, that is—what it was. It offered nothing in the way of entertainment—using the word in its broadest sense—that other towns had not provided. But in some intangible way the Texans found it different. Perhaps it was the manner in which it conducted itself, its spirit, that made it appeal to them as no other Kansas town had. Abilene, Ellsworth, Newton, Wichita, Caldwell were not "Western"; Dodge was. Maybe that made the difference.

The buffalo hunters had made it prosperous and cocky long before the Western Trail brought it fame and fortune. If it came through the transition from buffalo hides to beef on the hoof without losing its boisterous frontier character, it was largely due to the little group of men, not more than a dozen, who charted the course it was to take. Robert M. (Bob) Wright, foremost among frontier traders and outfitters, was one. He was easily the richest and foremost citizen of Dodge, several times mayor and member of the state legislature. Charlie Rath, his partner at one time in the firm of Rath and Wright, and Judge H. M. Beverley, who joined him when the firm became Wright and Beverley, belonged to the inner circle that made Dodge City strong. Others were James (Dog) Kelley,[1] its first mayor, sportsman and saloonkeeper; George Hoover, wholesale liquor and tabacco dealer and banker; A. B. Webster; Chalkley (Chalk) Beeson, the organizer of the Dodge City Cowboy Band and sheriff of Ford County; Will Harris, its leading gambler. And, of course, Deacon Cox and his Dodge House, fifty rooms no less and the best "table" on the plains. Little that was significant happened in Dodge in which one or more of them did not have a hand.

Much of what occurred in Dodge City would have attracted no more than local interest if it had happened elsewhere. Abilene and the other cow towns were largely unknown outside of Kansas and parts of Texas; Dodge's newspaper reputation was country-wide. Almost without exception, these stories and articles followed the lurid, wild and woolly pattern of the Wild West fiction typical of the period. It was what the readers wanted, and they did not question that in Dodge the streets ran red with gore and the six-gun was never silent.

If one is to be guided by police court records and the columns of the Ford County *Globe* and the Dodge City *Times,* and Robert M. Wright's *Dodge City: The Cowboy Capital and the Great Southwest,* still the best book on Dodge, Dodge wasn't more lawless than the cow towns that had preceded it. This was too tame for the aficionados of the fictional Dodge; they wanted violence and more Boot Hill.

Many towns had their "boot hills," but Dodge City lays claim to the original; Tascosa, down in the Texas Panhandle, is another claimant. But it is Dodge City's Boot Hill that is famous.

Tales of the scores of men who were wrapped in a blanket

and buried without ceremony in its yellow clay, within shouting distance of Front Street, are numerous. Mostly, they are
imaginative, melodramatic fiction. The most widely accepted
story is that in the summer of 1875, two cowboys camping on
the hill engaged in a gunfight. One was killed and the other
fled. The dead man was rolled up in his blankets and buried
where he had fallen, nameless and unknown. The tale is be-
lievable to me; the hill was handy, treeless, and at the time
Dodge City had no cemetery. A man had to be of some consequence to be interred in the old military cemetery at Fort
Dodge.

It is not true, as fiction has it, that all of the men who were
buried on Boot Hill died by gunfire; nor is it true that most
were buried in their blankets. "In 1879, when Dodge City
leveled part of Boot Hill to erect a school on the site, the bodies
were dug up and moved to the new Prairie Grove Cemetery,
north of town, and reburied side by side in four rows. There
was one exception—Alice Chambers, a dance-hall girl, and the
last person known to have been buried on Boot Hill, who was
placed in a grave apart from the others." [2]

The haphazard manner in which the original graves were
dug led to some confusion over the number of skeletons ex-
humed. It was agreed, however, that the figure did not exceed
twenty-five by more than one or two. So much for stories of
the scores that Wild West fiction said were buried there.

The Santa Fe tracks cut the town in two, leaving a wide
plaza between the north and south sides. The section south of
the tracks soon acquired the name of South Side, later South
Dodge. Dodge had the usual ordinance against carrying firearms. No attempt was made to enforce it on the South Side.
With its numerous cheap saloons, variety theatres, the Comique and Lady Gay, its dance halls, gamblers, pimps and
prostitutes, it was tough. When a man crossed the tracks to
the North Side and Front Street, where the big action was, he
was supposed to hang his pistol on a gunrack in any one of
several saloons or on the rack in Wright and Beverley's store.
However, the history of Front Street reveals that whenever

a man found that he needed a gun, he invariably had one on his person.

The police of Dodge were never averse to publicity. They got a bountiful helping of it when E. Z. C. Judson, known to the eastern half of the United States as "Ned Buntline," author of a hundred lurid Wild West tales, many of them featuring Buffalo Bill Cody, arrived in town with some presentation copies of a six-gun that the Colt Patent Firearms Company had made for him. He called it the "Buntline Special." The only way in which it differed from the standard .45 Colt Peacemaker was in the length of its barrel, which measured twelve inches. Judson had stopped off in North Platte and presented his friend Bill Cody with a "Buntline Special."

In Dodge City at a ceremony calculated to produce the maximum amount of publicity for himself, with Billy Petillon of the Ford County *Globe,* the local Associated Press correspondent and other reporters present, the recipients of Judson's generosity were Masterson, Earp, Tilghman, Neil Brown [3] and Sheriff Charley Bassett. Photographs were taken. Eastern newspapers used the story with pictures, and the "Buntline Special" took its place in frontier history. It is still with us, the genuine being a rare collector's item. As a pistol, it was a monstrosity. Masterson and the rest, except Wyatt Earp, promptly had the barrel sawed off to standard length; Earp claimed the long barrel was a decided advantage when it was necessary to buffalo a prisoner, which amounted to clipping a man on the side of the head with a pistol. He must really have liked the gun. If he can be believed, which I find hard to do, he was wearing it when he stepped through the ropes in San Francisco in 1896 to referee the Fitzsimmons-Sharkey fight. "I had completely forgotten how I was dressed," he recalled, "and there on my right hip, the old Buntline forty-five, with its twelve-inch barrel and the walnut butt, stuck out like a canon." [4]

The photograph of Front Street seen most often is of early, false-front vintage and shows it as it was in its cow town infancy. By the beginning of the following shipping season it presented a different appearance; most of the ramshackle buildings had been replaced by substantial structures, many of them housing saloons that were to become famous—the Long Branch, the Alhambra, Ab Webster's Alamo and the Opera House saloon. Wright and Beverley's new two-story brick emporium at the corner of Front and Second was open for business. More whisky barrels filled with water, the town's only protection against fire, were set out at intervals along the edge of the plank sidewalk.

Rivalry among the saloons was intense, and it erupted finally in the celebrated "Dodge City war," which kept the town on the front pages of local and out-of-state newspapers for five weeks. The seeds of it were planted when little Luke Short, the dapper, big-stakes gambler from Fort Worth, Texas, purchased Chalk Beeson's one-half interest in the Long Branch, with Will Harris, Beeson's erstwhile partner, retaining his half.[5]

In the spring election of 1883, in a bitter, mud-slinging campaign, gargantuan Larry Deger, marshal of the town during Wyatt Earp's first hitch as assistant marshal, was elected mayor over Will Harris, Short's partner, on April 3. Three weeks later, the new city administration passed two ordinances that precipitated the so-called war.

Ordinance No. 70 was entitled: "An Ordinance For The Supression of Vice And Immorality Within The City of Dodge City." It was the usual ordinance against bawdy houses, houses of assignation and the proprietors and inmates of such, together with fines against those found guilty.

No one thought much about it; there were ordinances already on the books that covered the same ground. It was Ordinance No. 71, "An Ordinance To Define And Punish Vagrancy," that mattered, especially Section 2, reading:

"Any person who may be found loitering around houses of ill-fame, gambling houses or places where liquors are sold or drunk, without any visible means of support or lawful vocation, or shall be the keeper or inmate of any house of ill-fame or gambling house, or engaged in any unlawful calling whatever, shall be deemed guilty of vagrancy under this ordinance, and may be fined in any sum not less than Ten nor more than One Hundred Dollars."

Special police were added to the force, and on Saturday night, April 28, two days after the ordinances became effective, arrests were made. The first arrests were of women ostensibly employed as singers or entertainers in the Long Branch Saloon. No one questioned that the real occupation of these women was prostitution, and that they used the saloon in which to solicit business. What roused the ire of Luke Short and his friends was that only the saloons owned by men who had opposed the election of Larry Deger were raided; the establishments of others, including the Alamo, owned by ex-Mayor Webster, who had managed Deger's campaign, were not molested.

It appeared to be a bit of base political skulduggery. Short held no brief for the women, other than they were good for business, but if he couldn't have entertainers in the Long Branch, he vowed that none of his competitors should have them. He tried to have the three females who had been taken out of his place freed on bail, but they were forced to spend the night in the calaboose—not the old roofed-over hole in the ground on the plaza, but a "modern" jail in which the police court was also housed.

Later in the evening, he encountered special policeman L. C. Hartman, who had made the arrests in the Long Branch, and fired several shots at him. Hartman dropped down behind a convenient fire-barrel and fired back. Short had seen Hartman fall, and believing he had wounded or killed him—neither was wounded—he surrendered himself and was freed in two thousand dollars bail. In the morning, he and five others, without a hearing, were informed that they were *persona non grata* in Dodge City and were given their choice of trains, east or west. They were marched down to the depot; Short, Johnson Gallagher and Tom Lane chose to go east; the others went west to Cimarron, eighteen miles away, where they might launch a counterattack against this highhanded usurpation of their legal rights.

In Dodge, bands of armed men searched every train that arrived, making sure that the banished men did not return. The *Times* applauded the measures the city government was taking;

referred to the men searching the trains as officially deputized police. The Ford County *Globe* blasted Mayor Deger and his associates; cried that the orderly processes of law and justice had disappeared from Dodge City and that the town was at the mercy of an organized mob. "If Luke Short returns, he will be murdered in cold blood," it charged. "Tension is growing hourly. Business is at a standstill. The feeling is spreading that Deger and his henchmen have gone too far. . . . Dodge City stands at the brink of war."

Rot and nonsense, screamed the Republican-owned *Times*, and the war—at least of words—between the rival papers was on. "The city has been under an intense commotion for several days, growing out of the ordinance in relation to the suppression of gambling and prostitution. Mayor Deger, learning that a conspiracy had been formed, which had for its object the armed resistance to the enforcement of the law and consequent murder of some of our best citizens, organized a police force on Sunday, and on Monday the plan was carried out. . . . As a precaution, about one hundred and fifty citizens were on watch Monday night, and a large police force is still held on duty night and day. . . . No half-way measures will be used in the suppression of either lawlessness or riot. Mayor Deger is a resolute, fearless and obstinate officer. All good and law abiding citizens are standing by him in this trying emergency."

To keep the rest of the state from learning what was transpiring in Dodge City, Sheriff George T. Hinkle ordered the Western Union operator not to accept for transmission any message regarding it. He could not interfere with the mails, however. Short had established himself in Kansas City and was receiving daily reports from Dodge. To present his side of the case, he began writing long communications to the Kansas City and Topeka newspapers. He then addressed himself to the Honorable George W. Glick, the first Democratic Governor of Kansas, reiterating the statements he had made in his letters to the press, to wit: that he had been unlawfully deprived of his property and unlawfully banished from Dodge City; that if there were any charges pending against him he was ready and willing to face them and accept the verdict of the court, provided the Governor would guarantee his personal safety.

By now the Dodge City "war" was attracting so much attention that Glick invited Luke to come to Topeka and present his side of the case in person. What he had to say must have impressed the Governor, for shortly thereafter Glick alerted two companies of the Kansas National Guard, Company H at Sterling and Company K at Newton, to be ready to entrain for Dodge on notice.[6]

The Governor's next move was a very lengthy letter to Sheriff Hinkle in which he reminded him that as sheriff of Ford County his authority in maintaining the peace exceeded that of Mayor Deger and Marshal Bridges, and that he (the Governor) would hold him personally responsible in the situation. "The peace of the city is with you, Mr. Sheriff, and I expect it to be safe in your hands."

Telegrams between Hinkle and the Governor began to come thick and fast. Hinkle, willfully it seems, continued to misunderstand the Governor's position and refused to face up to the fact that "driving persons out of town rather than trying them for their crimes, whether real or imaginary, in the courts," was an unlawful act.[7]

By mail and in person Glick heard from "committees" of reliable Dodge citizens, including such notables as Bob Wright, Ham Bell and George Hoover, who assured him that he had been grossly misinformed regarding conditions in Dodge; that the town was peaceful and going about its business in an orderly manner; that it could work out its own problems without any intervention by the state.

Being a practical man, Short realized that all this backing and filling was not getting him anywhere, so he began writing letters again—to old friends this time, not to the newspapers. The first to respond was Bat Masterson, who reached Kansas City on May 13.

Bat himself had once been told to get out of Dodge and not to come back, a pronouncement that no one took seriously. That had occurred on April 16, 1881, when he had been summoned from Tombstone, Arizona, by his brother Jim, who was in a hassle with A. J. Peacock, his partner in the Lady Gay Saloon, and Al

Updegraff, a bartender employed by them. It was Jim Masterson's contention when he sent for Bat that Peacock and Updegraff were planning to do him in. The four men met out on the plaza, and in a noonday gunbattle, Updegraff was struck and seriously wounded by a bullet from Bat's gun, but he recovered. For his part in this fracas Bat was fined eight dollars and "banished." Jim settled his affairs in a few hours, and the two of them departed for Colorado.

There was a great amount of running back and forth to Topeka by Short and Bat for several days, and then Bat hurriedly left for Colorado, passing through Dodge City in a locked Pullman, late at night. The purpose of this trip was to locate Wyatt Earp. Following the O.K. Corral fight, Wyatt had killed Frank Stillwell in the railroad yard at Tucson, believing him to be the man who had shot his brother Morgan Earp. Subsequently, a warrant charging him with murder was sworn out, and he dusted out of Arizona for Colorado. When extradition papers on him arrived, Colorado Governor Pitkin refused to honor them, stating that Earp would be marked for death if his political enemies in Arizona Territory got their hands on him.

Bat found Earp in Silverton, where he was supporting himself by gambling. Some say that Doc Holliday was with them. This I doubt; I believe Doc was in Denver at the time. That Wyatt readily agreed to recruit a number of "reliable" gunmen and be in Kansas with them at the right time is certain. With their plans made, Bat returned to Kansas City. The wheels began to turn faster now. On Thursday, May 31, Earp arrived at Dodge City. When he left Colorado he was accompanied by the promised "reliable" men, including Shotgun Collins, the notorious Rowdy Joe Lowe of Wichita fame, Johnny Millsap and others of equal reputation. Only Earp left the train at Dodge, the others continuing on to Kinsley, in adjoining Edwards County, where the Short forces were to rendezvous for the grand entry into Dodge City.

In view of his local reputation and the recent notoriety he had acquired in Tombstone, the unexpected presence of Earp, Short's long-time friend, was regarded with dire significance by the Deger faction, especially when coupled with such rumors as may have reached them of the gathering at Kinsley, some thirty-five miles away. Earp says he sent word to Ab Webster demanding that the mayor and town council meet him in executive session, at which time he gave them the terms for peace. "Luke Short is at Kinsley. I'll wire him to come on. He'll stay in Dodge as long as he wants to, to continue in business, or close out. . . . Over Ab Webster's protests, the council agreed. Luke and Masterson came into Dodge on the next train. Luke contended that the marshal's force was stacked against him. This resulted in selection of what became known in frontier history as The Dodge City Peace Commission, eight men appointed to select, in turn, a new set of peace officers. . . . They functioned for ten days, after which I returned to Silverton." [9]

No such meeting occurred. He did confer with George Hoover, Chalk Beeson and Bob Wright, among others. All that was agreed to was what had been offered Short at a meeting in Kansas City on May 15, to wit: that he could return home to settle up his private business within ten days or until official release of his bond in the city case against him and that he would be protected from public attack.

Short, Bat and Billy Petillon, the last an anomalous character who had been tagging along at Luke's coattails for several weeks, was a reporter for the Ford County *Globe* and also clerk of the district court, arrived at Kinsley on Saturday. Earp joined them on Sunday morning, and that evening the whole party boarded a train for Dodge City.

Sheriff Hinkle, a sick man, with a posse of forty men, organized on Governor Glick's orders, was on hand to meet the invaders. There was high tension but no violence. Hinkle seems to have got the jitters, however, and wired the Governor to send someone to Dodge at once with authority to organize a company of militia to protect the town. Glick responded by rushing Adjutant General Thomas Moonlight to Dodge. Moonlight took steps at once to organize what came to be known as "the Glick Guards." It played no part in the Dodge City war. Mayor Deger took a more positive step by issuing a proclamation closing all gambling places in the city. An agreement had been reached with Short, allowing him to remain in town on condition he would order his gunfighters to leave. This he failed to do. Closing the gambling rooms was ordered for the dual purpose of easing tension and showing the Short faction that the city government was not backing down.

But it was. It was ready to sue for peace—without losing face, if possible, and so were Short and his friends. When things looked the darkest and it seemed that only gunfire could settle their differences, both sides agreed to take the advice of Adjutant General Moonlight that a committee of eight reputable men be selected to sit down and discuss the matter at length and that whatever their findings, they were to be accepted without further argument.

It brought the much-publicized "Dodge City Peace Commission" into existence. The "statesmen" who composed it—Will Harris, Bat Masterson, Wyatt Earp, Neil Brown, Luke Short, Charlie Bassett, Frank McLane and Billy Petillon, the last acting as secretary, though if he put anything on paper it has never come to light—were hardly noted for their legal or judicial background, but their deliberations were eminently successful. Peace returned; the war was over. No one had been wounded. In fact, not a shot had been fired. Perhaps Bat was correct when he wrote: "I think the inflammatory reports published about Dodge City and its inhabitants have been greatly exaggerated and if at any time they did 'don the war paint' it was completely washed off before I arrived here."

Two months later, Short sold his interest in the Long Branch and returned to Texas. He was back in Dodge a year later and brought suit against the town for $15,000 for the damages he alleged he had suffered by being run out of town that spring. Incredible? Not for Dodge City. The suit was settled out of court for some undisclosed amount.

A year later, you will recall, Ab Webster put the town on the front pages again with his bullfight. But the episode that Dodge City has never forgotten was the killing of beautiful Fannie Keenan, alias Dora Hand, in 1878. As Dora Hand, the best-loved of its "Fairy Belles" (a localism for the girls who sang or danced at the Lady Gay and the Comique), she has been enshrined in the cow town history of Dodge. Song, verse and reams of romantic fiction have made her place secure, and she is mentioned with affection in Dodge City today.

Though alleged pictures of Dora Hand have been presented over the years, no authentic photographs of her are known to exist.[10] It lends piquancy to the mystery surrounding her. If Fannie Garretson, likewise a "Fairy Belle" and her closest associate, was acquainted with her background, who she really was and why she was in Dodge City, she was silent. According to the most widely believed tale, Dora Hand was a former Boston opera singer who had come west in the hope of staying the ravages of what used to be called "consumption" in the dry air of the high plains. The only evidence to support the story is that she is known to have had a trained soprano voice, which was not a requirement of singers in Western variety theatres of the period. Of course, unrequited love has often been given as the reason for her presence in Dodge.

Her admirers have her leading two lives: by night, entertaining drunken cowboys and their prostitute companions at the Comique, or singing in some Front Street saloon, the air she breathed foul with obscene humor and profanity; by day, a ministering angel, succoring the unfortunate, crossing the tracks to instruct the choir at the First Methodist church.

But some facts get in the way of these legends. Fannie Keenan (her maiden name) was not, as she is usually pictured, a young girl; she was thirty-four at the time of her death. She had been married to and divorced from a honky-tonk musician named Theodore Hand and had appeared for years in variety theatres in New Orleans, Memphis and other Southern towns as "Dora Hand." For two years prior to coming to Dodge City, she had appeared off and on at Esher's Varieties and the Tivoli Varieties in St. Louis. Originally, she may have come from Boston. There is no evidence that the state of her health had anything to do with her going to Dodge City. A far more likely reason is that her old friend Fannie Garretson, with whom she had worked and lived in St. Louis, was there and doing well.

It leaves only the question of her relations with "Dog" Kelley, owner of the Alhambra saloon and three times mayor of Dodge, to be explained. They could have been only friendly, or of a more intimate nature. Whatever they were, they led directly to her death.

On the night of August 17, young Spike Kenedy, the son of Miflin Kenedy, a Quaker and the partner of Captain Richard King of the famous King Ranch at Corpus Christi, drunk and obstreperous, had been forcibly ejected from the Alhambra. He had put up a fight but he was no match for Kelley. Determined to have revenge, young Kenedy hung around the South Side for a week, watching Kelley's two-room cabin at the rear of the Western Hotel. After he had made sure that Kelley always slept in the front room, that it would be an easy matter to ride up to the cabin and fire several shots through the window, killing him as he slept, Kenedy took a train to Kansas City, where he bought the fastest horse he could find. He was not back in Dodge until Friday night, October 3.

In the meantime, Kelley had fallen ill and had to be taken out to Fort Dodge for a minor operation and a stay in the military hospital. Before leaving, he told Fannie to use the cabin while he was away. Some commentators say he rented it to her, which is hard to believe of a man who was as open-handed and as free a spender as "Dog" Kelley. However that may have been she moved in, along with Fannie Garretson. The latter was sleeping in the front room when Kenedy, ignorant of the fact that Kelley was five miles away, rode up between three and four o'clock in the morning of October 4 and fired four shots through the window. Two of the balls plowed into the floor; the third knifed through the front-room bedclothes, barely missing the sleeping girl; the fourth pierced the thinly plastered partition between the two rooms and struck Fannie Keenan in the right side under the arm, killing her instantly.

Shots at that hour, even on the South side, attracted attention. Kenedy was recognized as he headed up the river, which was believed to be a ruse to throw off pursuit, that as soon as he had swung around town he would strike south.

When it was discovered that Fannie Keenan had been killed, a small posse consisting of Sheriff Masterson, Earp, Tilghman and Charlie Bassett left Dodge and headed for Wagon Bed Springs crossing on the Cimarron, seventy miles to the southeast, believing that with hard riding they could intercept the fugitive there.

They saw nothing of Kenedy during the day. A heavy hailstorm delayed them for an hour, and the sluicing rain that followed slowed them further. The short October day was fading into evening when they reached the soddy at the crossing and were told that no rider had passed. Realizing that they were in time if Kenedy were coming that way, they hid their horses and waited. As night was closing down, they saw him riding in. He was within a few yards of the soddy when he realized what awaited him. Foolishly, he tried to flee. Though a slug from Bat's rifle smashed his right arm, Earp had to kill the man's horse before he surrendered. Kenedy was astounded on learning that he was wanted for killing a young woman, not "Dog" Kelley.

He was taken to Dodge and charged with murder in the second degree. An emergency operation saved his arm, but he never regained full use of it. In the meantime Dodge City prepared to give Dora Hand such a funeral as the town had not witnessed since the slaying of Marshal Ed Masterson.

On October 28, Kenedy was physically able to undergo a preliminary arraignment by Judge R. G. Cook, which was held in the sheriff's office, no spectators admitted. No record of the evidence offered exists, only the cryptic fact that he was acquitted for lack of evidence to convict. Dodge howled its disgust, and it was the general feeling that, through friends, Spike Kenedy's wealthy father had dug deep into his pocket to save his son.

Miflin Kenedy arrived in town on December 8 and had Spike removed to the hospital at Fort Dodge for a second operation on his shoulder, which was performed by the post surgeon, assisted by Dr. McCarty, of Dodge City, and Dr. B. E. Fryer, from Fort Leavenworth. Fragments of shattered bone were removed. By the first of the year, young Kenedy was sufficiently recovered to undertake the long trip to Texas.

That closed the book on Dora Hand. But where history ends, the myths and legend begin. Dora Hand is not likely to be forgotten.

19

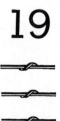

California and the Goodnight Trails

WHEN THOUSANDS OF MEN were rushing to the gold diggings of California in the early 1850's, perhaps as many as fifty thousand Longhorns were trailed out of Texas, across present New Mexico and Arizona to the West Coast. It was a hazardous undertaking. Not only were the Apaches a constant menace, but on the long waterless stretches of desert, hundreds of cattle became so weak that they had to be abandoned. Herds of straight steers fared best. They moved faster and no time had to be lost destroying calves that were dropped on the way. In the late years of the Chisholm and Western trails, many of the outfits carried calf wagons. That was not feasible when a herd was bound for California, with three times as far to go.

Though the prices the Texans received at first were high, when measured against the losses that had been sustained, little profit was left. There were thousands of black Spanish cattle in California. The native owners, of Spanish and Mexican descent, had never bestirred themselves to drive their herds long distances to market, but they took a leaf out of the *Americanos'* book and began moving their cattle up the San Joaquin to San Francisco and the gold camps. With supply catching up with demand, prices fell. It convinced the Texas drovers that the California game wasn't worth the candle. In the late sixties and throughout the seventies some Texas cattle reached California, but they were trailed north through Colorado and across Wyoming and Nevada.

This westward movement of Texas cattle established no definite trails. That was particularly true of the herds that crossed
New Mexico and Arizona. In the north, in Wyoming, there was
no beaten track that all followed. At widely separated points,
some outfits cut into the emigrant Oregon Trail and stayed with
it over South Pass and on to old Fort Hall; others struck southwest into Utah and then down the Humboldt River to Reno and
the Carson Valley.

Beyond Fort Hall the drover had his choice of the several routes
to California that had been pioneered by the forty-niners. They
were plainly marked, but needing grass and water, he couldn't
stay with them. After weeks of wandering, he eventually found
himself on the Humboldt. He still had some three hundred miles
of desert and sagebrush flats to cross before he could put his
emaciated herd on good grass.

Though driving cattle to California never became important
with Texans, they turned eagerly to the trails that Loving and
Goodnight had blazed up the Pecos River, through eastern New
Mexico. Over it thousands of Longhorns grazed their way to
Colorado and Wyoming.

Of all the hundreds of men who were connected with the
Texas cattle trade—ranchers, stockmen, trail drivers—none rate
higher than Oliver Loving and Charles Goodnight and their
closest associate and at one time partner, John Chisum, who was
unrelated to Jesse Chisholm. They were bold, intrepid men. Almost ten years before McCoy opened his cattle market at Abilene,
Oliver Loving trailed a herd in 1858 across No Man's Land (the
Oklahoma Panhandle), through eastern Kansas, northwestern
Missouri and into Illinois, where he disposed of them at a satisfactory profit. It well may be that Loving's success convinced
McCoy that Texas cattle could be driven to a convenient market
in Kansas, once a railroad crossed it.

That Oliver Loving was the first to drive Longhorns north
from Texas is not open to question. In 1859, he made another
long drive; leaving the Texas frontier on the upper Brazos with
another herd, he took a northwest course until he struck the

Arkansas River, near the mouth of Walnut Creek, and followed it to the vicinity of Pueblo, where he wintered.

Of the first herds that reached the Pecos at Horsehead Crossing one was owned by John Chisum, another by Goodnight and Loving. They trailed north as far as today's Roswell and then turned west up the Hondo to Fort Stanton, where the government was buying beef for the post and the nearby Mescalero Reservation. Between cattle needed for military supply and the reservation, there was an excellent market.

This, the original Goodnight Trail, was extended to Fort Sumner. It began at old Fort Belknap on the Brazos, in Texas. Properly speaking, the Goodnight-Loving Trail ran from Fort Sumner to Wyoming. After Oliver Loving's death, Goodnight blazed another trail from Almagordo Creek to Granada, Colorado, and down the Apishapa River until east of Haystack Peak and then north in the direction of Pueblo. He had a holding ranch on the Apishapa and a permanent one just north of Pueblo. After he located in Palo Duro Canyon, he blazed still another trail from the Palo Duro to Dodge City. Part of this trail was the old Dodge Trail. When he began driving cattle over it, it became in popular usage the Goodnight, or the Dodge-Goodnight, Trail.

In the sixties it was wild country along the Pecos, exposed to attack by bands of Comanches sweeping in from the Llano to the east. In at least three instances whole herds were lost to them. They were as cruel and ferocious as the Apaches, perhaps even better horsemen, and the excuse can be offered for them, as it has for the Apaches, that in their raiding and killing they were only fighting to preserve the freedom and ownership of their homeland. Even when traffic on the Goodnight-Loving Trail reached the point where several outfits could travel together for greater protection, the hit-and-run warfare continued.

Early in July, 1867, they jumped Loving and his companion, one-armed Bill Wilson, and inflicted wounds from which Loving died. It was not until 1874, seven years later, that the military launched its great offensive against the Comanches, culminating in the battle of Palo Duro Canyon and their subjugation. By then the Goodnight-Loving Trail had been opened all the way to Cheyenne. From Fort Sumner it ran up the Pecos to Las Vegas, up the old Santa Fe Trail to Raton Pass and on through Trinidad to Pueblo and the north.

Turn back to John Chisum. As he grew old and rich and powerful, he became the perfect image of the cattle baron, the unscrupulous range lord, the oppressor of the "little fellers" who tried to move into his domain. He was all those things, and more. The house he built at the South Spring, below today's Roswell, with its looped windows and thick walls was as much fort as house. The men who worked for him were not hired for their riding ability; they were his fighters, his warriors, and he made no bones about it. In the Lincoln County War, he opposed the Murphy and Dolan faction and gave his backing, which was considerable, to Billy the Kid and his friends.

In the town of Lincoln, the county seat, Murphy and Dolan had some thirty gunmen in their employ. They sent them out to convince the enemies of the King of the Pecos—by persuasion or by stronger means if necessary—that the time had come for them to square their grudges against John Chisum. Farmers and small ranchers from the Rio Feliz, the Ruidoso, the Bonito and the mountains around White Oaks flocked to the Murphy and Dolan banner.

And now there was war on the flatlands. They ambushed and killed Frank McNab, Chisum's foreman, but he fought back and held them off as he had held off the Comanches. The old saying, "No law west of the Pecos," lost some of its meaning when Sheriff Brady, the hand-picked creature of Murphy and Dolan, was ambushed and killed in Lincoln. Had he been a private citizen when he was struck down it would have been regarded as just another killing. But the emblem he wore on his vest made it vastly different, and it changed the complexion of the Lincoln County War. What had been a factional fight, no quarter asked and none given, suddenly became a battle between the so-called forces of law and outlawry, though from this distance one side appears to have been as bankrupt of virtue as the other. However, Billy the Kid and his friends were branded outlaws, and found not only local "law" but the military and even the federal government arrayed against them.

President Hayes appointed General Lew Wallace Territorial Governor for the express purpose of ending the killings and depredations of the Kid and his gang. But they were not to be stopped until all were cut down. When it was all over, John Chisum was still boss of the narrow Pecos River Valley, two hundred miles of level grasslands lying between the low mesas that closed it in from the east and west, and stretching all the way from Fort Sumner to the Texas line. He had appealed to President Grant to give him a patent to it, and though the request had been denied, he managed by ruthless violence and intimidation to maintain de facto ownership.

Chisum had not always been an arrogant, immovable block of granite, with his holdings at their peak, a hundred thousand head, making him the biggest owner of cattle in the world. He came to Texas from Tennessee and settled originally in Paris, where he served as clerk of Lamar County for a time. Soon after the war, he drove two small herds (not over a thousand head in all, says Charles Goodnight) to Little Rock, where he had an interest in a small packing house. The enterprise failed and he filed papers in bankruptcy. Out in what was then unorganized Runnels County, he had a ranch between the Concho and Colorado rivers, and some wild cattle, which were not accessible to attachment and could not be converted into cash. It was there that he began his famous Jingle-Bob outfit—a long "rail" for a brand, both ears split vertically. If the ears did not "jingle" they at least "bobbed."

Goodnight says: "John Chisum followed the Goodnight Trail up the Pecos in 1866, reaching Bosque Grande on the Pecos about December, wintering right below Bosque Grande, with 600 Jingle-Bob steers. We wintered about eight miles apart. In the spring of 1867 he disposed of those steers to government contractors, and returned to his Colorado and Concho ranch and began moving his cattle west. In 1868 I formed a partnership with him on the following basis: He was to deliver to me all cattle he could handle at Bosque Grande, I allowing him one dollar per head profit over Texas prices for his risk.

"During this contract or agreement, he lost two herds to the Indians. I handled the rest of his drives from Bosque Grande west, disposing of them in Colorado and Wyoming. This continued for three years, and I divided profits equally with him. These profits enabled him to buy the 60,000 head he held on the Pecos.

"Chisum never drove a herd north, and never claimed to have done so." [1]

This should scotch the often-heard story that John Chisum was a noted trail driver. He had no need to be one, not with experienced men like Loving, Goodnight and others ready to take the risk and danger of getting a herd through to Colorado and the North. And yet, Goodnight calls him "a good trail man, and the best counter I have ever known. He was the only man I have ever seen who could count three grades accurately as they went by. I have seen him do this many times." [2]

Chisum squatted at Bosque Grande and built his headquarters ranch at the South Spring. After his death in 1884 and liquidation of his estate, the ranch changed hands several times and was then purchased by Cornell University to be conducted as an experimental station on range control and the diversification of crops for the area. In the past twenty years federal reclamation projects and dams have miraculously enhanced the agricultural possibilities of the Pecos Valley.

Why Oliver Loving's name does not appear among the Texans who drove their cattle up the Chisholm and Western Trails to Kansas is easily explained. In 1867, when McCoy opened his market at Abilene, Loving and Goodnight were out on the Pecos, moving their herds over the trail that bore their name. Less than a year later, Loving lay dead at Fort Sumner, killed by a Comanche bullet.

He was in Pueblo when the War between the States began, and he required the assistance of Kit Carson, Lucien Maxwell and Dick Wooten to make his way back to Texas. During the war he was one of many cattlemen, as has been noted, who drove cattle to Shreveport, Louisiana, to supply the armies of the South. He had been one of the most prosperous men in Parker County, but with the defeat of the Rebel cause everything was swept away, leaving him with only worthless Confederate currency to show for his labors. A year later he was on the upper Brazos with Good-

night, rounding up wild cattle and pointing them through In-
dian-infested country for Horsehead Crossing and the Pecos.

Goodnight, the chronicler of their years together, repeatedly
voices his respect and affection for his quiet, soft-spoken partner.
His narrative dealing with the events leading up to the Indian
attack on Loving and his companion Bill Wilson, a trail man of
no mean stature in his own right, and Loving's death is a tribute
to the courage and tenacity of the two men. It is a tale of bravery
and physical endurance unequaled in frontier history.

"In 1867 we started another herd west . . . and struck the Pecos
the latter part of June," says Goodnight. "After we had gone up
the river about one hundred miles it was decided that Mr. Loving
should go ahead on horseback in order to reach New Mexico and
Colorado in time to bid on the contracts which were to be let in
July, to use the cattle we then had on the trail, for we knew that
there were no other cattle in the west to take their place.

"Loving was a man of religious instincts and one of the coolest
and bravest I have ever known, but devoid of caution. Since the
journey was to be made with a one-man escort I selected Bill
Wilson, the clearest-headed man in the outfit, as his companion.

"Knowing the dangers of traveling through an Indian infested
country I endeavored to impress on these men the fact that only
by traveling by night could they hope to make the trip in safety.

"The first two nights after the journey was begun they followed
my instructions. But Loving, who detested night riding, persuaded Wilson that I had been over-cautious and one fine morning they changed their tactics and proceeded by daylight.
Nothing happened until 2 o'clock that afternoon, when Wilson,
who had been keeping a lookout, sighted Comanches heading toward them from the southwest. Apparently they were five or six
hundred strong. The men left the trail and made for the Pecos
River which was about four miles to the northwest and was the
nearest place they could hope to find shelter. They were then on
the plain which lies between the Pecos and the Rio Sule, or Blue
River. One hundred and fifty feet from the bank of the Pecos this
bank drops abruptly some one hundred feet. The men scrambled
down this bluff and dismounted. They hitched their horses
(which the Indians captured at once) and crossed the river where

they hid themselves among the sand dunes and brakes of the river. Meantime the Indians were hot on their tracks, some of them halted on the bluff and others crossed the river and surrounded the men. A brake of *carrea,* or Spanish cane, which grew in a bend of the river a short distance from the dunes, was soon filled with them. Since this cane was from five to six feet tall these Indians were easily concealed from view of the men; they dared not advance on the men as they knew them to be armed. The Indians on the bluff, speaking in Spanish, begged the men to come out for a consultation. Wilson instructed Loving to watch the rear so they could not shoot him in the back, and he stepped out to see what he could do with them. Loving attempting to guard the rear was fired on from the cane. He sustained a broken arm and bad wound in the side. The men retreated to the shelter of the river bank.

"Toward dawn of the next day Loving, believing that he was going to die from the wound in his side, begged Wilson to leave him and go to me. . . . He gave him his Henry rifle which had metallic cartridges, since in swimming the river any other kind would be useless. Wilson turned over to him all of the pistols—five—and his six-shooting rifle. How he expected to cross the river with the gun I have never comprehended for Wilson was a one-armed man.

"It happened that some hundred feet from their place of concealment down the river there was a shoal, the only one I know of within a hundred miles of the place. On this shoal an Indian sentinel on horseback was on guard and Wilson knew this. The water was almost four feet deep. When Wilson decided to start he divested himself of clothing except underwear and hat. He hid his trousers in one place, his boots in another and his knife in another all under water. Then taking his gun he attempted to cross the river. This he found to be impossible, so he floated downstream, about seventy-five feet where he struck bottom. He stuck down the muzzle of the gun in the sand until the breech came under water and then floated noiselessly down the river."

Bill Wilson has left a spine-tingling account of those breathless moments when his life as well as Loving's hung in the balance and what followed. He had just seen the Indian sitting on his horse out in the river—

"He was sitting there splashing water with his foot, just playing. I got under some smart weeds and drifted by until I got far enough below the Indian where I could get out. Then I made a three days' march barefooted. Everything in that country had stickers in it. On the way I picked up the small end of a tepee pole which I used for a walking stick. The last night of this painful journey the wolves followed me all night. I would give out, just like a horse, and lay down in the road and drop off to sleep and when I would awaken the wolves would be all around me, snapping and snarling. I would take up that stick, knock the wolves away, get started again and the wolves would follow behind. I kept that up until daylight, when the wolves quit me.

"About 12 o'clock on that last day I crossed a little mountain and knew the boys ought to be right in there somewhere with the cattle. I found a little place, a sort of cave, that afforded protection from the sun, and I could go no further. After a short time the boys came along with the cattle and found me."

The "short time" he mentions was actually the better part of a long June day. He does not mention the pitiable condition of his bleeding, lacerated feet, the sun blisters that covered his body or that he had gone three days and three nights without food.

"When I reached him," Goodnight recalled, "I asked him many questions, too many in fact, for he was so broken and starved and shocked by knowing he was saved, I could get nothing satisfactory from him. I put him on the horse and took him to the herd at once. We immediately wrapped his feet in wet blankets. They were swollen out of all reason, and how he could walk on them is more than I can comprehend. Since he had starved for three days and nights I could give him nothing but gruel."

Wilson says: "As soon as I was able to tell Mr. Goodnight what had happened, he took a party of about fourteen men and pulled out to see about Mr. Loving. After riding about twenty-four hours they came to the spot where I had left him, but he was not there. They supposed the Indians had killed him and thrown his body into the river. They found the gun I had concealed in the water (also his boots and clothing) and came back to camp.

"About two weeks after this we met a party coming from Fort Sumner and they told us Loving was at Fort Sumner. The bullet which had penetrated his side did not prove fatal and the next night after I had left him he got into the river and drifted by the Indians as I had done, crawled out and lay in the weeds all the next day. The following night he made his way to the road where it struck the river, hoping to find somebody traveling that way. He remained there for five days, being without anything to eat for seven days. Finally some Mexicans came along, and he hired them to take him to Fort Sumner and I believe he would have fully recovered if the doctor at that point had been a competent surgeon. But that doctor had never amputated any limbs and did not want to undertake such work.

"When we heard Mr. Loving was at Fort Sumner, Mr. Goodnight and I hastened there. As soon as we beheld his condition we realized the arm would have to be amputated. . . . Goodnight started a man to Santa Fe after a surgeon, but before he could get back mortification set in, and we were satisfied that something had to be done at once and we prevailed upon the doctor to cut off the affected limb. But too late. Thus ended the career of one of the best men I ever knew. Mr. Goodnight had the body of Mr. Loving prepared for the long journey and carried it to Weatherford, Texas, where interment was made with Masonic honors." [3]

Colorado is not all mountains; the eastern third of the state is a continuation of the plains of western Kansas. After reaching Trinidad, cattle that had been driven up the Goodnight-Loving Trail were pointed for one of three destinations: the lively market at Pueblo, which supplied the mining camps; Ogallala, Nebraska, on the Union Pacific; or were contracted for range delivery at Cheyenne. All went down the Purgatoire until they struck the Arkansas River east of Las Animas. There, herds bound for Pueblo turned up the Arkansas; the rest trailed on north or somewhere east of north by way of Trail Town and Kit Carson, on Big Sandy Creek, then across the creeks that form the headwaters of the Republican. Another thirty miles brought them to the Arickaree. With the North Star pointing the way, they reached the South Platte and turned down it to Ogallala. If bound for Cheyenne, they crossed to the North Platte and followed it to their destination.

This long, rambling trail was well watered and grassed. Cattle that moved over it customarily reached their destination in excellent condition. But whether they originated in west Texas or New Mexico, they were exclusively Longhorns, and they were tick carriers. If no cry was raised against their passing it was due primarily to the fact that Colorado had no livestock industry of its own much before 1880. It grew rapidly after that, with Colorado stockmen devoting themselves unanimously to breeding Shorthorn cattle. Inevitably, as it had in Kansas, growing demands were raised for a quarantine law against the entry of Longhorns.

This agitation in the North, especially in Kansas, roused Texas cattlemen to action. Instead of waiting until the door had been closed in their face, they began clamoring for the establishment of a National Cattle Trail, Congress "to set aside a strip of public lands through the national domain in Kansas, Nebraska and Dakota, such lands to be withheld from private entry, and held by the Government as a great free highway for the especial purpose of a cattle trail." Counting on the support of the Democratic South, a bill to that effect was written, but before it could be introduced, Kansas congressmen got wind of it and raised such violent objection that Representative James F. Miller, of Texas, its author, deemed it advisable to reroute the proposed trail and locate it in Colorado along the western boundary of Kansas and to extend it to Canada.

In its revised form it was introduced on January 17, 1885. It provided, "That said quarantined national live-stock trail may be of any practicable width, not exceeding six miles, and said quarantined grazing-grounds (at convenient points on the trail) shall not exceed twelve miles square at any one place." [4]

The Texas Legislature voted to grant the right-of-way for such a trail across state-owned public lands. But that was as far as it got. On March 12 the Kansas Quarantine Law closed the borders of that state. Eight days later, on March 20, Colorado banned the entry of Longhorn cattle. It was the death of the National Cattle Trail. Some thousands of Longhorns used the proposed route but they were native Colorado cattle.

Joseph Nimmo, Jr., states in his famous report that the amount of public lands asked for in the bill would have amounted to 1,324,000 acres, which he holds would not have been excessive when compared with the 14,807,800 acres granted the so-called Pacific Railroads.

To get back to Goodnight. He had made a fortune and become famous in the world of cattle and cattlemen. In September, 1873, he was in Pueblo with 8,000 steers. Prices were low, and they went lower as he and a score of other trail men waited for an upturn. He estimates that at least 30,000 head were being held around Pueblo that fall. There was nothing in the daily news reports being received from the East to justify the hope that the market would bounce back shortly. Two New York banks had been forced to close; prices on the New York Stock Exchange began to sag. Around Pueblo the more timid among the Texans began to offer their cattle for sale at bargain prices.

Goodnight, who never hesitated to back his own judgment, began buying, it being his intention to winter what he bought, confident that he could dispose of them in the spring at a handsome profit. On September 20, the great banking house of Jay Cooke and Company failed. The panic of 1873, the worst in the country's history, swept the United States. Before it was over, he had lost everything. Though for the next two years he was in greatly reduced circumstances, he was still a comparatively young man and he believed he could win another fortune if he could find capital for a new start. It came seeking him, in Denver, and through circumstances that read like fiction.

John G. Adair, a young, landed Irish aristocrat, from Rathdair, had come to New York City and, apparently just to have something to do, became engaged in the brokerage business. There he met Cornelia Wadsworth, the daughter of James Samuel Wadsworth, a banker prominent in national politics and the father of soon-to-become United States Senator James Wadsworth. They were married two years later, and after spending a year at Adair's Castle Glenvaugh in County Donegal and on his estates in County Leix, they returned to the United States.

General Phil Sheridan, a friend of Mrs. Adair's father, interested them in making a buffalo hunt along the South Platte and named Colonel Richard I. Dodge, one of the Army's top frontier officers, to accompany them with a suitable escort. The Adairs were so captivated by the West and its opportunities that Adair moved his brokerage business from New York City to Denver, and they made the Colorado capital their home. Both of the Adairs were wealthy, and they were prepared to make a large investment in land and cattle if they could find a man of character and experience to take charge of the enterprise. In Charles Goodnight they found the man for whom they were looking.

Goodnight was well-acquainted with the Palo Duro Canyon, where Mackenzie had dealt the Comanches a crushing blow, and it was his opinion that there was no better place in the Texas Panhandle for establishing such a ranch as the Adairs had in mind. They did as he advised, and in the spring he drove 1,700 head of cattle, many of them full-blood Durhams and Herefords, from his ranch four miles north of Pueblo to the Palo Duro. It was the beginning of the famous J A Ranch, second to none in Texas.[5]

I have said elsewhere that there wasn't the scratch of a pen binding the two men to anything, and it was not until the following June, 1877, that they signed a formal partnership agreement to run five years; Goodnight to operate the J A for a one-third interest in the land, cattle and horses, with a drawing account of twenty-five hundred dollars a year, and to repay Adair his third of the original investment at 10 per cent per annum at the end of the five-year period.

"The enterprise proved to be far more profitable than either had anticipated. The original agreement was renewed, and the J A continued to expand. Goodnight bought, fenced and leased thousands of acres, including large tracts of 'school lands' which belonged to the State of Texas. At one time, he controlled almost a million acres, on which ranged sixty-five to eighty thousand head of cattle wearing the J A brand. John Adair died before the second agreement expired. Amicably, Mrs. Adair and Goodnight divided their interests, and Mrs. Adair became the sole owner of the J A." [6]

With the vast holdings that remained to him, Goodnight continued to dominate the policies of the Panhandle Cattlemen's

Association in its battles with the big Eastern land companies that were bent on colonizing the Panhandle.

Though he strongly supported the twin causes of religion and education—he established Goodnight College, at Goodnight, Texas, the first institution of its kind in west Texas—he was, admittedly, a ruthless fighter who, when the law got in his way, did not hesitate to pack a jury or bribe a judge.

Though his legs were bowed from his life in the saddle, he was a massive, broad-shouldered man, catlike in his movements. His head, with its shock of hair and shaggy brows, was larger than life-size. Those who knew him well, even as an old man, say there was something in his eyes that demanded and got respect and attention. For over forty years, first as a young ranger serving without pay, he had fought Indians and pitted himself against the hard life of the plains. To the very end—he was ninety-three when he died in 1929—he retained the vigor that sustained him for almost a century. Two years before his death, he remarried. Even at that advanced age he became the father of a child which, unfortunately, did not survive.[7]

No man did more to improve the quality of Texas range cattle than Charles Goodnight. Through his selective experimentation in cross-breeding the native Longhorn with his blooded Shorthorn stock, he produced an animal that put on more weight, was more easily worked and still retained the Longhorn's ability to rustle a living.

Only Timothy Dwight Hobart, with his windmills and earthen tanks in which water could be held, who, after an interval of several years, followed him as manager of the J A Ranch, has left a comparable mark on the Texas Panhandle. But it was Goodnight who pioneered the way. "He is," as J. Evetts Haley, his excellent biographer, has said, "generally recognized as the most representative cowman that the West has known."

20

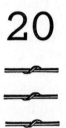

Sea of Grass

In wyoming, eastern Montana and Dakota there was a vast area of potential rangeland greater than in all of Texas. Adequately watered, carpeted with buffalo grass on the open plains and rich with gramma and bluejoint on the benchlands, it justifiably could be called a cowman's paradise. It was the hunting land of the Sioux, Northern Cheyenne, Crow and other tribes. Save for Indian treaty restrictions barring white cattlemen from that part of Wyoming lying north of the Platte and east of the Bozeman Trail, it was all in the public domain, and from the center of it there wasn't a fence in five hundred miles.

Within that great circle, reaching from the Missouri River on the north to the Yellowstone on the south, the total white population, other than military personnel located on the various forts, could not have been more than two or three thousand, including Cheyenne and Miles City. Over that grasslands empire roamed the last of the great herds of buffalo, both white and blacktail deer, elk and thousands of antelope. If they could survive the long cold winters, it was presumed that hardy range cattle could. The gramma and bluejoint held their seeds after they withered and lost none of their nutriment. There were few extended periods in which herbivorous animals could not reach the succulent heads, for save in those regions where the sage grew so thick that snow could not blow off in a day or two, the open range was usually bare.

Some cattle, numbered only in the hundreds, were trailed from Colorado into Montana as early as 1860. They were fattened and then driven down to the Emigrant Trail to Oregon and exchanged for footsore cattle. Granville Stuart, the dean of Montana stockmen and its most influential leader, recalls that he and his brother engaged in this primitive business of trading fat, strong cattle for worn-out animals on the Emigrant Trail.

"In the fall of 1860," says he, "we drove in sixty head of cattle and Robert Hereford brought in seventy-five head from the Emigrant Road. At that time there was a small herd at St. Ignatius, a few at Fort Owen, and about two hundred head in and near Fort Benton. These herds all increased rapidly and when gold was struck at Alder Gulch every emigrant train brought in a few cattle, ranches were established and by 1863 cattle growing had become an industry of considerable importance.

"Nelson Storey of Bozeman drove the first herd of Texas cattle into Montana in the spring of 1866. Storey purchased six hundred head of cattle at Dallas, Texas, and started north with them, arriving in the Gallatin valley on December 3 and camped where Fort Ellis was later located." [1]

During the second year of the Abilene market, 1868, perhaps as many as 75,000 stock cattle were trailed north from that point. Many of them got no further than Nebraska; the rest went on to Wyoming over what came to be called the Texas Trail, or Texas-Montana Trail, with range delivery being made in the vicinity of Lusk, which was about as far north as any got that year, the Indians being a constant menace.

Throughout the early seventies, the number of Longhorns that entered Wyoming increased from year to year, except for 1873 and 1874, when the Kansas market shifted to Wichita. As soon as stock cattle began coming up the Western Trail to Dodge City the upward trend was resumed, in addition to which a not inconsiderable number of Iowa, or so-called pilgrim, cattle reached Ogallala by rail and were driven north into Wyoming. These Iowans were largely farm-bred Durhams and Herefords. Among the many references to them made by early-day stockmen, very few are favorable, the general feeling being that never having had to rustle a living, they were unsuited for the open range. It was said that at the first sign of a storm they would make a bee-line for the ranch yard, looking for a haystack. They were more prone to lung cancer than the Longhorn. Of a herd of twelve hundred that was wintered in well-protected Goshen Hole, only a handful were alive in the spring.

Despite the contempt expressed in dubbing them "pilgrim cattle," the big outfits must have found the Iowans profitable, for as late as 1883–84, John Clay, perhaps Wyoming's foremost stockman, in his annual report of cattle purchased for the year, lists a total of 5,659 head, for which he paid an average of $30.00.[2] A quarter of a century later the Hereford, whether or not his forebears came from Iowa, had become king without a rival of all range cattle breeds.

The Texas Trail is appropriately marked today by several historical monuments. After reaching old Camp Clark it crossed the North Platte to Ogallala. From there it followed the Sidney and Black Hills stage road north to Cottonwood Creek and Hat Creek, passing to the east of today's Lusk, then on north to Belle Fourche Crossing, west of Moorecroft. From there it struck westward to the Little Powder and down that stream to its mouth, where it crossed Tongue River, down which it ran to the Yellowstone, crossing that river just above Fort Keogh. Its course then lay up Sunday Creek to the Little Dry and on to the Big Dry, where it turned down Lodge Pole Creek to the Musselshell. There it ended. This route, had its advocates been successful, would have been incorporated in the National Trail.

In the early sixties, when thousands of gold-crazed men and women of varying shades of honor and morality were rushing to Virginia City and the Montana diggings, a shorter and more practicable way of getting there had to be found than following the Emigrant (Oregon) Trail across Wyoming, over South Pass and then north via old Eagle Rock (today's Idaho Falls) to Monida Pass and a second crossing of the Continental Divide before coasting downhill into the Beaverhead and Deer Lodge valleys.

Jim Bridger attempted to fill the need by breaking a trail that took off from the Red Buttes on the North Platte for Wind River, then north to the Stinking Water (Shoshone), up Pryors Fork to Clarks Fork, up Clarks Fork to the Yellowstone and on to the Gallatin Valley. It was shorter and, by keeping to the west of the Big Horn Mountains, was reasonably safe from Indian attack. It had its advantages, especially for the bull train freighters, but for some reason it never caught the fancy of Virginia City.

John Bozeman and John Jacobs fared better when they blazed the Bozeman Trail (the Bozeman Road). It too began at old Fort Laramie, but it kept to the east of the Big Horns. It was fast, having few streams to cross, and it was well watered and grassed. Though it ran through Sioux country and was wide open to attack, the freighting outfits used it. To offer some protection, the Army built forts along the way: Fort Reno, on Powder River; Fort McKinney, on Piney Fork of the Powder (near today's Buffalo); Fort C. F. Smith, on Bighorn River, and Fort Fetterman. The debacle at Fetterman, in which eighty-two soldiers were slaughtered by the Sioux, led to the abandonment of these under-manned and undersupplied posts.

On April 16, 1867, several miles below the old Crow Reservation on the Yellowstone, John M. Bozeman, noted frontiersman that he was, mistook five renegade Blackfeet for friendly Crows and paid for his mistake with his life. Which, story has it, led old Jim Bridger to remark caustically some time later: "The Bozeman Road is known to everybody, and the Bridger Road is forgotten. But that's all right with me; I've still got my hair."

The Bozeman Road and the Bridger Road were not cattle trails, though some cattle were driven over them. Nor did they have any noticeable effect on the main artery of commerce of the gold camps; it continued to go over Monida Pass and down the eastern fringe of Idaho to Eagle Rock and on south to the Union Pacific Railroad at Kelton, Utah. Fewer stagecoaches and jerkline freighters used the road after the little narrow-gauge Utah and Northern put its rails into the Beaverhead and Deer Lodge valleys in 1881, for that was the route it followed. The Mormons had profited greatly from the Montana diggings. By wagon, they had freighted tons of sodium chloride (common salt) to the mines. Stump Creek was the principal source of their supply, though other creeks in the neighborhood were heavily impregnated. The water was turned on the land, and by solar evaporation the brine was reduced to salt. In fact, so much salt was shipped north that the road in popular parlance was called the "Salt Road."

But far more important than the stampede to Virginia City and Alder Gulch were the plodding trains of oxen and bobbing covered wagons, jolting across the undulating plains of uninhabited Wyoming. For a decade and a half they had been pressing westward, and still they came, seemingly without end. The iron horse had not yet broken out of its stable east of the Missouri River to go galloping across mountain and Western wastelands to the Pacific Coast. No one had yet dared to dream that this empire of grass, stretching from the Platte to the Canadian boundary, was destined to become one of the great stock-raising areas of the world. It is equally certain that among the few white men gathered at such outposts of semicivilization as old Fort Laramie and Bridger's Fort none realized that what they saw passing before their eyes every day was the greatest mass emigration of people this country was ever to see.

They came from many states, these bearded men and sunbonneted women who passed. Mostly they had been strangers when they gathered for the take-off from one of the Missouri River towns. Tragedy had overtaken some already. But they pressed on, the majority bound for the Oregon country, about which they knew so little that the prospect was limited only by the fertility of their imaginaion. Some were for California and would turn to the west at Fort Hall. But to the buckskin-clad traders and trappers the Mormons, trudging across the trackless plains with their handcarts, to escape religious persecution and found their State of Deseret, were even more of an enigma.

The animals that drew the heavy Conestoga-type wagons (many of them were Murphy or Schuttler wagons) are usually referred to collectively as oxen. An ox is a castrated bull. That a considerable percentage of the bulls that reached Oregon were unaltered is obvious. It was from them and the cow or two that the emigrants trailed into the country that Oregon cattle were bred. Almost without exception they were Durhams or Durham-Herefords.

Very little has been said about the farm-raised cattle from Iowa,

Missouri, Illinois and other Midwestern states that supplied the motive power for the thousands of emigrant wagons that, beginning in 1843 and continuing for more than a score of years (contrary to popular belief the covered wagon did not disappear from the Oregon Trail with the completion of the transcontinental railroad), reached the Pacific Northwest. Even less has been said about the family cow. She not only was the source of fresh milk but could, when one of the team went lame or was otherwise incapacitated, take its place and keep the heavy wagon creaking toward its destination.

The reason why so little has been said about the family cow of the Oregon pioneer undoubtedly is due to the fact that there appeared to be so few of them, never more than one or two to a wagon. But when the driblets of twenty years or more are added together, the total becomes impressive.

Looking back, even today, it seems incredible that the cattle the covered wagon pioneers took to eastern Oregon and Washington could have so multiplied in the following thirty years that thousands of them were trailed back across the Continental Divide into Montana and Wyoming in the first, and last, great west-to-east movement of range livestock. Equally incredible is the fact that when they had been east of the Rockies long enough to be considered native, they were responsible for the almost total disappearance of the Texas Longhorn from Northern ranges.

But during the intervening years three-quarters of a million Longhorns were to overrun the great unsurveyed grasslands north of the Platte.

Following the Indian uprising of 1876, Indian resistance ended with the signing of the treaty with the Sioux and Cheyennes at the Red Cloud Agency on September 26, 1876. Under its terms stockmen were free at last to graze their herds north from the Platte to the Missouri. Texas cattle began to stream into the Powder River country, in eastern Wyoming. Over what was soon to become the established Texas-Montana Trail, other thousands were driven to the Yellowstone and Musselshell. It was as though a dam had burst, and there was no end to it. A few years later Granville Stuart was complaining that Montana ranges were being overstocked.

Though I am telling the story of the trails, the purpose they served and the men who followed them, and not the history of the range cattle business of Wyoming, Montana and parts of Dakota Territory, it should be noted that in addition to the men I previously have mentioned there were a score or more who became the giants of that trade, among them Con Kohrs, Zeke and Henry Newman, Nick Bielenberg, Pierre Wibaux, John T. Murphy, the Englishman Moreton Frewen and John Clay, the guiding genius of the Great Swan Land and Cattle Company.

The Texas trail crews liked the North. The pay was better, and so was the grub—with some outfits you actually got white bread twice a day. So many of them remained in Montana and Wyoming that it became a commonplace to hear the Texas drawl on the streets and in the saloons of Cheyenne and Miles City. Presently the broad English "a" and the Scotch burr began to be heard in the posh Cheyenne Club, for news of the beef bonanza had traveled across the sea and titled foreigners were clamoring to invest their money in American stock raising.

Some were shamefully begowked; others made fortunes. Absentee ownership became so popular that the speculators had a field day. Some were unscrupulous enough to rent a herd for a few days and mix it with what cattle they owned before showing their "holdings" to a prospective buyer. The vigorous campaign that the Wyoming Stock Growers' Association waged against such fraudulent dealings saved more than one gullible foreigner from disaster. With or without trickery being involved, the book counts of even the biggest and most reputable outfits were invariably higher than actual range count. The discrepancy was attributed to losses from predatory animals, Indians or rustlers, losings which the distant owner could not question, no matter what his suspicions.

When the Red Cloud Treaty, opening Wyoming to settlement, was signed in 1876, the white population of the Big Horn Basin was limited to a handful of old-time trappers and mountain men like Pat O'Hara. Why slightly more than three years were permitted to pass before the first cattle, a herd of 2,800 Longhorns belonging to Judge Carter, of Fort Bridger, was trailed into the basin and a ranch established on Carter Creek, a branch of the

Stinking Water, can be explained only by the fact that cattlemen found such an immensity of excellent range open to them that it was unnecessary to look beyond the Powder River and its tributaries to find what they wanted.[3]

In miles, Big Horn Basin was no more distant from a railroad shipping point than much of eastern Wyoming. Nowhere was there better grass. The Big Horn, Stinking Water and Greybull rivers and their forks and creeks gave it an adequate supply of living water. It was high country and wooded with black ash, fir and mountain cedar beyond the needs of a ranching country. No other region in Wyoming Territory had so much natural, mountain-protected winter range.

A few months after the Carter cattle were sent into the Basin, John Chapman, of Douglas County, Oregon, came in from the north (from Montana) with 1,200 Durham and Durham-Hereford cows and 80 big Oregon horses and established a ranch on Pat O'Hara Creek. The horses were the first of Oregon origin to reach Wyoming in any number. Chapman's Durhams were the first of that strain to be turned out on Wyoming grass, I believe. This was nine years after 450 pure-bred Durham bull calves, purchased in Omaha, were trailed north from the Union Pacific, at Kelton, and over Monida Pass into the Gallatin Valley of Montana.[4]

Two other Big Horn Basin pioneers who brought in Oregon cattle and horses were Henry Belknap and Captain R. H. Torrey. Torrey's outfit, the famous M Bar, on Owl Creek, trailed in 4,000 Oregon stock cattle in 1880. In that same year little Otto Franc, a greenhorn from New York, who had grown rich in the wholesale banana business, organized the Franc Cattle Company and established himself on the Greybull. Shrewd to his fingertips, his Pitchfork brand soon decorated thousands of Oregon cattle and Oregon horses. When the first post office was established, it was on his ranch and was named Franc, in his honor. It was later changed to Frank, and then, much later, to Meeteetse, when that little settlement, the only town in the Basin, came into existence.

Otto Franc was, I believe, the first Wyoming-Montana stockman to switch away from the Durhams and other cross-bred stock to straight white-faced Herefords—a step that all others were to follow eventually.

Trailing livestock across the harsh, often waterless lava-rock deserts of Idaho, from the great gash of the Snake River that forms a great part of the boundary between it and Oregon, and climbing over the Great Divide into Montana and Wyoming were a grueling undertaking that, in many ways, made driving a herd up from Texas tame by comparison.

Stockmen east of the Rockies had been aware for years that there was a great reservoir of cattle and horses in Oregon and Washington for which the owners had no market, and which could be bought for a song. Nothing was done about it because the belief was widespread that cattle and horses could not survive being trailed over a nearly grassless country for weeks on end, their hoofs cut to ribbons by jagged lava-rock and their strength drained away getting through miles of deep sand. As the crow flies, it was more than five hundred miles from Baker City, Oregon, to any of the passes over the Divide, and half again as far by the twisting, devious route a trail herd would have to take.

Granville Stuart, who made a habit of doing the impossible, was the first to try it. As usual, he knew what he was doing.

21

The Oregon and the Northern—
Last of the Cattle Trails

AFTER STUART AND HIS PARTNERS had decided on a location for a large ranch (the famous D-S) near Fort Maginnis, Montana, in present Fergus County, east of Lewistown, he took a small crew out of the Beaverhead Valley and over Monida Pass to Baker City and the Grande Ronde Valley. This route soon came to be called the Northern Trail. Stuart found that he could buy a horse for ten to twelve dollars in Oregon that was worth a hundred in Montana. Cattle were correspondingly cheap—eight to twelve dollars, depending on their age.

The venture was so profitable that it was repeated again and again. In time most of the big D-S herd was of Oregon origin. Very likely it was Stuart's successful operations that led John Chapman to go over Monida Pass with the horses and cattle that he drove into the Big Horn Basin in 1869. It was a year later before Oregon cattle began reaching Wyoming over what, for want of a better name, was called the Old Oregon Trail. For part of the way the route followed was the original emigrant trail but cut away from it to the north after crossing Big Camas Prairie and did not come back to it until it neared the Snake, west of old Fort Hall.[1]

Bypassing Fort Hall, it crossed the river at Blackfoot. If a herd was to be wintered west of the Divide, and many were, it was driven up the Blackfoot River, sometimes as far as Grays Lake. If a herd was going through, usually it took the Lander Cutoff, east of Blackfoot, which was good for a saving of between fifty or sixty miles to South Pass. But not all, some trail bosses preferring to stay with the old, main-traveled trail. Once east of the Continental Divide, the routes converged and followed the old emigrant trail to the west fork of the Sweetwater and on to the Three Crossings. After 1881, when Oregon cattle were coming through in a passing parade, many herds went all the way east to the Sioux (Pine Ridge) Agency, in South Dakota. Some were trailed into Nebraska.

Whether a trail herd was bound for Montana or Wyoming, it was necessary to cross the lower Snake as it moved up to the Oregon-Idaho line. It was a dangerous crossing at any time; when the savage river was running high, it was folly to attempt it. Above the mouth of Burnt River, which flowed into the Snake from the Oregon side, there were riffles and a bar, also a wire ferry. It was used extensively as a livestock crossing, being regarded as the best on the river. There was another much-used crossing at the mouth of Sucker Creek, on the Oregon side, where pens had been built for holding stock and a chute cut down to the water's edge. But whichever one of the two crossings was used, a herd still had to cross the Weiser, Payette and Boise rivers, usually without difficulty, before it swung around to the south of the town of Boise and struck off to the southeast for Little Camas and Big Camas prairies and across the lava-ash plains to the old stage-station at Arco, on Big Lost River.

The Northern Trail and the Oregon (cattle) Trail ran parallel courses as they left the Boise region, and continued to do so halfway across Idaho, with seldom more than fifteen to twenty miles separating them. This was scarcely a matter of choice, for whether you were bound for Monida Pass and Montana or for South Pass and Wyoming, you needed grass and water and a suitable place to lay over for a day or two to give your stock an opportunity to recuperate. That made you point your herd for Little Camas and Big Camas prairies, for you couldn't be sure you would find water in Big Wood River or Little Wood River. If the Little Wood was dry, your difficulties would multiply in a hurry. Ahead of you you would have the Giant Lava Beds (today's Craters of the Moon National Monument) and a hundred miles of barren lava ash.

What is difficult to understand about these two paralleling routes is why the Montana outfits, whose ultimate destination lay far to the north, elected to move across those wastelands to the south of those that were headed for South Pass. I have never seen a satisfactory explanation for it. The two trails crossed when they reached Big Lost River. The Montana men either drove on east to Eagle Rock and the well-traveled north-south road or angled off to reach it by way of Mud Lake; the herds pointing for South Pass struck off down the river for the Snake and Blackfoot.

If emphasis has been put on Monida Pass, it is because it got the bulk of the traffic over the Northern Trail. But there were other passes into Montana. Swinging around from east to west, they were Targhee, Raynolds, Monida and Medicine Lodge. All four had been important Indian passes, but aside from Monida, only Targhee was used by the herds from the Northwest, and such as used it were invariably bound for the Big Horn Basin. After going through Targhee Pass you dropped down to the south fork of the Madison, followed that stream to within a few miles of its junction with the Gallatin. Turning east up the Gallatin to the new town of Bozeman, you went over a low pass and down to the Yellowstone. Along it you trailed until you reached Clarks Fork, which opened the way into the Basin.

It is not likely that more than 60 per cent of all the Oregon-Washington stock that was trailed over Monida and Targhee passes remained in Montana; thousands were driven into Wyoming, and not only into Big Horn Basin; others went over the International Boundary into Canada. Since no records were kept, it is impossible to say how many head crossed the Snake River Plains in the six years from 1869 to 1875 which embraced the beginning and virtual ending of the movement of cattle from the West. From such figures as are available, a conservative estimate would put the number at a quarter of a million. This seems like a trifling figure when compared with the six million or more Longhorns that were trailed north out of Texas. And yet, for all its lack of numbers, it was to have a far greater effect on cattle

raising in the United States. In fact, our modern livestock industry can be said to have been based on the lessons learned in Wyoming and Montana in those crucial years.

Traffic on the old Wilderness Road and Three Mountain Trail
had moved from west to east, but driving cattle and horses out
of Oregon and Washington across the Idaho wastelands was the
first mass movement of livestock in that direction, and it was the
last. The hazards that were part of it—thirst, choking dust and
extremes of heat and subzero cold—were as hard on men as any
that were faced on the Chisholm or Western trails. For the
owner, bringing a herd out of the Northwest into Wyoming or
Montana was not the speculative business that characterized
trail driving out of Texas. The cattle he bought were for himself. The men that he dispatched by rail to Kelton, Utah, and
on to Baker City by stage were his own ranch crew. More often
than not, he accompanied them. If not, he sent his foreman to
attend to the purchase and act as trail boss on the way home.
The brand he burned was his ranch brand, not a road brand.
There were exceptions but they were few.

Several herds of young, tick-free Texas stock cattle that had
been wintered in Nebraska were brought into the Big Horn
Basin in 1880–81. It was claimed by their owners that they were
hardier and better rustlers than the cattle being trailed in from
the Pacific Northwest. Range comparison proved that not to be
the case; the chunkier and more easily handled Shorthorns could
sustain themselves every bit as well, the cows equally able to
protect their young against predatory animals.

It needed only time to prove them superior to the Longhorn
in many ways. At the end of the long drive to the railroad at
shipping time, he was easier to load, and when he reached a
Midwestern feed lot, he took up less room in a pen. But most
important of all in the economics of stock raising, he put on
more weight than the Longhorn, and he produced a better grade
of beef. For reasons not yet understood (Theobald Smith's dis-
coveries were still some years in the future) he was a stranger to
Texas fever.

Judged by today's exacting standards they were "rough" cattle,
lacking the highly prized uniformity of color and conformation

that have been achieved through years of careful upgrading. But the introduction of the hardy, range-bred Oregon-Washington Shorthorn into Wyoming and Montana marked the end, or at least the beginning of the end, of the long, undisputed reign of the Texas Longhorn over the cattle trade of the West, which, with a mighty assist from the cruel winter of 1886, was to lead to the virtual disappearance of the Longhorn from Northern ranges.

During this period, 1869–86, thousands of Oregon broncs were driven across the Rockies. They were so cheap around Baker City that they could be sold for ten times their cost, once they were east of the Rockies. Not only were herds of six to eight hundred head trailed across Idaho, but every outfit carried forty to fifty extra head in its cavvy. They were fine, big horses and they began to supplant the Texas cow pony. Of them, John K. Rollinson, the first historian to give them their due, says:

"Oregon was raising some fine, large-sized horses, and as they were of native mustang stock from blackhawk or graded-up sires, the three- and four-year-old geldings, often weighing twelve and thirteen hundred pounds, were as active as cats. Being desert-bred horses they had remarkably fine feet, and their hoofs were as tough as those of mountain sheep; and with their sure-footedness and the splendid lung capacity of their well-ribbed, short-coupled barrel chests, they had the traditional stamina and endurance of the clay-bank stock from which they originated." [2]

Unquestionably the white breeders of the so-called Oregon horse profited by what they had learned from the Palouse and Nez Percé. It was intelligent and made an excellent roping or cutting horse. The Spanish pony of Texas was its equal in everything but size. You will recall that in the early years of the Abilene market that Northern stockmen would not buy the little mustang because it was small. Their preference for the Oregon horse, a dozen years later, was perhaps in some degree a reflection of that old prejudice.

Sheep had begun to appear on the Laramie Plains, and in a dozen directions the homesteader was digging in on his quarter-section. They weren't the immediate problem of the free-range cattlemen; they were providing that themselves by blindly overstocking the grasslands of Wyoming, Montana and the Dakota Bad Lands. As more and more outfits drove in with their cattle and horses its first effect was to create a situation that enabled the stock rustler to raise his activities to the level of an organized business. The outlaws had the active support of many small ranchers (nesters) who concealed stolen stock, provided false evidence in the rustler's favor, when an arrest occurred, and packed a jury so that a conviction could not be secured.

At the spring meeting of the Montana Stock Growers' Association in 1884, the figures submitted showed that there had been a loss of 4 per cent to rustlers, mostly horses. Stolen horses could be moved more quickly than cattle, and they were more profitable to the thieves. An animal stolen in Montana or Wyoming could be driven into Dakota and sold without too many questions being asked. The best market was across the boundary in Canada. To be handy to that market, the rustler rendezvoused along the Missouri River, below the mouth of the Musselshell.

No course of action having been agreed on at the spring meeting in Miles City, the rustlers continued their activities. A second meeting took place at the D-S Ranch at the close of the fall roundup. Stuart says fourteen men were present. Plans were made for the swift and secret elimination of the outlaws. This resulted in what went into history as "the great horse-thief round-up." The number of men hanged has been put as high as twenty-eight; using Granville Stuart's own figures, I can account for only nineteen, hanged or killed by gunfire. A hundred and sixty-five stolen horses were recovered at Bates Point and one hundred and nineteen at other places.

Stuart was the self-admitted leader of this sanguinary reprisal, and he was severely criticized for it, and still is by a few. It was vigilante law, without any semblance of legality, but its effectiveness cannot be questioned; it ended organized horse stealing along the Missouri. There was more rustling, but it was largely perpetrated by the large bands of Cree Indians who had been permitted to cross the international boundary after the collapse of the Riel Rebellion in Canada. Their only means of subsistence was stealing cattle on the range and their "only source of amusement," as Granville Stuart put it, "was stealing horses."

By the spring of 1885 (speaking from the vantage point that hindsight gives) it should have been apparent to all concerned that the free-range cattle business could not continue indefinitely on the scale it had reached. To beat the Kansas embargo on the Longhorns, Texas owners had hustled no less than a hundred thousand head into Wyoming, Montana and the Dakota Bad Lands. The influx of Oregon cattle continued, though in reduced numbers, for they no longer could be bought at bargain prices, the fast-growing cities of Seattle, Portland and Tacoma beginning to provide a home market. In the short space of two years the number of sheep spreading out over Wyoming rose from practically nothing to fifty thousand. Almost as many more were grazing grass to the roots in Montana. A growing stream of homesteaders were settling down on their government claims, fencing themselves in. In self-defense the big outfits were illegally stringing miles of wire on the public domain, to which they had no right, title or interest other than they were "using it." These facts were not unrelated, but it was not until after an extended drouth lasting ten weeks burned out the grass and dried up the creeks, making it necessary to move many herds north of the Missouri River, that it was generally acknowledged that Wyoming-Montana ranges were being asked to carry more stock than they could support.

But nothing was done to rectify the situation. In fact, the reverse occurred when the fall shipping normally would have relieved the range of thousands of beeves. Due to the condition of the grass, the shortage of water and the incessant fires, cattle were in such poor condition that many owners decided not to ship at all; others trimmed their drives to the railroad pens by 50 per cent or more. Several factors over which they had no control justified this reluctance to ship. The failure of the corn crop in the Midwest had forced many feed lots to close. On the Chicago market the price of Western range beef had dropped to $1.80 a hundredweight—barely enough to defray freight charges. Though stockmen, big and small, were undoubtedly justified in holding back as much as they could, it left the range clogged with cattle to face the oncoming winter.

There were signs that it was going to be severe. The birds and wildlife had migrated southward earlier than usual. Cattle and horses put on an extra heavy coat of hair. In the Judith Basin and other places, white Arctic owls were seen for the first time in years.

An early November storm, bringing snow and icy temperatures, set the stage for what was to follow—the terrible "die-up" of 1886, extending from the Canadian border to the Texas Panhandle, in which more than a million head of starving, helpless cattle, horses, mules and sheep were to freeze to death in the worst sub-Arctic winter ever experienced on the high plains.[3]

In Bozeman and Billings ghostly, ice-incrusted cattle staggered into the business streets and died where they stood. On the North Platte and its tributaries, on Powder River and in the Lander Valley of Wyoming, the losses were greatest. On the Kansas prairies livestock perished in such numbers that the following spring men working out of Dodge City made a living gathering up the bones.

Big Horn Basin and other mountain-protected areas fared better, but even there fortunes were swept away.

The first severe storm began on November 16. The thermometer fell to two degrees below zero, with an icy blast from the northeast continuing for three days. On the seventeenth and eighteenth six inches of snow fell and drifted badly. It was followed by a second storm on December 5, bringing more snow and the temperature dropping to twelve degrees below zero. The wind was from the north. The cattle went with it until they piled up against a fence, where they died miserably. "Conditions were so changed from what they were in 1880–81," Granville Stuart comments. "The thick brush and tall rye-grass along the streams that afforded them excellent shelter at that time was now all fenced in and the poor animals drifted against those fences and perished."[4]

The second storm lasted three days without let-up and then snowed and blew intermittently until December 14. The sun shone wanly then. The temperature moderated, and men dared to hope that the worst was over. Much worse was to come. On January 9, 1887, it began to snow and snowed heavily for sixteen hours, in which sixteen inches of snow fell on the level.

The thermometer plunged to twenty-two below zero, then to twenty-seven below, then to thirty; on January 15 it stood at forty-six degrees below zero. Eighteen inches of fresh snow fell in the ten days that the storm lasted. Piling up on top of the high drifts left by previous storms, it buried bunkhouses and ranch buildings.

February brought another series of storms, not so severe but they came when the cattle were least able to withstand them. Weak, shrunken, starving, they perished by the thousand. "One of the killing features," says Rollinson, "was a snowfall followed by a chinook wind which blew warm and melting, sending men's hopes out of their boot tops. Then they found, by morning, that the chinook had played the Judas and betrayed them with another Arctic blast, with more zero weather, which caked the snow with a crust so hard it would even bear the weight of a steer." [5]

Months passed before even a rough estimate of the losses suffered could be made. Some cattle had drifted as much as three hundred miles from their home range and were not returned for a year. Stuart placed the over-all loss to the livestock industry at $20,000,000. It was among the Longhorns that had been driven north the previous year (1885) that the greatest losing occurred. In some instances an entire herd was lost; with the more fortunate, 35 to 40 per cent survived. The Pioneer Cattle Company, the Swan Land and Cattle Company, Granville Stuart's D-S and practically all of the big outfits reported losses of 50 to 60 per cent. In Big Horn Basin, with its preponderance of Oregon cattle, the average loss was not over 15 per cent.

The big "die-up" sounded the knell of the range cattle business as it had been conducted in the past. It left some outfits in a position where they could not continue. Those that did realized that they dared not risk being caught again without some means of feeding and sheltering their cattle in an emergency; putting up just enough hay for the riding stock wouldn't suffice.

The little outfits, running a few hundred cows, had come through the appalling winter of 1886–87 in much better shape than most of the old established companies. If some of the latter had to be broken up, it was obvious that the scramble for range would be greater than ever. In self-protection, it was going to be necessary to begin buying government land. This was heresy to men who had waxed rich on the free range. But it had to come, for the era of free grass, of ripping out a fortune in a hurry and of control of the territorial governments of Montana and Wyoming vested in the powerful stock associations was nearing its end. Never again would thousands of Longhorns come pounding up the trail from Texas. No new trails would be opened; the old ones would be abandoned. Trail driving, as a business and as an occupation, was finished. The railroads would make certain of that. When the Matador, the Pitchfork and other big Texas outfits moved into the Cheyenne and Sioux reservations, they would come lock, stock and barrel by rail. Moving cattle on the hoof would be confined to the long drive to the railroad pens in the shipping season.

If time has all but obliterated the old cattle trails, the part they played in the development of this country was far too great for them ever to be forgotten. Nostalgically they will always wind through the fabric of American history.

Notes

CHAPTER 1.

1. Thomas Speed: *The Wilderness Road,* New York, 1886 and Charles A. Hanna, *The Wilderness Trail.* New York, 1911.
2. Reuben Gold Thaites: *Daniel Boone,* New York, 1902.
3. Harry Sinclair Drago: *Wild, Woolly and Wicked,* New York, 1960.
4. Minnie Dubbs Millbank: *The Three Mountain Trail,* the *N.Y. Westerners Brand Book,* Vol. 5, No. 2, 1958.

CHAPTER 2.

1. Harry Sinclair Drago: *Red River Valley,* New York, 1962.
2. Grant Foreman: *Down the Texas Road,* Norman, Oklahoma, 1936.
3. Chouteau's Verdigris River trading post should not be confused with his main establishment at La Saline.
4. John Francis McDermott: *A Tour on the Prairies,* Introduction, Norman, Oklahoma, 1956.
5. Washington Irving: *A Tour on the Prairies,* 1956 edition, Norman, Oklahoma.
6. *Ibid.*
7. *Ibid.*
8. Washington Irving: *The Western Journals of Washington Irving,* edited by John Francis McDermott, 1944 edition, Norman, Oklahoma.
9. Washington Irving: *A Tour on the Prairies,* 1956 edition, Norman, Oklahoma.
10. V. V. Masterson: *The Katy Railroad,* Norman, Oklahoma, 1952.
11. For a list of Butterfield Stations in Oklahoma see map prepared by Oklahoma Historical Society, price $1.00.

CHAPTER 3.

1. As to Chouteau's participation in the Missouri Fur Co., this from Chittenden, pages 137–38:

The return of Lisa in the summer of 1808 [from the upper Missouri] was followed by the formation of a trading company that included nearly all the prominent men in St. Louis. It was incorporated under the name of the St. Louis Missouri Fur Company but it was known generally as the Missouri Fur Company. Included among the members were Benjamin Wilkinson, Pierre Chouteau Sr., Manuel Lisa, Auguste Chouteau Jr., Reuben Lewis, William Clark and Sylvestre Labadie. . . .

The Articles of Association for the St. L. M. Fur Co. were signed May 9, 1809.

2. *The Western Journals of Washington Irving,* edited by John Francis McDermott, 1944 edition, Norman, Oklahoma.
3. *Oklahoma, A Guide to the Sooner State,* Norman, Oklahoma, 1941.
4. A quarter of a century ago, in a belated acknowledgment of the Chouteau family's contribution to the development of the state, the Oklahoma Legislature proclaimed October 10, the anniversary of Major Pierre Chouteau's birth, as "Oklahoma Historical Day." It was first celebrated at Salina in 1940.
5. Grant Foreman: *Down the Texas Road,* Norman, Oklahoma, 1936.
6. *Marcy and the Goldseekers,* edited by Grant Foreman, Norman, Oklahoma, 1939.
7. Harry Sinclair Drago: *Red River Valley,* New York, 1962.
8. His annoyance at the Cherokee Indian tolls, when the Missouri, Kansas and Texas Railroad was building down through Indian Territory in 1872, led General Manager Robert S. Stevens to bypass Fort Gibson and strike out for the Creek Nation. It made Muskogee and left Fort Gibson to wither on the vine.

CHAPTER 4.

1. Frank Cunningham: *General Stand Watie's Confederate Indians,* San Antonio, Texas, 1959.
2. Angie Debo: *The Five Civilized Tribes,* Philadelphia, 1951.
3. Grant Foreman: *A History of Oklahoma,* Norman, Oklahoma, 1939.
4. Burton Rascoe: *Belle Starr, the Bandit Queen,* New York, 1941.
5. *Kansas, A Guide to the Sunflower State,* New York, 1939.
6. He was principally engaged at the time in gathering up small herds of prairie cattle (not Texan) and trailing them to Fort Riley and Fort Scott.
7. U. S. Highway 81 throughout its course in Oklahoma has the Chisholm Trail for its historic background. The Oklahoma Historical Society, in cooperation with the state, has erected a number of stone markers to identify it as the route of the old trail.
8. Harry Sinclair Drago: *Wild, Woolly and Wicked,* New York, 1960.

CHAPTER 5.

1. Harry Sinclair Drago: *Wild, Woolly and Wicked,* New York, 1960.
2. *Wyoming Stock Growers' Association, Annual Report 1884.*
3. Joseph G. McCoy: *Historic Sketches of the Cattle Trade,* Kansas City, Missouri, 1874.

4. Floyd B. Streeter: *Prairie Trails and Cow Towns,* Boston, 1936.

5. *Act of Kansas State Legislature, March 12, 1885.*

6. Included in *Nimmo Report, March 3, 1885,* U. S. Archives.

7. Paul de Kruif: *Microbe Hunters,* New York, 1926.

8. *Ibid.* I am indebted for much of the foregoing to Paul de Kruif and his *Microbe Hunters,* called by H. L. Mencken, "One of the noblest chapters in the history of mankind."

CHAPTER 6.

1. John Joseph Matthews: *Wah'Kon-tah: The Osage and the White Man's Road,* Norman, Oklahoma, 1932.

2. The Five Civilized Tribes signed treaties with the United States in 1866, freeing their slaves and ceding their "reserve lands" in the western half of Oklahoma for the settlement of other Indians (Southern Cheyennes, Kiowas and Comanches), and agreeing to a proposed intertribal organization. Reservations were assigned to the Plains Indians the following year.

3. Harry Sinclair Drago: *Outlaws on Horseback,* New York, 1964.

4. Joy's construction crews were decoyed into crossing the Indian Territory line into the Quapaw Reservation which had been whittled off the great Cherokee Reservation and was no longer part of the lands of the Five Civilized Tribes, into which a railroad had to enter to be eligible for the land grant. This bit of trickery, perpetrated by the Katy, turned the Border Tier's apparent victory to defeat.

5. Grant Foreman: *Down the Texas Road,* Norman, Oklahoma, 1936.

6. Harry Sinclair Drago: *Outlaws on Horseback,* New York, 1964.

7. Charles E. A. Gayarre: *A History of Louisiana,* New York, 1854.

8. Fanny Cora Potter: *History of Montague County,* Austin, Texas, 1912.

9. Glen O. Wilson: *Southwest Historical Quarterly,* January, 1958.

10. Harry Sinclair Drago: *Red River Valley,* New York, 1962.

CHAPTER 7.

1. Harry Sinclair Drago: *Wild, Woolly and Wicked,* New York, 1960.

2. J. Frank Dobie: *The Mustangs,* Boston, 1952.

3. J. Frank Dobie: *The Longhorns,* Boston, 1941.

4. Álvar Nuñez Cabeza de Vaca, the royal treasurer of the ill-fated Narvaez Expedition, is noted for his Western wanderings and is seldom given credit for having discovered one of the mouths of the Mississippi River.

5. *Narrative of the Career of Hernando de Soto* (2 vols.), edited by Gaylord Bourne, New York, 1922.

6. Nez Percé is a misnomer. They never pierced their noses. The French pronunciation has been dropped by such modern historians as Alvin Josephy, Jr., and others.

7. John K. Rollinson: *Wyoming Cattle Trails,* Caldwell, Idaho, 1948.

CHAPTER 8.

1. *The Trail Drivers of Texas;* J. Marvin Hunter, editor, San Antonio, Texas, 1920.

2. Louis Nordyke: *The Roundup,* published by the Western Writers of of America, July, 1960.
3. Joseph G. McCoy: *Historic Sketches of the Cattle Trade,* Kansas City, Missouri, 1874.
4. A. T. Andreas: *History of Kansas,* Wichita, Kansas, 1883.
5. *The Trail Drivers of Texas:* J. Marvin Hunter, editor, San Antonio, Texas, 1920.
6. *Ibid.*
7. *Ibid.*
8. Harry Sinclair Drago: *Wild, Woolly and Wicked,* New York, 1960.

CHAPTER 9.

1. Harry Sinclair Drago: *Wild, Woolly and Wicked,* New York, 1960.
2. Joseph G. McCoy: *Historic Sketches of the Cattle Trade,* Kansas City, Missouri, 1874.
3. *Ibid.*
4. *Ibid.*
5. Stuart Henry: *Conquering Our Great American Plains,* New York, 1930.
6. Floyd B. Streeter: *Prairie Trails and Cow Towns,* Boston, 1936.

CHAPTER 10.

1. Stuart Henry: *Conquering Our Great American Plains,* New York, 1930.
2. *The Trail Drivers of Texas:* J. Marvin Hunter, editor, San Antonio, Texas, 1920.
3. J. Frank Dobie: *The Longhorns,* Boston, 1941.
4. *The Abilene Chronicle,* Abilene, Kansas.
5. "It was due to Charles F. Adams, descendant of Presidents John and John Quincy Adams, that Kansas City became a meat packing center. Adams acquired several large tracts of land in the Kansas River Valley, now occupied by Armourdale and the central industrial district, and built the first of the stockyards. He then persuaded Plankington and Armour to remove the packing house they had set up in Missouri to Kansas that it might be convenient to his stockyards. This they did in 1871. . . . Today Kansas City has eleven packing houses, including those of the 'Big Four'—Armour, Swift, Cudahy and Wilson." *(Kansas, a Guide to the Sunflower State.)*
6. Harry Sinclair Drago: *Wild, Woolly and Wicked,* New York, 1960.
7. Stuart Henry: *Conquering Our Great American Plains,* New York, 1930.
8. Floyd B. Streeter: *Prairie Trails and Cow Towns,* Boston, 1936.
9. *The Theodore C. Henry Collections:* Kansas State Historical Society, 1905–6.

CHAPTER 11.

1. Stuart Henry: *Conquering Our Great American Plains,* New York, 1930.
2. Charles Gross' letter to J. B. Edwards, April 13, 1922. Gross in his many letters is as omnipresent as Fred Sutton in his *Hands Up,* both claiming to have a part in whatever happened.
3. Eugene Cunningham: *Triggernometry,* Caldwell, Idaho, 1941.

4. Harry Sinclair Drago: *Wild, Woolly and Wicked,* New York, 1960.
5. Bill Lake was killed by a local tough named Jack Killian, at Granby, Missouri, in an argument over the latter's unwillingness to produce a ticket for admission to the circus.
6. Floyd B. Streeter: *Prairie Trails and Cow Towns,* Boston, 1936.

<h2 style="text-align:center">CHAPTER 12.</h2>

1. Ben Thompson, his wife and young son were involved in an accident in Kansas City as they were leaving for Texas. The buggy in which they were riding overturned. Mrs. Thompson's arm was so badly broken that it had to be amputated.
2. Adolph Roenigk: *Pioneer History of Kansas,* Lincoln, Kansas, 1933.
3. Harry Sinclair Drago: *Wild, Woolly and Wicked,* New York, 1960.
4. R. W. Muse: *A History of Harvey County,* Wichita, 1883.

<h2 style="text-align:center">CHAPTER 13.</h2>

1. Floyd B. Streeter: *Prairie Trails and Cow Towns,* Boston, 1936.
2. George Jelinek: *Ellsworth, 1867–1947,* Salina, Kansas, 1947.
3. Chris Emmett: *Shanghai Pierce: A Fair Likeness,* Norman, Oklahoma, 1953.
4. This shotgun, a gift to Ben Thompson from Cad Pierce, can be seen in the Beeson Museum at Dodge City. Hard up, Ben borrowed $75 on it from Chalk Beeson and never reclaimed it.
5. Ellsworth *Reporter,* August 18, 1872.
6. Stuart N. Lake: *Wyatt Earp: Frontier Marshal,* Boston, 1931.

<h2 style="text-align:center">CHAPTER 14.</h2>

1. *The Trail Drivers of Texas:* J. Marvin Hunter, editor, San Antonio, Texas, 1920.
2. Kansas Historical Quarterly: *Cowtown Police Officers and Gunfighters,* Autumn, 1960, Topeka, Kansas.
3. Records of City of Wichita, Journal B., pp. 55–100.
4. Frank W. Blackmar: *Kansas: A Cyclopedia of State History,* Chicago, 1912.
5. William Allen White: *Woodrow Wilson, The Man, His Times and His Task,* Boston, 1924.
6. Floyd B. Streeter: *Prairie Trails and Cow Towns,* Boston, 1936.
7. Stewart Holbrook: *The Story of the American Railroads,* New York, 1947.

<h2 style="text-align:center">CHAPTER 15.</h2>

1. Wayne Gard: *The Great Buffalo Hunt,* New York, 1959.
2. *The Trail Drivers of Texas:* J. Marvin Hunter, editor, San Antonio, Texas, 1920.
3. Stewart H. Holbrook: *The Story of American Railroads,* New York, 1947.
4. V. V. Masterson: *The Katy Railroad and the Last Frontier,* Norman, Oklahoma, 1952.
5. *The Trail Drivers of Texas:* J. Marvin Hunter, editor, San Antonia, Texas, 1920.

6. *Ibid.*
7. *Ibid.*
8. *Ibid.*
9. Harry Sinclair Drago: *Red River Valley,* New York, 1962.
10. Office of General Freight Agent, Santa Fe Railroad, Topeka, Kan.
11. *The Nimmo Report,* Appendix 4, March 3, 1885, U. S. Archives, Washington, D.C.
12. *The Nimmo Report,* Appendix 50, March 3, 1885, U. S. Archives, Washington, D.C.

CHAPTER 16.

1. Harry Sinclair Drago: *Epitaph for a Marshal,* New York, 1963. A novel that dwells at some length on the Red Light.
2. *Caldwell Commercial,* July 1, 1880.
3. *Ibid,* July 8, 1880.
4. *Caldwell Post,* December 22, 1881.
5. Nyle H. Miller and Joseph W. Snell: *Some Notes on Kansas Cowtown Police Officers and Gun Fighters,* Kansas Historical Quarterly, Summer, 1960.
6. *Caldwell Post,* January 4, 1884.
7. *Medicine Lodge* (Kansas) *Cressett,* May 1, 1884.

CHAPTER 17.

1. *The Trail Drivers of Texas:* J. Marvin Hunter, editor, San Antonio, Texas 1920.
2. E. C. (Teddy Blue) Abbott and Helena Huntington Smith: *We Pointed Them North,* New York, 1939.
3. Mr. McDonald is head of the American History Department of the New York Public Library.
4. *The Trail Drivers of Texas:* J. Marvin Hunter, editor, San Antonio, Texas, 1920.
5. *Kansas Cowtown Police and Gunfighters:* edited and compiled by Nyle H. Miller and Joseph W. Snell. It is now available in book form, published by the Kansas Historical Society, Topeka, Kansas. A monumental work, indispensable to anyone interested in Kansas cow town history.
6. *Ibid.*
7. Whether Earp served two hitches as assistant marshal of Dodge City or three, as he claims, is in dispute. The editors of *Kansas Peace Officers and Gunfighters* doubt it, mainly, I take it, because they were unable to find any newspaper reference to him between July 6 and November, 1877, the period Earp gives as his second term. The well-known Stanley Vestal in his *Dodge City: Queen of Cow Towns* accepts Earp's figures. So must I, for I have found no record of his having been anywhere else between July and November, 1877.

CHAPTER 18.

1. In Hays City, before he came to Dodge, Jim Kelley was called "Hound "Dog," which sprang from the pack of hounds with which he hunted.

Two of his pack were said to have been a gift from Colonel Custer, when he was commandant at nearby Fort Hays.

2. Harry Sinclair Drago: *Wild, Woolly and Wicked,* New York, 1960.
3. Neil Brown was a competent police officer. When Bill Tilghman went to Guthrie after the "opening," Brown followed. Tilghman and he were together when the marshal blundered into the hide-out of the Doolin Gang at the Will Dunn ranch. He was half Cherokee.
4. Stuart N. Lake: *Wyatt Earp: Frontier Marshal,* Boston, 1931.
5. If you have wondered why the Long Branch Saloon was so named, Will Harris, one of the proprietors, hailed from Long Branch, New Jersey.
6. Nyle H. Miller and Joseph W. Snell, editors and compilers, *Kansas Cowtown Police Officers and Gun Fighters,* Kansas Historical Quarterly, Topeka, Kansas, Spring, 1962.
7. *Ibid.*
8. When Wyatt Earp left Dodge City for Tombstone, Ed Masterson was appointed to his place as assistant marshal of the town.
9. Stuart N. Lake: *Wyatt Earp: Frontier Marshall,* Boston, 1931.
10. Mrs. Merritt Beeson told me several years ago that the Beeson Museum had a standing offer of $100 for an authentic photograph of Fannie Keenan.

CHAPTER 19.

1. *The Trail Drivers of Texas:* J. Marvin Hunter, editor, San Antonio, Texas, 1920.
2. *Ibid.* Also *Pioneer Days in the Southwest:* Charles Goodnight and others, Guthrie, Oklahoma, 1909.
3. *Ibid.* See also *Charles Goodnight, Cowman and Plainsman* by J. Evetts Haley, New York, 1936, and *A History of the J A Ranch,* by H. T. Burton, Austin, Texas, 1927.
4. *The Nimmo Report,* Appendix 30, 1885, U. S. Archives, Washington, D.C.
5. Harry Sinclair Drago: *Red River Valley,* New York, 1962.
6. *Ibid.*
7. On roundup and on the trail the chuck wagon improved the quality and variety of the grub a cowpuncher ate, and for it he could thank the ingenuity of this grizzled veteran: Charles Goodnight had "invented" it. Goodnight College or "Academy" was no more than a primitive highschool, but considering the time and place, a monument to its founder. For an authentic account of how Goodnight removed the buffalos from Palo Duro Canyon and brought in his Longhorns, see J. Evetts Haley's *Charles Goodnight, Cowman and Plainsman.*

CHAPTER 20.

1. *Forty Years on the Frontier as seen in the Journals and Reminiscences of Granville Stuart.*
2. *My Life on the Range,* by John Clay.
3. *Wyoming Cattle Trails,* by John K. Rollinson.

4. *Forty Years on the Frontier as seen in the Journals and Reminiscences of Granville Stuart.*

CHAPTER 21.

1. *Fort Hall,* by Frank C. Robertson.
2. *Wyoming Cattle Trails,* by John K. Rollinson.
3. The Indians suffered untold hardships. Forty percent of their pony herds died. Those that survived did so by subsisting on the bark of the red willow and the cottonwood. Along the river bottoms the trees were stripped bare as high as an animal standing on its hind legs could reach. Among white men cases of frozen hands and feet were too numerous to be recorded. Near Fort Washakie a stage driver and a passenger (a woman) were frozen to death.
4. *Forty Years on the Frontier as seen in the Journals and Reminiscences of Granville Stuart.*
5. *Wyoming Cattle Trails,* by John K. Rollinson.

Bibliography

BOOKS

Abbott, E. C. (Teddy Blue): *We Pointed Them North*, New York, 1939.

Bandelier, Fanny: *The Journey of Cabeza de Vaca*, Austin, Texas, 1904.

Burton, H. T.: *A History of the J A Ranch*, Austin, Texas, 1927.

Brayer, Herbert O. and Garnet M.: *American Cattle Trails*, New York, 1952.

Carter, Capt. R. G.: *On the Border With Mackenzie*, New York, 1961.

Chittenden, Hiram M., *The American Fur Trade of the Far West*, New York, 1903.

Clay, John: *My Life on the Range*, Chicago, 1924.

Debo, Angie: *And Still the Waters Run*, Princeton, N. J., 1940.

Dixon, Olive K.: *The Life of Billy Dixon*, Dallas, Texas, 1927.

Dobie, J. Frank: *The Longhorns*, Boston, 1941.

—— *The Mustangs*, Boston, 1952.

Drago, Harry Sinclair: *Wild, Woolly and Wicked*, New York, 1960.

—— *Red River Valley*, New York 1962.

—— *Outlaws on Horseback*, New York 1964.

de Kruif, Paul: *Microbe Hunters*, New York, 1928.

Foreman, Grant: *A History of Oklahoma*, Norman, Oklahoma, 1937.

—— *Down the Texas Road*, Norman, Oklahoma, 1936.

—— *Advancing the Frontier*, Norman, Oklahoma, 1933.

Gard, Wayne: *The Chisholm Trail*, Norman, Oklahoma, 1954.

Haley, J. Evetts: *Charles Goodnight, Cowman and Plainsman*, Boston, 1936.

Hanna, Charles A.: *The Wilderness Trail*, 2 vols. New York, 1911.

Howard, George P.: *Coronado's Seven Cities*, Albuquerque, N.M., 1940.

Hulbert, Archer B.: *Boone's Wilderness Road*, Cleveland, Ohio, 1903.

Hunter, J. Marvin, editor: *The Trail Drivers of Texas*, San Antonio, Texas, 1920.

Irving, Washington: *A Tour on the Prairies*, edited by John Francis McDermott (reissue), Norman, Oklahoma, 1956.

—— *Western Journals,* edited by John Francis McDermott, Norman, Oklahoma, 1944.

Lake, Stuart: *Wyatt Earp: Frontier Marshal,* Boston, 1931.

Masterson, V. V.: *The Katy Railroad,* Norman, Oklahoma, 1952.

McCoy, Joseph G.: *Historic Sketches of the Cattle Trade,* Kansas City, Missouri, 1874.

Millbank, Minnie Dubbs: *The Three Mountain Trail,* N.Y. Westerners Brand Book, Vol. 5, No. 2, 1958.

Miller, Nyle H., and Snell, Joseph W.: *Kansas Cowtown Police Officers and Gunfighters,* Topeka, Kansas, 1964.

Nimmo, Joseph A., Jr.: *The Nimmo Report,* Washington, D.C., 1885.

Parkman, Francis: *The Oregon Trail,* Dodd, Mead, editorial with introduction by Harry Sinclair Drago, 1964.

Price, Con: *Memories of Old Montana,* Pasadena, California, 1945.

Robertson, Frank C.: *Fort Hall,* New York, 1964.

Rollinson, John K.: *Wyoming Cattle Trails,* Caldwell, Idaho, 1948.

Russell, Charles M.: *Trails Ploughed Under,* New York, 1932.

Sandoz, Mari: *The Cattlemen,* New York, 1958.

Sharp, Paul F.: *Whoop-Up Country,* Minneapolis, Minnesota, 1955.

Smith, Buckingham: *Alvar Muñez de Vaca,* a translation from the Spanish, Washington, D.C., 1851.

Speed, Thomas: *The Wilderness Road,* Louisville, Kentucky, 1886.

Streeter, Floyd B.: *Prairie Trails and Cow Towns,* Boston, 1936.

Stuart, Granville: *Forty Years on the Frontier,* Cleveland, Ohio, 1925.

Thwaites, Reuben Gold: *Daniel Boone,* New York, 1902.

Wright, Robert M.: *Dodge City: The Cowboy Capital and the Great Southwest,* Wichita, Kansas, 1913.

PERIODICALS

Montana, the Magazine of Western History
Chronicles of Oklahoma
Kansas Historical Quarterly
Southwestern Quarterly Review
Panhandle-Plains Review
Louisiana Historical Quarterly
Oklahoma Today
Annals of Wyoming

Index